*The State and Rural Transformation in
Northern Somalia, 1884–1986*

The State and Rural Transformation in Northern Somalia, 1884–1986

Abdi Ismail Samatar

The University of Wisconsin Press

The University of Wisconsin Press
114 North Murray Street
Madison, Wisconsin 53715

The University of Wisconsin Press, Ltd.
1 Gower Street
London WC1E 6HA, England

5 4 3 2 1

CIP to come

To my parents Halimo and Ismail, to those women of my mother's generation who gave up so much of their personal lives for the collective improvement of their communities, and to the oppressed people of the globe.

It would be erroneous to believe that revolutionary classes always have sufficient strength for the accomplishment of the overturn at the time at which conditions of the socioeconomic development have rendered the need for that overturn entirely ripe. No, human society is not arranged so rationally and so "conveniently" for its progressive elements. The need for the overturn may be ripe, but the strength of the revolutionary creators may turn out to be inadequate for carrying it out. Under such conditions society rots and this rotting sometimes lasts entire decades.

V. I. Lenin
quoted in Paul A. Baran,
The Political Economy of Growth

Contents

Illustrations

Maps

Figures and Tables

Preface

This book is about the making of the contemporary northern Somali society. It probes into the dynamic and dialectical, internal and external, processes responsible for the creation of the peripheral capitalist Somali social formation. In doing so, it acknowledges the central contributions of I. M. Lewis, the chief Somalist, to Somali studies, while at the same time challenging the principal thrust of his analysis of the (de)composition of precolonial Somali society and the contours of its current social geography. Our differences are fundamentally conceptual, as they pertain to the transformation of precapitalist societies caught in the web of the world market. I single out Lewis because his modus operandi and writings have had such fundamental influences on Somalist scholarship.

In the main, the Lewisian interpretations of Somali social history assume that the evolution of northern Somali society has been quantitative in nature despite its articulation to and integration into the colonial empire and the world capitalist system. Symptomatic of this view is the unproblematic deployment of such important and theoretically loaded concepts as the state, tribalism, and pastoralism transhistorically. My use of such concepts is historically specific. For example, I view pastoralism under the postcolonial state as qualitatively different from precolonial pastoralism, since the social environment within which pastoralists produce and reproduce has changed enormously over the last hundred years. This applies to tribalism and the state as well. Such conceptual differences are not "academic." They lead to contrasting analyses of the nature of Somali underdevelopment, and ultimately to development policies that affect people's lives.

Somalia is one of the least studied societies on the African continent. The sparsity and/or lack of basic data make writing Somali social history exceedingly difficult. Lewis's numerous contributions, dating back to the 1950s, are the central pillars of Somali studies. I have pieced together bits and pieces of archival, oral, and survey data, using the materialist historical method as an organizing tool, to reconstruct the dialectical relationships between domestic economy, politics, and ecology, and the international political economy.[1]

The data on which this book is based were gathered during a year-long field study in Britain and the Horn of Africa in 1983–84 and subsequent

xiii

visits in 1986 and 1987. Four techniques were employed at different stages of the fieldwork. These were survey research (interviews), participant observation, archival research, and oral history. There is no need here to lay out the details of the strength and weakness of these techniques.[2]

I would, however, like to highlight some of the principal characteristics of the oral history tradition. Vansina notes that oral histories are "testimonies of the past which are deliberately transmitted from mouth to mouth. They concern past events, and are distinct from rumors, which always bear the character of sensational 'news,' and are not deliberately transmitted from generation to generation in the same way."[3] Furthermore, he adds that this method is quite different from eyewitness reports, since the latter method involves no oral transmission. Although I share the general definition of the technique, my use of the technique was slightly broader to include eyewitness reports. This extension was essential, since part of the study period was so recent and since my informants had been both eyewitnesses and transmitters of historical data from the preceding generations.

Person and Vansina point out that oral tradition involves individuals specializing in keeping oral tradition (*griot*) and insuring its proper transmission.[4] Since there were no such specialists in the research area, I made use of the alternative approach suggested by Vansina, that of collecting testimony from variant sources. Since it is impractical to collect all such possible sources, Vansina suggests that the researcher use a sample.[5] In my case the sample included all adults who were willing to engage in conversations open to all.

Oral tradition or history may be classified either as tribal, village, or family history. This research focused primarily on the latter two. Oral history poses a host of problems. Some of the major ones are time depth and falsification of information. Time depth means that since time is not mathematically recorded but based on ecology, the further back the historical event is, the more difficult it becomes to validate the accuracy of the testimony. Falsification of information can be minimized by enlarging the sample size. I was able to minimize falsification by making the discussion open to everyone. The authenticity of the information is enhanced if the researcher speaks the language of the original sources.[6] Moreover, one should have a good understanding of the sociocultural context one seeks to explore, and one should avoid adopting a "detective" attitude.

In gathering data for this study, I was able to use five principal sources:

1. *Colonial reports.* These are divided into two categories: published and unpublished documents. The former include the annual Colonial Reports of Somaliland Protectorate from 1901 to 1959 (interrupted during World War II). Most of these and other published literature, including

newspapers, were available in libraries and centers in England: the British library, the Commonwealth and Foreign Office Library, the London School of Economics Library, and Rhodes' House Library in Oxford. Almost all the unpublished reports and notes (usually in the form of correspondence from the Colonial Office or the Foreign Office to the protectorate government, and vice versa) are housed in the Public Record Office at Kew Gardens in London.

2. *Somali state publications.* These are scattered in the documentation centers of various ministries—Planning, Local Government and Rural Development, Agriculture, Education, Livestock, Somali Central Bank, and the Somali Institute of Development Administration—all of them in Mogadishu.

3. *United Nations publications.* These documents are housed in the libraries of the Food and Agriculture Organization, the U.N. Development Program, and the U.N. Children's Education Fund, all in Mogadishu.

4. *Unprinted material.* These include a variety of sources. One of the chief sources of information were discussions I had with peasants and rural elders. Here I made extensive use of oral history methods. I conversed with (and in some cases taped) state officials, such as district commissioners, local government executives, and members of the Somali Socialist Revolutionary Party. I participated in such official state functions as a rural "development" campaign, the fourteenth anniversary of the "revolution," receptions, and conferences. I recorded most of the information from such events in a diary after leaving the event.

5. *Interviews.* I interviewed a sample of peasant households in the farming settlements around the town of Gabileh (Gabileh District). The sample of peasants interviewed was not, statistically speaking, randomly selected. Rather, I interviewed all those peasants in the settlement who volunteered to participate. The seven settlements under study were, conversely, randomly selected from thirty-four settlements around the town of Gabileh. Gabileh District was chosen as the focus of this part of the study because of its unique mix of pastoral and peasant population.

There are two aspects of this study reflected in the major divisions of the book. After an introduction, chapters 2 and 3 explore historically the precolonial pastoral political economy, the arrival and establishment of the colonial state, the articulation of the pastoral economy to the regional mercantile system, and the impact of this linkage between the pastoral society and the colonial state (late 1880s–1960). Chapters 4 and 5 examine the postcolonial state development strategy, its impact on pastoral and peasant production, and finally, its impact on rural underdevelopment

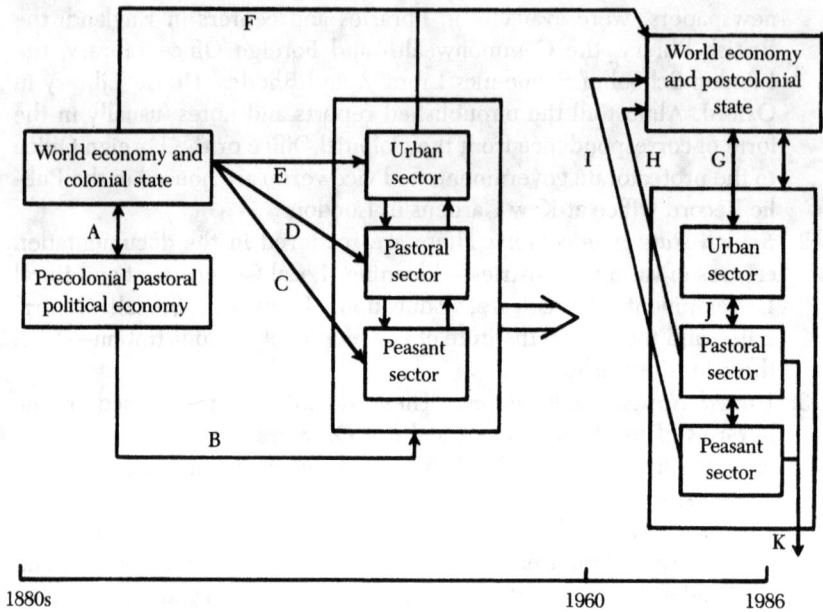

Figure 1. Schematic Diagram of the Study

Legend:
   A. The interaction between the incoming colonial state and the precolonial pastoral political economy
   B. The development of the colonial economy
   C. The emergence of the peasant economy and colonial state policy on pastoral production
   D. The colonial state, the market, and pastoralism
   E. The development of the urban sector
   F. The route to independence
   G. The role of the urban sector in postcolonial policy formulation
   H. The postcolonial state and the pastoralists
   I. The postcolonial state and the peasantry
   J. The merchant-pastoral relationship
   K. The crisis of peasant and pastoral production as a product of the development of a disarticulated capitalist economy
   [ABCDEF] The colonial era, 1880s–1960
   [GHIJK] The independence era, 1960–present

and poverty (1960–84). The processes outlined above are schematically depicted in Figure 1. The solid lines bearing letters indicate the historical factors and junctures that are central to this research.

Chapter 1 maps the core relationships in the rural development process, using theoretical advances in African and Third World studies. The remaining five chapters of the book are more Somali specific, although the analysis is informed by the conceptual tools explicated in Chapter 1. In a long historical sweep, Chapter 2 brings us to the late 1930s. This chapter lays bare, historically and theoretically, (*a*) the impact of the articulation of the precolonial pastoral political economy to the regional mercantile system (e.g., the development of the peasant sector); and (*b*) the political economy of colonization: what forms early colonial state rule took, what the reaction of the precolonial social structure was to colonialism, and how this reaction conditioned further state intervention into the pastoral society. Chapter 3 registers the development of the colonial economy between the late 1930s and the end of the colonial era (1960). More specifically, it delineates (*a*) the impact of World War II on the colonial state, the colonial society, and the relationships between the state and society; and (*b*) the emergence of an urban economy and its rural base. This chapter contrasts the socio-economic condition of the rural sector at the time of independence to its condition during the stateless era.

Chapter 4 is a study of the interaction between the postcolonial state, dominated by the petite bourgeoisie, and pastoral and peasant producers, and rural producers' continued incorporation into the commodity economy (1960–69).

Chapter 5 examines the agrarian development strategy of the military regime and suggests that it has contributed to the underdevelopment and marginalization of the agrarian sector. Further, the chapter evaluates the responses of the peasants of the northwest region to the deteriorating condition of rural production. Chapter 6 concludes the study by attempting to assess what all this means for rural development in the future.

Many institutions have contributed immensely to the writing of this book. The University of Iowa and the University of California provided me with stimulating intellectual environments. The Social Science Research Council in New York, The Center for International and Comparative Studies at Iowa, The Institute of International Studies, and the Graduate College at the University of California supported me financially during the life of this project. My thanks go to the working people of the states of Wisconsin, Iowa, and California, whose resources support their respective public universities where I did all my postsecondary education.

I have immeasurably benefited from the intellectual and material generosity of many people in three continents, whom I cannot mention here. I am grateful to them. However, there are a handful of them whose contributions deserve a special mention. Many thanks to the peasant families in Gabileh and Borama districts, who gave me so much during the fieldwork, and also to Galbeedi, who helped me in the latter phase of the project. I am extremely grateful to the Abib family for their kindness and friendship during my many field visits to Mogadishu.

Several colleagues and friends read some or all the chapters in various stages of development. Their criticism significantly helped me rethink some of the issues even though I did not accept all of their suggestions. I would like to thank my colleagues Dave Reynolds, Rebecca Roberts, and Carol Parsons, and my friends Mike Halderman, James Lafky, Charles Geshekter, Micky Lauria, and Caroline Tauxe. Special thanks to Elias Mandala and Lee Cassanelli for reading the entire manuscript and offering valuable suggestions, and to Gail Hollander for proofreading the manuscript. The constant and constructive critique of my brother, Ahmed, significantly sharpened my analysis both in this book and elsewhere. Over the years, I gained enormously from my intellectual association with Mike Watts, without whose encouragement and support this book, as it is, would not have seen the light of day. I also benefited from the generous and critical advice of Jack Potter and Dick Walker. I am grateful to Carol Evans, Betty Breazealle, and Sonia Sunstadt for patiently and skillfully typing and retyping the manuscript. Thanks also to Dave Bennett, Jeff Hansen, and Lance Salisbury for helping me with the graphics. I am deeply indebted to Marlene Guzman and Betsy May for their invaluable support. Finally, for their superb professional support I am grateful to Barbara Hanrahan of the University of Wisconsin Press and my copy editor, Carolyn Moser.

Lastly, this book is not the product of a research visit to the country and the region by an expatriate researcher who was unwittingly oblivious to the intricacies of local tradition. I was born in a pastoral camp in the region in the early 1950s. I learned the chemistry of pastoral and peasant culture first hand. In fact, my parents granted me a she-camel at birth— Mandeeq was its name—in keeping with pastoral tradition, so that I could start my own herd when I came of age. My parent's livelihood, like that of so many of their kinfolk, changed with the times, as a result of the transformations discussed in Chapters 2 and 3. Through these serendipitous circumstances I left pastoral life. My parents settled in the farming village of Gabileh, where I attended Koranic school. There I began the sojourn that took me to the industrial midlands of England as a migrant worker in a steel factory in Scunthorpe in the 1970s, then to La Crosse, Wisconsin, Ames, Iowa, and finally Berkeley, California, where I did my graduate work.

This biographical note is motivated by Professor Goran Hyden's recent claim to an authentic understanding of African peasant behaviour because he has internalized African culture "both through professional work and family life." As a result of this deep personal and professional experience,

Hyden asserts, his conceptualization of village culture and of the peasant's mindset—what he terms "the economy of Affection"—is a more accurate representation of African reality than Western (liberal or Marxian) analysis of the African social formation. My brother and I have argued elsewhere that Hyden's *Beyond Ujamaa* is an imaginative rehearsal of the theology of modernization.[7] In sharp contrast to Hyden, I have come to the conclusion, through close and careful study of northern Somali social formation, that the (nondeterministic) materialist method is most appropriate in explicating the labyrinth of underdevelopment in an African society like Somalia. The ultimate value of any social scientific theory is not to predict social processes, but rather to engage and explain human phenomena. One can claim the inapplicability of the materialist method to Africa on two grounds: first, that the method is bereft of the necessary conceptual tools to grasp the totality of social processes on the continent; and second, that African social processes and social relationships are qualitatively different from those of other contemporary agrarian societies in the periphery such that they are beyond the purview of *Europe and the World without History*.[8] On both accounts, I believe Professor Hyden to be mistaken.

Iowa City, Iowa
March 1988

The State and Rural Transformation in Northern Somalia, 1884–1986

1

Introduction

The independence of data from theory is always relative. . . . We always approach the world with some well-honed conceptual apparatus, the capital equipment of our intellect, and interpret the world broadly in those terms. Yet there are, fortunately, moments, events, people, and experiences that impinge upon imagination in unexpected ways, that jolt and jar received ways of thinking and doing, that demand some extra imaginative or theoretical leap to give them meaning.

David Harvey
The Urbanization of Capital

Since the late 1970s, Somalia, like many other countries in Africa, has earned the unenviable image of being the home of poverty, starvation, and human debasement. Attempts to explain the Somali problem, both in the popular media and in academic discourse, have produced what amounts to a barrage of hollow pronouncements regarding the origin and nature of this human calamity. Accordingly, the causes assigned to poverty are either climatic aridity, poor resource endowment, and/or a corrupt public sector. None of these scenarios are acceptable, in the forms in which they are presented. They fall far short of providing a coherent and purposeful analysis of the genesis of the Somali predicament, analysis which would help in the formulation of more practical ways out of the paralysis. In no way am I arguing that inclement nature and corruption are not important in shaping the development process; rather, they constitute a secondary constraint to it.

The foremost purpose of this book is to *retheorize* the nature of Somali economic (under)development, locate the social forces that form the principal constraints to development, and consequently assess the prospects for the future. A reformulation that goes beyond the currently dominant methodological framework is essential, as political economist Samir Amin argued more than a decade ago in his analysis of modern migration in West Africa, in order to bring research questions in consonance with social reality.

3

The rewriting of Somali social history, historical geography, and political economy is just under way.[1] The first task in this effort is to deconstruct the ghettoization of Somali studies as a backwater area in African studies. In spite of the revolutionary theoretical advances in the latter field in the last twenty years, which was stimulated by the crisis of peripheral capitalist development in the continent, Somali studies seem marooned to the earlier phases of modernization theory. The previous infertile analyses of Somali social life and their redeployment as in the recent work by Laitin and S. S. Samatar are not capable of producing sharp insights into the deepening crisis of the Somali postcolonial state, material life, and ecosystem.[2] It is therefore high time that the theoretical and methodological innovation in the study of African underdevelopment penetrate and inform the Somali condition. This is not a call for an indiscriminate application of theories and concepts developed elsewhere but for their selective and critical utilization to unravel the essence of the Somali predicament.

Social relations in agriculture is a central concept in understanding the contours of agrarian change. It captures the character of relations between state and rural producers, which I contend, is an appropriate point of departure in studying development or underdevelopment. By starting here, one inherently focuses attention on the motor of development, that is, surplus extraction and its redeployment in order to expand society's productive capacity. The extraction of resources from rural producers by the state and other dominant classes is as old as class society. Yet Somali scholarship is notable for its silence on this matter. By contrast, the centrality of state-peasant relations in the process of rural development and agrarian change is the principal axis of current theoretical discussion in Africa. There are two dimensions to this debate.[3]

1. The neoclassical-liberal position, as reflected in the works of Bates, Lofchie and Commins, and Hart, argues that African states are committed to the modernization of their societies through import-substitution industrialization.[4] The state extracts, by market and nonmarket means such as cheap food prices, the necessary "surplus" from the rural sector. These policies undermine the rural sector's capacity to grow. According to this paradigm the state, ideally, has no identifiable *class* interest,[5] except the general public interest. The conflicts between different fragments of the peasantry (rich, middle, and poor) are considered immaterial.
2. The Marxian paradigm contends that the state must be grounded in the processes of capital accumulation and of class antagonism.[6] Marxists argue that state intervention in the rural economy has a differential impact and therefore contributes to the differentiation of rural society

into antagonistic classes. Furthermore, they insist that the *nature* of rural poverty can be understood only by scrutinizing the role that underclasses serve in the contradictory process of capital accumulation. It is the struggle between the state and the exploitative classes on the one hand, and rural producers on the other, that merits special attention if one is to clearly grasp the origins and the metamorphosis of rural poverty.

This research exposes the forms and the impact of colonial and postcolonial state interventions in the rural society of northern Somalia, and northwest Somalia in particular, in the light of the above theoretical introduction. There is no published work examining the role of the state in agrarian change and (under)development in Somalia. Most publications on Somalia do not critically examine state-peasant/pastoral relations.[7] I. M. Lewis, the leading Somalist, pays no attention to the importance of the colonial state to the transformation of precapitalist Somali pastoralism.[8]

The following three issues, overlooked in past studies, constitute the core of this investigation:

1. The nature of precolonial society and economy, and the organization of production and distribution on the eve of colonial conquest.
2. The foundations of the colonial and postcolonial states, including the growth of the colonial economy, the forms of state intervention in the rural economy, and the consequences of such intervention.
3. Finally, given the constitution of the colonial Somali economy at the time of independence, the social class(es) that inherited the state (1960–85) and the consequences of their development strategy to the peasants and pastoralists who account for the overwhelming majority of the Somali population.

The aforementioned issues constitute the fundamental process wherein precapitalist northern Somali society was *articulated* into the world capitalist system. Articulation is a contradictory and eventful process which straps together various social actors such as the state, capital, and precapitalist society during pivotal transitions. Somalist scholarship is bereft of the conceptual and theoretical tools necessary to study the articulation-transformation thesis. Because of the dearth of such tools I devote the next few pages to a review of the current theoretical debate regarding the state and the agrarian question in Africa. Some traditional scholars may question the relevance of this debate to the unique northern Somali case. The rationale behind this review is not to mechanically impose an alien theory on Somalia data but to underscore the fact that the relationships conceptualized in the African debate are the issues which demand immediate attention in Somalia.

State and Rural Development: Theoretical Thrust

A plethora of explanations have emerged to explain the malaise that characterizes African underdevelopment and its root causes. In recent years, however, liberal neoclassicalism and Marxism have become the main theoretical poles of research on the African agrarian crisis.[9]

Liberal Neoclassicalism

In spite of its appeal to the majority of Western researchers and development experts, the liberal neoclassical model is inherently incapable of conceptualizing a coherent development program. This limitation is systemic.[10] Well-meaning liberal writers on African and Third World underdevelopment often conclude their studies with a list of policy recommendations.[11] Such well-intentioned suggestions rarely become the core objectives of the central social actor in the development process, the state, beyond the public relations realm. The glaring incongruence between development rhetoric and the reality of state action reflects untenable liberal assumptions about the nature of the state and the development process.

Bates's recent important contribution, *Markets and States in Africa,* significantly advances the explanatory power of the liberal paradigm. Focusing on the role of the state in African agricultural underdevelopment, he argues that the economic interest of the state-urban constituency is in contradiction to the development needs of the vast majority of rural producers. The accumulation requirements of industrial-urban development and the desire of the state's elite to remain in power, which are the central objectives of African governments, demand surplus extraction from rural producers. These twin purposes determine both agrarian policies and the (il)logic of state intervention in the rural sector. The accumulation needs of the urban-industrial complex necessitate lower costs of production inputs such as labor, raw materials, and import products. Government, industry, and business, as employers and sponsors of industry, jointly shape development policy. The domination of development policies by these classes has the effect of reducing the cost of wage labor and raw-material inputs by suppressing the prices paid to producers of food and other rural products. In essence, Bates argues that the commitment of African governments to industrialization requires resource transfer from producers. Such policies consequently deprive peasants of the necessary material incentives to increase agricultural production and productivity.

Other variants of the same general philosophical camp contend vehemently that it is the peasants' incapacity and unwillingness to participate in the market economy that is impeding rural progress. In a powerful re-introduction of modernization theory, Hyden argues that such "reactionary" market-averse characteristics are endemic to the peasant mode of production (the so-called economy of affection).[12] He suggests that the peasant-based economy of affection (read "tradition") must be destroyed (captured) if Africa is to achieve economic and social progress. Hart reiterates this position by contending that a weak decentralized state and technological backwardness is at the heart of the production problem.[13] Furthermore, this technological inertia exists because capitalism has yet to penetrate the agrarian sector. Hart is absolutely clear about the consequences of industrial capitalist penetration of West African agriculture: the dispossession of the majority of the peasantry. Unlike Hart, Bates and Hyden are conspicuously silent on the shape of the social terrain that would result from capitalist development in the countryside. The logical conclusion of Hart's and Hyden's arguments comes around full circle to Bates's position, in that state policies (or the lack thereof) are seen as the culprit.

The dichotomization of society into state, industry, business, and workers on the one hand, and rural people on the other (Liptonian Urban bias—what Henry Bernstein calls neoclassical populism), is obviously conflict-ridden, even in the liberal paradigm. The former group constitutes a class alliance against the latter. To ward off the social and political confrontation that is inherent in this context, the state uses resources at its disposal (both the carrot and the stick), first by "buying" allies in the rural areas (recipients of subsidized modern agricultural inputs), second by providing minor subsidies to various groups, and finally by resorting to sheer coercion. It is this urban-industrial bias of state policy that is seen as the root cause of the African crisis. To alleviate rural poverty and underdevelopment, the liberal paradigm contends, the political-economic relations in African societies must change to allow the vast majority of the dispossessed peasants to overcome the destitution that has heretofore been their fate.[14] In other words, the dominant social classes are asked to give up some important portions of their privileges; Hyden is an exception in this regard. The more conservative Berg Report arrives at a similar conclusion. That is, it urges African states to free the market and to concentrate on "small" farmers, although it also reserves a fundamental role for large-scale farming.[15]

Apart from being ahistorical, these discussions of the African rural condition are at best baptismal. There are two main shortcomings of this particular version of the neoclassical view. First, it presumes the "good will" of African governments or states and consequently their responsiveness to political pressure.[16] That this is a mistaken conception of the essence of the postcolonial state is clear to any serious student of African development. Moreover, the social basis of the state class and its historical roots belie such belief: "Opposition to colonialism was based on an imperfect alliance of three major interest groups of farmers, traders and wage-earners, all of whom shared a degree of commitment to the exchange economy which distinguished them from the bulk of the population. Political leaders were drawn from the higher, more affluent echelons of these groups. . . . This explains why nationalism lacked a sharp break with the past." [17]

This assumption explains the tension present in Bates's analysis. In other words, it is a reminder of his underlying pluralist conception of the state. Second, the belief implicit in neoclassical analysis—that is, the uncontradictory nature of capitalist development and class formation in the countryside—is not credible and crumbles under rigorous analytical scrutiny. [18] Moreover, the assumption that all urban workers are part of the exploitative alliance against rural producers is untenable. [19]

The making of African political economy cannot be understood without recognizing its role in, and relations to, the development of the world capitalist system. I will argue that it is in fact the world system which has strongly conditioned the nature and the dynamics of African peripheral capitalist economies and the relationship between the so-called urban-industrial interest and the "tradition"-dominated peasantry. The superimposition of capitalism over precapitalist society, using all the might of the colonial state, gave birth to an incoherent economy that denied Third World societies the development of what Samir Amin called autocentric capitalist development. The reproduction of peripheral capitalism and its social relations perpetuates underdevelopment. The liberal paradigm seems content with reforms of the peripheral capitalist economy. However, such reforms fall far short of the necessary transformation that will progressively liberate the peasantry and other producers from their subordinate status.

Marxism and African Development

Materialist discourse provides a sharper analysis of the roots of current crisis by tracing the evolution of colonial and neocolonial development strategies since the rise of colonial capitalism. It also specifies the roles played by different and often antagonistic social classes created and reproduced in the process and therefore avoids rhetorical policy recommendations, since the dominant social forces champion concerns other than those of most rural producers.

One's analysis must proceed *historically,* in order to comprehend the essence and the growth of contemporary rural underdevelopment in Africa. The logical first step in such an analysis is the study of the social structures and organizations of precolonial, precapitalist societies, for the constitution of such societies influenced the course of their transition to colonial-capitalism. Second, one must uncover the nature of the confrontation and interaction between these precapitalist social formations and imperial and colonial capitalism. Third, one must consider the explicit and implicit role of the colonial state in the process. Watts takes up the transformation issue using an historical and dialectical framework.[20] He demonstrates how the colonial capitalist state confronted, captured, and restructured the precolonial state system in northern Nigeria. Of course, the colonial state did not have a free hand in the process. It had to play a dialectical role in the restructuring process.[21] The colonial exercise was set on transforming the economic orientation of these societies so that they would yield "surplus" to the dominant capitalist structure, in the form of labor or other commodities. Such restructuring of the economic organization, and consequent surplus extraction, was problematic. On the one hand, capital, either merchant or industrial, was interested in maximizing these extractions, and this involved destroying the socio-economic logic of the captured society. On the other hand, these precapitalist Africans did not simply submit to this violence but responded vigorously against it. In some instances, as in British Somaliland (Chapter 2), the resistance was vigorous enough to derail the agenda of the state.

It was the tension between the two imperatives which defined the role of the colonial state. It had a contradictory role to play. First of all, it had to guarantee the establishment and perpetuation of an exploitative social setting. Secondly, it had to maintain social order and peace. Such order could be attained through the continuous use of coercion, but since that was too costly, the colonial state had to restrain some of what it considered the excesses of capital. For example, in British Somaliland, the Colonial Office curbed the zeal of some of its agents in the field and unwillingly absorbed tremendous costs in the process. Such constraints on capital and the colonial field staff were vital in order to maintain its image of "impartiality" before the African masses. Caught in this contradictory bind, the state had to muddle through. The manifestation of such a "neutral" facade should not be misinterpreted to mean a genuinely neutral stance by the colonial state. The role of the state in the creation and the dominance of a colonial social system whereby (metropolitan) capital could dominate African producers was unquestionable.

The logic of the subsistence economy was disarticulated once colonialism prevailed and commodity production penetrated precapitalist production. There were instances of precapitalist resistance to commodity production. However, through taxes and land and labor laws, significant segments of these societies were commoditized. Where land and other means of production could not be appropriated, commodity production, such as the production of cotton, was often forcefully introduced.[22] Such penetration may not have been pervasive, and some have suggested that Africa's rural sector was only marginally affected by colonial and commodity penetration. Bernstein underlines how futile such analysis is if it implies that the African peasantry were not qualitatively reformed by colonialism:

Once commodity relations are incorporated in the reproduction cycle of the peasant household as an economic necessity, the question of how much of its resources, in terms of labor-time or of land, are devoted to the production of use values and of commodities is secondary, though still important. . . . Simple quantitative measures which might show, say, that only 20 percent of labor time . . . is devoted to commodity production, are misleading if they imply that the household is still basically a subsistence unit, and for this reason is only marginally involved with commodity relations and can, therefore, easily withdraw from them.[23]

Mamdani's recent research in northern Uganda corroborates Bernstein's work.[24] The Somali case, examined in the next five chapters, is a most vivid manifestation of the claim that commoditization is fundamentally a qualitative process.

The simultaneity of the processes of articulation and commoditization refutes the dual-economy notion of mechanical coexistence between different modes of production. In the course of these processes the "subsistence" logic of the precapitalist society was profoundly altered: "In short, the social nature of the subsistence system and the qualities of the moral economy were severely ruptured. Reciprocity and solidarity and hence the nature of inequality itself had changed."[25]

The encapsulation of the precolonial society by the capitalist-colonial system undermined its capacity to reproduce itself. This subjugation of the precapitalist society was a major milestone in the creation of the present conditions of the peasantry and the particular forms of rural underdevelopment. Furthermore, the growing demands of colonial capital and state gradually "squeezed" and undermined the means through which the peasantry reproduced itself. These demands were met either through direct or indirect state and capital intervention in the production process.[26]

The institutions and the policies of the (colonial) state are central to understanding the evolution and the nature of rural underdevelopment. What is both implicit and explicit in the above analysis is that the destitution of tropical Africa is not because of its "traditional" nature. In fact, some go so far as to argue that the colonial state was the real culprit.[27] Meillassoux goes still further and suggests that the demands of the world capitalist system were assuaged by the extraction of resources (i.e., labor) from the precapitalist community, and that continued exploitation of the community depends very much on *constricting* the pace of imminent dissolution of the precapitalist community which buttressed this exploitation.[28] The extraction of the community's resources, the continual growth of population, and hence the stagnating productive capacity of the community reveal the historically specific nature of contemporary rural underdevelopment. Two issues are left out of this discourse: (*a*) It does not explain how far this "conservation-dissolution" process can last before the bottom falls out from the remnants of the precapitalist social formation; and (*b*) the discussion assumes that the precapitalist community was passive while it was being distorted and dismantled by colonial capitalism.[29]

My own analysis of Somaliland demonstrates how much the colonial state had to accommodate the precapitalist order in the face of stiff resistance. Marx and Lenin suggest that the precapitalist modes do influence the speed with which capitalism can penetrate and the forms the new order takes, but warn that there can be no specific and predictable path or schedule.[30] The Somali pastoral case (Chapters 2 and 3) clearly supports this position.

This theoretical conceptualization of colonial and precolonial Africa illuminates the issues much more clearly than neoclassical development theory or its derivatives. Moreover, the materialist approach illustrates the partiality of the state rather than its plurality. Although there is a vigorous debate among materialist analysts on the exact specificity of the capitalist state, there is no question as to the class nature of the state.[31] Hence, the state is not readily subject to popular pressure and therefore will not significantly and *voluntarily* change the socio-economic equation.

Colonial capitalism was predicated on the development of commodity-producing economies. What form(s), then, does capitalist development take in the countryside, what influences do precapitalist forms have on such development trajectories, and what roles does the state play in this process? Borrowing partially from Lenin, DeJanvry's work in Latin America is most insightful.[32] The development of commodity relations in the rural areas takes three main forms depending on the character and composition of capital and the social practices in the precapitalist society:

1. The Junker Road. In this course of capitalist development, feudal peasants are transformed into rural semiproletariat while the feudal lords become capitalist farmers.
2. The Farmer Road. This is the so-called American or petite bourgeoisie road. Farmers or free peasants are created either by violent elimination of the feudal landowning class through revolution or land reform, or through the colonization and homesteading of new lands.
3. The Merchant Road, or the Gentleman-Telephone Farmer Road, as it is known in Kenya. Here urban merchant capital invades the rural sec-

Precapitalist social classes	Transitional classes	Classes under capitalist agriculture

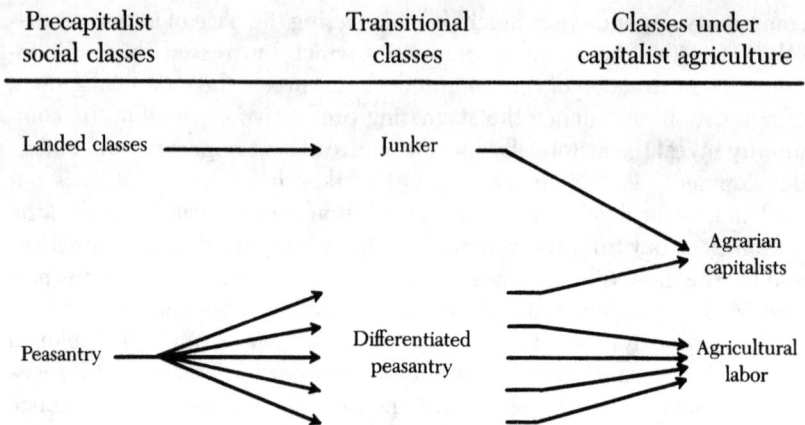

Figure 2. Lenin's Model of Capitalist Development in Agriculture

tor. Historically, the merchant road is not as progressive in terms of widening and deepening the domestic market and consequently improving the means of production on a wide scale, as my discussion of the Somali pastoral sector will demonstrate.

As commodity production becomes more generalized in the countryside, rural producers differentiate into laborers and capitalist farmers, in both the merchant and the farmer roads (see Fig. 2).[33] Lenin notes that the rural proletariat at certain stages and in certain forms of capitalist development in agriculture could still possess small plots of land. However, such plot ownership will not stymie the trend toward capitalist agriculture in the long run.

The commoditization of agricultural production and the resulting class differentiation noted in the preceding discussion has been the "classic" course of capitalist development in the countryside. Of course, this does not mean that commoditization inherently takes *linear* forms under all circumstances (as some crude interpretations of Lenin's analysis suggest), given the conditioning effect of contrasting precapitalist societies. As the penetrating writings of Kitching, Bernstein, and Gibbon and Neocosmos bring to sharp focus, commodity development in the countryside can take a variety of forms and need not, in the short run, lead to the classic differentiation. Petty-commodity production (peasant or otherwise) need not vanish from the social terrain even under conditions of generalized commodity development. Capital continuously creates "spaces" for petty commodity: "The classic statement of capitalist development itself maintains that *certain forms of capitalism* actually produce petty commodity production while others destroy it. . . . Lenin also saw petty commodity production as a permanent feature of capitalism which was reproduced even at its highest stage of development."[34]

The contingent nature of the process of social differentiation is, at least in the short run, largely a product of social struggles in which real people— in our case, peasants and pastoralists—scramble to ward off their dispossession despite their membership in the market economy. The outcome of these struggles is not easily predictable, particularly since they need not be open and violent, as James Scott has lucidly demonstrated in his latest work.[35] Where such struggles are sufficiently strong and endanger the social system, capital and the state may accommodate and hence create "spaces." The emergence of contract farming in many Third World regions is a notable demonstration of such strategy. This in no way implies that such "spaces" are free from contradictions and are therefore stable.

The profile of agrarian transformation is unmistakably shaped by the development agenda of the state. In fact, some scholars allude to state-induced transitions.[36] The form of state intervention in the process of agrarian transformation very much depends upon the morphology of the dominant classes who are in command of the state apparatus in any specific historical juncture and the requirements of the capital accumulation process.[37] In the junker road model, for instance, the landlord class remains dominant at the state level but is transformed over time into capitalist farmers, whereas the tide of history turns against landlords in the American road. This elucidates the fact that in the cases where the landowning classes remain dominant but appear in "modern dress," the state cannot be expected to introduce structural changes that will subvert its material base. This would in effect amount to self-destruction. The instances where land reform has been implemented in order to restructure the rural economic and social landscape demonstrate the irreconcilable conflict between a "nascent" urban-bourgeoisie (or a coalition between the bourgeoisie and workers) whose interest is served by land reform and the agrarian oligarchy. State intervention in this case is premised on the creation of a rural economy dominated by nonoligarchic producers. In colonial societies, as I noted earlier and as I will empirically show in the coming chapters, the colonial state intervened on behalf of metropolitan capital, while the postcolonial state does not act at the behest of peasants and other rural producers (see Chapters 2–5).

The above discussion of the agrarian question is not meant, of course, to suggest that the contours of Somali transition from precapitalism to peripheral capitalism can be read simply from the pages of this debate. On the contrary. I do recognize the uniqueness of the Somali historical context, yet I am convinced that conventional scholarship has failed to grasp qualitative changes in Somali social structure owing to the limitations of its theoretical tools. The materialist discourse on agrarian transition yields five analytical concepts capable of capturing the comprehensive nature of the transition and the process of underdevelopment: precapitalism, articulation, colonial capitalism, social classes, social relations, and the state. These concepts—the core of current analysis of the African development crisis—are virtually missing from the annals of Somali scholarship. This is so despite the fact that Somalia has been in the midst of crisis (in the full sense of the word).[38]

A final word about my interpretation of the term *underdevelopment* is in order. Underdevelopment need not be only an all-impoverishing process. Rather, it entails gross and uneven distribution of productive and consumption resources. In essence, underdevelopment is a relationship of inequality. It is one such relationship—between the (colonial) state, rural producers, and the world capitalist system—which I seek to unravel.

Somalia: Geographical and Historical Context

The Land and Its Resources

The northern portion of Somalia (former British Somaliland) lies in the area known as the Horn of Africa. This region lies between 42°35' and 49° east longitude, and between 8° and 11°27' north latitude. Northern Somalia, or just the north (as the region will be designated), consists of three main topographic zones (Map 1).[39] These zones are the coastal plain, the coastal range, and the plateau, known in Somali as the Guban, the Ogo, and the Haud.

The Guban is a region of high temperatures and low rainfall (the word *Guban* means "charred" in Somali). Summer temperatures in the region easily average over 100°F. Summer rains are scanty; the only precipitation of any significance occurs in winter, when the rest of the country is suffering from seasonal drought. Temperatures are relatively moderate in winter, and it is during this season that both humans and livestock are concentrated in the zone. Despite the scant rainfall, there is fairly abundant underground water a few feet below the bed of the intermittent rivers.

The Ogo is a high plateau to the immediate south of the Guban. Its elevation ranges between 6,000 feet in the north to 3,000 feet in the south. Rainfall is heavier than in the Guban, although it varies tremendously within the zone. Underground water is much harder to find here, and wells have to be sunk to much greater depth. Such wells are used for domestic purposes by the people who inhabit the Ogo. During years of normal precipitation, these wells provide sufficient water for both human and animal needs during the long winter.

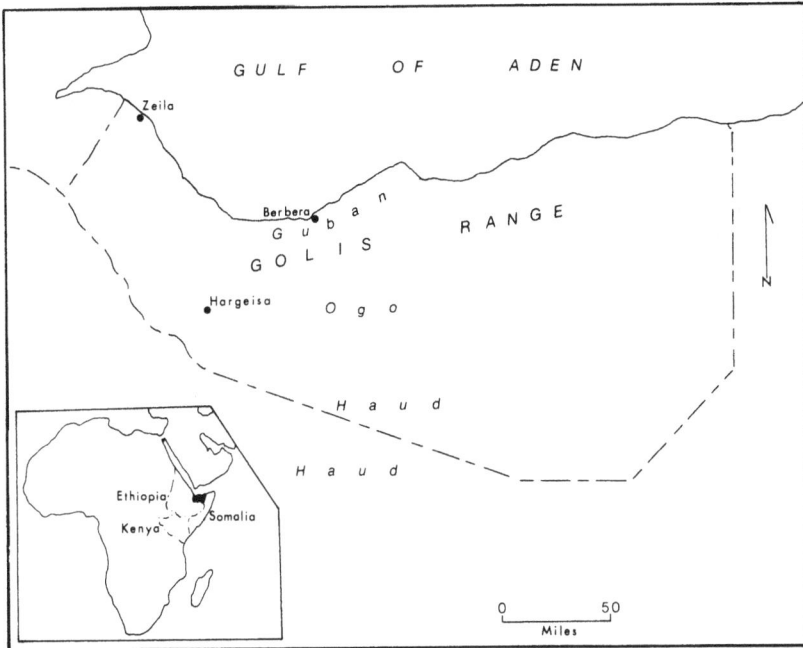

Map 1. Topographic Features of Northern Somalia

The last region is the Haud, which lies to the south of the Ogo. Here rainfall is meager, and underground water is nearly unavailable except at extreme depths. During rainy years grazing is excellent, and in spite of the usual scarcity of water, this zone is the most important grazing region. It is generally well populated during the wet season, when surface water is available.

Climatologically, Somalia is semiarid. Somalis recognize four seasons in the year, defined by rainfall patterns.[40] These are called JiLaal, Gu, Hagaa, and Der. Gu and Hagaa are the summer seasons, and JiLaal and Der, the winter. Climatological records are poor or nonexistent; from the little that is known, the amount of rainfall in any given year varies from a few inches along the coast to as much as over 25 inches in a few places in the Ogo and Golis range. Most of the region receives between 5 and 15 inches of rainfall annually. The summer rains fall between April and September. Gu, which is the first part of the summer (late March, April, and May), witnesses the heaviest rainfall in the Ogo and the Haud. This is the season of fresh grazing and abundant surface water. It is also the breeding season for livestock. Winter (JiLaal and Der) is the season of dearth and thirst. The onset of the dry season starts in October and lasts until the end of March or early April. The Ogo and the Haud receive virtually no rainfall in winter; the Der rains fall in the coastal zone between January and March.

The vegetation cover, broadly speaking, follows the same pattern as the rainfall. The Guban is covered by poor scrub, and only during unusually heavy Der rains does it provide sufficient grazing. The Ogo is mostly covered by various species of acacia and savana grasses. The Haud supports primarily savana grasses with a few acacia thickets.

The climatic and topographic zones complement each other. When rainfall and water are scarce in the higher elevation, the Der rains fall in the coast. Conversely, when the coastal zone is devoid of grazing and the temperatures soar above 100°F, the higher elevations are relatively cool and well watered. It must also be noted that there are no permanent lakes or rivers in northern Somaliland, and rainfall largely determines conditions on the ground. Most of the region receives far less than 20 inches of annual precipitation.

As is the case in many semiarid regions in tropical Africa, rainfall in northern Somalia is not only meager, but also highly cyclical and unreliable. Consequently, recurring droughts are a salient characteristic of the country.[41] Another climatic feature worth noting is the variability of rainfall within a short distance. For instance, in certain years one may witness contrasting conditions of drought-stricken and lush growth within a small area.

Historical Overview

The Somali society that developed in response to these arid conditions was fundamentally pastoral and dependent on the products of its own pastoral economy. Products necessary for consumption which could not be procured locally were obtained through simple trade (barter). This trade was an essential but not a dominant factor in the precolonial pastoral economy.[42] The household was the basic unit of herd ownership. Conversely, the grazing lands and water resources were collectively utilized by the members of the clan. Although the clan (and clan elders) was a very important social unit, it nevertheless had very little economic control over the household, at least in normal times. Some of the social functions of the clan through the clan elders were to (*a*) mediate petty conflicts within the clan, and between its members and those of other clans; (*b*) serve as a forum and an "organization" through which the exploitation of nature by its members was managed—that is, exploring new grazing areas and/or designating range areas and prohibiting grazing during particular seasons (*xidmo*); and (*c*) mitigate the effects of natural and personal tragedies. These functions notwithstanding, the clan had no standing committee or organizational structure, and all members were engaged in subsistence production. The clan forum was open to all mature males. Although there were variations in the size of herds between households, nevertheless this was an ahierarchical society: there was no resource extraction through involuntary means by nonproducers from producers. This should not be misconstrued to mean that economic exploitation was absent among the producers, that is, within the household. There is very little data to warrant discussion of this matter. In short, this was a stateless society.

This description of the precapitalist pastoral societies should not be seen as a romanticization of the virtues of the past; rather, it should be seen as a way of providing a historical benchmark. Generally speaking, this was the society which British colonialism confronted and captured.

The British occupation of Aden in 1839 brought an expanding world capitalist economy to the doorsteps of this pastoral society. After the opening of the Suez Canal, the British moved to the Somali coast. The conquest was aimed at satisfying two needs. First, the strategic location of the Somali coast was deemed necessary to the British possessions in the East,[43] and second, there was the need to secure full supplies for the British garrison in Aden.[44] In fact, Berbera, the Somali port, supplied all the animals consumed by the garrison in the late 1860s. Although the absolute number of animals involved in this trade was large compared to the animal trade prior to that date, it was not significantly large enough to immediately and seriously affect the subsistence base of the pastoralist. What this trade did, however, was to lay, intensify, and expand the commercial organizational infrastructure into many corners of the country that were originally beyond the reach of such trade. It was primarily through this trade that the precolonial pastoral society was articulated to the regional mercantile system. This growth was interrupted by the twenty-year war of resistance (1898–1920) against the British. At one point the British government had to abandon the entire territory except the port of Berbera to Sayyid Mohamed and his Dervishes. Livestock trade did not become a central factor in the pastoral economy until the late 1930s.[45]

The commoditization of livestock and the imposition of colonial rule had three major consequences for the pastoral economy and society. In the first place, the development of the colonial economy gradually began to erode precolonial methods of mitigating natural calamities, as the new economy nurtured the emergence of elite livestock traders.[46] Second, because of the provision of veterinary services and water reservoirs,[47] livestock population increased. From the early 1930s on, the colonial state expressed concern that such growth was having a detrimental impact on the range. The lack of simultaneous improvement of land and labor productivity compounded the pressure on the environment. This enhanced the susceptibility of the pastoral society to drought and hence famines.

Somali Women in Traditional Pastoral Attire Celebrating International Women's Day

Thus the very "progress" of commercialization—increased herds, new commodities for consumption, access to urban areas, possible accumulation of money wealth or stock capital, and destruction and restructuring of precapitalist ideology—may have begun incurring its own penalty on the pastoral society.

Third, the increased livestock trade also brought the emergence of markets and villages throughout the region. The best example of such a marketing town is Hargeisa, the second largest city in the country today. The elite traders, their agents, the entourage of the colonial state, and spillover population from the countryside reside in these towns and villages. Until very recently, the urban population was very small, and many urban dwellers depended on the countryside for their living. (Lewis's groundbreaking research in *A Pastoral Democracy* clearly shows this linkage.) All parts of British Somaliland bore these consequences, but with different intensities.

Among the changes resulting from the social restructuring was a major transformation in the pastoral economy of the northwest region of Somaliland Protectorate around the turn of the century. Some of the pastoralists in this region turned to cultivation to supplement their subsistence, and over the years some of them came to depend on farming as their main occupation. Lewis suggests that this transformation was a product of the transfer of agricultural technology from the neighboring Oromo.[48] This is a simplistic explanation, however, because technological change must be situated in the political economy of the colonial pastoral economy. One must seek to locate the contradictions that gave life to this shift, particularly since the Oromo and the Somalis had long coexisted and known of each others' subsistence means. Writing on a different region, Lewis revised his earlier interpretation of such a transformation: "Some nomadic pastoralists have adopted cultivation because population pressure thrust them into areas where this was a sensible adaptation to better soil conditions, and rinderpest and other cattle scourges have often reinforced switches of emphasis away from pastoralism towards cultivation."[49]

Although this revisionist explanation goes a little further in situating the social and ecological context of change, one must yet ask, Why did the pastoralists in northwest Somalia shift at this point, particularly since these scourges have ravaged them many times earlier? Was it the intensity of these scourges and the consequent devastation after the turn of the century that finally tilted the balance? I hypothesize that three factors played a significant role in this change:

1. The herds of the pastoralists were decimated by rinderpest in the years around 1900.[50] The droughts of the first decade of the present century also did their share of damage.
2. The development of markets and villages and the gradual extension of merchant capital as a result of livestock trade and the war of resistance (1900–1920) created "opportunities" that did not exist before. Although little is known about the barter terms of trade, Lewis suggests that the dislocation caused by the war created a local market for locally grown grain (cheaper than imports).
3. The raids of the Ethiopian army on western Somaliland and the subsequent closure of parts of the pastoralists' traditional grazing lands, due to the demarcation of the Ethiopian–British Somaliland border, partially affected their free movement.

These three factors, I suggest, may have had the combined effect of making sedentary cultivation more attractive than pure pastoralism.[51] Clans in the northeast did not have this option, since the climate of most parts of the protectorate was not suitable for cultivation.

Although livestock trade had become a very crucial part of the national economy, there is very little detailed data on the degree of pastoral differentiation that has occurred since this trade became important in the 1950s.[52] At any rate, Lewis, who is the main authority on Somali pastoralism, contends that these pastoralists are "thick-skinned capitalists."[53] However one defines capitalists, what is of interest here is what became of the pastoralist "capitalists" turned peasants. Was the social frame of reference of these "capitalists" carried over to their new social environment? Were these cultivator-peasants capitalists? All prelimininary indications are that this was not so. What Lewis interpreted as capitalistic character, that is risk-taking, is not necessarily a quality confined to capitalists. In fact, what distinguishes a capitalist from others is not only private ownership of the means of production, but most importantly hiring labor and appropriating the products of that labor. This the typical Somali pastoralist did not do.

Since some of the demands of the capitalist colonial economy and the colonial state were met by the partially commoditized pastoral economy, and since Somaliland had offered little prospect for commercial colonial agriculture and industry, there was little need for direct and pervasive state involvement in the domestic economy. Moreover, the contradictions between the precapitalist society and the slowly emerging commercial sector were not severe enough to necessitate intense state intervention, say, of the magnitude of neighboring Kenya. In fact, some of the state's attempts to levy direct taxes on the pastoralists were resisted and had to be abandoned. An indication of the absence of such intervention was the glaring lack of the provision of basic state infrastructure. For instance, the first secondary school was established in 1953, seven years before independence. This is an illustration of the lack of need for local state bureaucracy to run the machinery of the state. Although the protectorate had a department of agriculture, up until the late 1940s it was mainly confined to the provision of veterinary services. In short, there were no state marketing boards, and the principal method of resource extraction from the rural producers was the open market and indirect taxes on consumer products that were imported. In the cultivated region of northwest Somaliland, no kulaks or budding capitalists emerged from agriculture, contrary to what "thick-skinned capitalists" might be expected to do. For only a handful of merchants did agriculture become the "cash cow" to be milked to supplement trade. The overwhelming majority of the peasants merely subsisted. The continual use of land, mono-cropping, the lack of modern agricultural inputs, and the increase in rural population gradually but surely undercut the peasant's capacity to eke out an existence from the marginal Somali environment. The steady rise of the prices of imported necessities foreshadowed the emerging problems of the rural economy.

After the Second World War, some livestock traders and the small (native) state bureaucracy began to organize political parties influenced by movements in Italian Somaliland, but the transfer of the Haud to Ethiopia in 1953–54 gave the Somali petite bourgeoisie a cause around which rural people could mobilize.[54] When Britain departed in 1960, Somaliland had very little economic progress to show for the eighty years of colonial rule.

The governing elite, an amalgamation of the products of the colonial economy and the remnants of precapitalists, inherited an underdeveloped economy. The institutions of the state were not changed but merely embraced. Somali state policies departed from those of the colonial state in two ways:

1. The state began to intervene more vigorously in agriculture and in industry.
2. The state bureaucratic machinery was vastly expanded.

Bates's contention of heightened intensity of state intervention in the postcolonial economy is on the mark. The stagnation and decline of the productivity and production of peasant agriculture, further commercialization of pastoralism without concommitant increase in the productivity of land and labor, and the significant expansion of a nonproductive urban population continually reinforced the underdevelment of the Somali rural economy. Meanwhile a small petite bourgeoisie was engulfed in internal conflict over which "fraction" was to capture the state, the state being, or having become, the main instrument through which one could either accumulate or at least indulge in what seemed conspicuous consumption. Unlike conditions in Mali as outlined in Meillassoux, the conflict of the petite bourgeoisie in Somalia was "ethnically" and "regionally" based.[55] These conditions, among others, precipitated the military coup of October 1969.

Immediately following the coup, direct state involvement in most sectors of the economy increased. Many more state farms—the so-called Agricultural Crash Programs—were created. Increasing taxes on peasants through price manipulation became the order of the day, and state monopoly over wholesale trade, except livestock, was established. State marketing boards were either created or strengthened.[56] Although the military government professed to be socialist, the relationship between the state and pastoral-peasant society had not radically changed. In fact, the state's development programs quite clearly illustrate that little investment was *directly* allocated for the improvement of peasant farming (see Chapter 5). Furthermore, no attempt was made at any level of government to restructure or reorient pastoralism, and livestock trade never came under the state marketing monopoly, although livestock had become the main export sector. In sum, the economic development strategy of the postcolonial Somali state (1960–85) bypassed rural producers and contributed to their marginalization. This study attempts to explain why this has been the case.

2

Somali Pastoralism and the Development of the Colonial Economy, 1880–1937

The Colonial State was indeed an interventionist, although not necessarily a strong, state whose 'function' was to establish the supremacy of the capitalist mode of production.

M. Burawoy
The Politics of Production

As incorporation proceeded, new markets for . . . [livestock] emerged across [northern Somalia]. Far from signalling the articulation, through the exchange of [livestock] . . . of a capitalist sphere with a pre-capitalist domain, these developments destroyed the integrity of the pre-capitalist mode of production, inserting social and political life into an extensive web of relationships that stretched beyond the boundaries of the region to the core areas of the world economy.

W. G. Martin and M. Beittel
"The Hidden Abode of Reproduction"

Many authors have recently called attention to the critical importance of the precolonial social history of the Third World in understanding the origins and the nature of the problems of underdevelopment that bedevil these societies.[1] The purpose of this chapter is twofold: First, in spite of the dearth of historical data on Somali society, it will attempt to draw an outline of the precolonial Somali pastoral society, given what is known about similar pastoral societies elsewhere in Africa. Second, it will highlight how the precapitalist Somali society was articulated to the British Colonial empire, how the British colonial state was established in Somaliland, and what its impact on the pastoral society was (1884–1937).

Precolonial Pastoral Economy

Over the centuries, Somali society developed a pastoral economy that made good use of the region's meager natural resource base. Lewis has elucidated how well this system was developed and how the movement of herds and humans were organized, so further discussion is not necessary here.[2] Although he describes the kinds of livestock Somali pastoralists raise, and the techniques employed in this process, Lewis does not define pastoralism. Synthesizing Kroeber's and Krader's definitions, Jacobs classifies pastoralism into two types: pure pastoralism and semi-pastoralism.[3] The distinction between the two categories is the degree to which pastoral livestock directly provide the dietary needs of the pastoralists. Again, this definition describes the form of pastoral production but neglects to give these categories any theoretical (that is, historically and socially specific) content.[4] In other words, how can one distinguish between pastoralists, say, of the 1600s and those that exist today? This difference is similar to the distinction between medieval peasantry and its contemporary counterpart. One has to turn to Saul and Woods for such a distinction.[5] Saul and Woods underline the similarity of the political and economic forces that impinge on peasants and pastoralists. The examination of the development of the pastoral economy can make sense only if sufficient attention is paid to its relationship with other social entities of the larger society of which pastoralists are a part. And as such, contemporary pastoralism is subject to forces that are vastly different from those that prevailed a century ago.

The external forces that impinged on the nineteenth-century pastoral economy were the British colonial state and merchants' capital. The efficacy of the colonial state and merchants' capital in reforming the precolonial pastoral economy depended largely on two factors. First, it depended on the capacity of the colonial state and merchants' capital to intervene in the pastoral economy. Second, it was contingent upon the internal coherence or articulation of the pastoral economy and its tenacity in resisting the intrusion of merchants' capital and the colonial state.[6]

In order to understand the present conditions of the rural economy of Somalia, one must recreate the logic of the precolonial pastoral economy and then trace subsequent evolution since colonialism. This brief analysis of the precolonial pastoral economy will be confined to three items: the nature of pastoral production, politics and social structure, and precolonial trade.

Pastoral Production

Pastoral production required mobility and flexibility in order to adequately utilize marginal ecological conditions. Given the precarious environment and precapitalist technology, units of pastoral production were small and widely dispersed to avoid resource depletion. In precolonial Somaliland, the nuclear family was the unit of production and herd ownership. The family herd consisted of sheep, goats, and camels, and was divided into two categories according to the animals' capacity to withstand the arid conditions of the region.[7] Sheep and goats and a burden camel were kept by the nuclear family, which usually stayed close to its home well. Camels, which can go without water for a long period of time, were taken some distance away by the unmarried young men, or camel boys, of the family. The concentration of many nuclear families in one area at any particular time depended principally on the availability of water and grazing. During the spring and summer, when the rains had fallen and grazing was plentiful, families were widely dispersed. At the height of the dry season, population density around the home wells increased tremendously. Another factor which affected families' concentration in one area was the level of harmony or conflict among various political units in the pastoral economy.

Since the pastoral family was not self-sufficient in terms of labor requirements for its survival, a number of families cohabited together in a kraal (*reer*). These households cooperated in tasks whose labor needs could not be met by any one family—for instance, well-digging. The social and political linkages between the household and the larger units of production were mediated by the particular needs of the production unit.

Because of the aridity of the Somali climate, droughts have been a characteristic feature of the Somali ecosystem. During this century alone there have been many catastrophic droughts. The drought of 1926–28 destroyed as much as 80 percent of the total sheep and goats of the pastoralists.[8] Climatological records indicate droughts of varying severity in the years 1925, 1926–29, 1933–34, 1938, 1943, 1950–51, 1955, 1959, 1965, 1968–69, 1973, 1981, and 1983.[9] Oral tradition has it that the frequency of droughts in this century has not been abnormal compared to the previous century.[10] In addition to the damage caused by drought, another scourge that frequently devastated the pastoral economy was animal disease epidemics.

The precolonial economic and social logic of the unit of production was oriented towards minimizing risk, in order to insure the preservation of the family.[11] Survival was the central preoccupation of the precolonial pastoral economy.[12] The centrality of "safety first" had conditioned the organization and management of the precolonial pastoral capital, the herd, and the family's response to drought. Four principal characteristics of pastoral production—diverse herds, large herd size, reciprocal stock exchange between families, and geographic dispersal—were elements of their risk-avoidance strategy.[13] This strategy was a coherent attempt aimed at maximizing the exploitation of the meager natural resources of the region and at establishing a reliable relationship with other production units that could be called upon during crisis.[14]

Politics and Social Structure

Precolonial Somali political structure consisted of a set of segmentary patrilineal groups, or clans (Fig. 3). The smallest of such political groups was the *Jilib,* or dia-paying group. *Dia* refers to blood money for blood compensation in feuds. The Jilib was the most fundamental and stable social unit and consisted of a number of families whose alliances were essentially based on the security needs of the member families.[15] The clan family in precolonial Somalia was so large and its members so widely dispersed that it had marginal impact on the family. The clan marked the highest limit of political cooperation and included anywhere from a few hundred to over a few thousand persons. Although the clan set the upper limit of any functionally meaningful political organization, below the clan level there was a continuous process of political realignment. As Cassanelli noted, "The effective unit of social and political cooperation in precolonial Somalia varied according to the circumstances. A man might identify with his entire clan when its wells or grazing lands were threatened by another clan but act on behalf of his own lineage or dia-paying group in a feud within the clan over access to dry season grazing reserves."[16]

This continuous shift of alliances in conjunction with characteristic migration of the production units negated the development of stable territo-

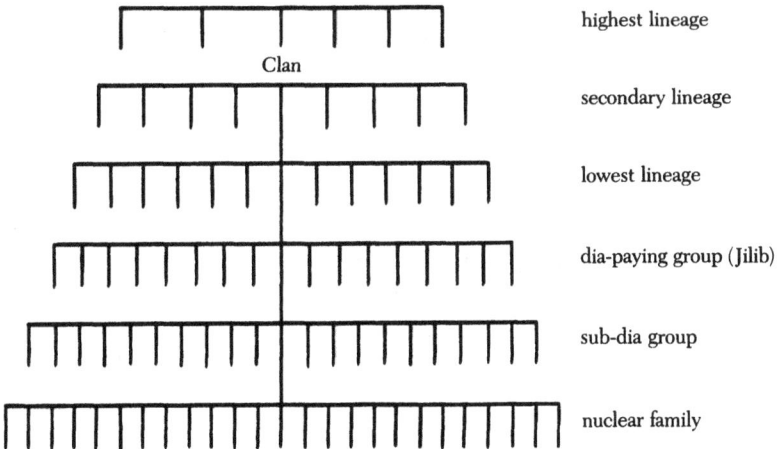

Figure 3. Precolonial Somali Political Structure
Source: Adapted from Lewis, *A Pastoral Democracy*

rial groups as well as of established political, economic, and administrative institutions. In his travels through Somaliland in the 1850s, Burton hinted at this lack of state institutions: "Every free-born man holds himself equal to his ruler, and allows no royalties or prerogatives to abridge his birthright of liberty."[17] Lewis echoed this statelessness almost a century after Burton's travels.[18] Stateless societies were found in a variety of ecosystems; some were agricultural while others were pastoral.[19] The variability of the ecosystems of stateless societies does not necessarily negate the significant role that the environment played in the development of stateless societies.[20]

In the absence of state institutions, what civil associations were there in the precapitalist society to mediate conflict? It has been noted that the Jilib (dia-paying group) was the most stable and fundamental political entity. Members of the dia-paying group were united by contract, or *heer.* This contract was a pledge of mutual support among the members against other dia-paying groups. Within the Jilib there was law and order. In precolonial Somalia there were no chiefs or any other form of standing official leaders. Everyone was a member of a production unit, and consequently no tribute or other forms of surplus extraction existed. When conflicts arose, elders from various levels of political segmentation gathered in a *Shir* (elders' council) to mediate between the concerned parties. The Shir was the forum in which the problems of the political unit(s) were discussed and settled. Theoretically, all adult men had equal access to the Shir, but, as Lewis clearly showed, that was not quite the case in practice: "Naturally, however, the opinions of different men carry different weights. . . . status differences refer to wealth, inherited prestige, skill in public oratory and poetry, political acumen, age, wisdom, and other personal characteristics."[21]

The relationships between various lineages, in terms of peace and war treaties, were decided in these Shirs. The council had no officials or standing committees, and the participants dispersed as soon as the matters at hand were resolved. Even though there were no officials in these gatherings, the lineage "heads" (wherever these lineage heads existed) served as group spokesmen without formal authority over the membership.

The learned men of Islam were another important element in the pastoral society. In this highly segmented (subdivided) society, Islam was the only social phenomenon that transcended the frequently developing, endemic social cleavages. Even so, the position of these holy men was not unambiguous. Some writers have suggested that the sheikhs were an integral part of the political unit, since they were the "bookkeepers" of their lineage.[22] Lewis, however, captured the unique and contradictory position of this group when he indicated that although sheikhs were ideally outside secular politics, their security base was the particular dia-paying group to which they belonged.[23] This partial freedom from clan politics and their supralineage position made them likely potential alternatives to lineage elders as a leadership group, as we shall see.

Precolonial Trade

Although the precolonial pastoral economy was geared to the production of use-values, it was far from being self-sufficient.[24] Only the camel boys lived on milk alone for extended periods of time. The pastoral society bartered pastoral and wild products such as ghee, skins, gum, incense, ostrich feathers, ivory, and livestock for grain and clothing. The trade between the pastoral society and the outside moved in two directions. The barter for grain was mainly westward with the grain-producing societies of eastern Ethiopia,[25] and the coast-bound trade involved the exchange of pastoral productions for commodities such as clothes. According to Pankhurst, in the year 1875–76 the Somali coast (Berbera) exported to Aden 65,000 sheep and goats and 1,100 cattle, and imported grain, sugar, dates, iron, beads, and cotton.[26] Coast-bound trade has a history going back to long before the nineteenth and twentieth centuries; the Somali coast was known to the ancient Egyptians as the land of incense, and Chinese and Arab travellers noted the lively trade of these ports.[27] Among the ports that dotted the Somali coast were Zeila and Berbera. Although Zeila was much older than Berbera, the latter eclipsed the former in recent history and became famous for its annual trade fair.

Despite the long history of this trade, no internal market centers developed in the interior of northern Somaliland before the dawn of this century.[28] To understand why not, one must bear in mind that the actual quantity and value involved in the overland caravan trade was very small, as shown in the estimates in Table 1. The small quantities of commodities involved in this trade (which included products from outside the territory of the precolonial pastoral Somaliland) must have been a significant factor in the lack of development of internal market centers.

Since there was no state system in northern Somaliland to safeguard the movement of pastoral products to the coast and of imported commodities inland, a system based on the local lineage political structure developed.[29] The passage of caravans from the interior to the coast and vice versa was conducted by a guide known as an *abaan*. This abaan led the caravan through territories that did not "belong" to his lineage, but the security of the caravan was assured by the abaan's lineage. The abaan received a commission on the merchandise based on its quantity and value. Little is known about the interlineage distribution of trade and the methods employed in the collection of pastoral products for the port-bound

Table 1. Exports from Berbera, 1840

Commodity	Quantity
Coffee	240,000 kg
Gum arabic	200,000 kg
Myrrh	100,000 kg
Wax	100,000 kg
Butter	100,000 kg
Ivory	40,000 kg
Ostrich feathers	200 kg
Civet	50 kg
Hides	8,000 skins
Sheepskins	5,000 skins
Goats	4,000 skins

Source: Richard Pankhurst. "The Trade of the Gulf of Aden Ports of Africa in the Nineteenth and Early Twentieth Centuries," *Journal of Ethiopian Studies* (Addis Ababa) 3, no. 1 (1965): 36–82.

caravan. Furthermore, it is not clear from the records of this trade how far inland Arab and Indian merchants ventured, despite their dominant role in the ports. Burton in his trip through the interior of western Somaliland made no mention of any foreign merchants in the interior. He did note, however, that pastoralists brought their own products to the ports.[30]

Although this trade was essential to the maintenance of the pastoral economy, little is known about the terms of the barter trade of pastoral products and imported goods. Burton indicated the existence of unequal exchange between these two sectors: "The Bedouin becomes the . . . guest of the townsmen, and he is bound to receive a little tobacco, a penny looking-glass, and a cheap German razor, in return for his slaves, ivory, hides, gums, milk and grain . . . ; of course the wild men are hopelessly cheated, and their citizen brethren live in plenty and indolence."[31]

Swift notes that earlier in the nineteenth century most of the pastoral products exported were the products of hunting and gathering, but included some sheep and goats. Using data from the nineteenth century he suggests that the pastoral sector lost ground in the exchange. For instance, in 1847 an adult sheep was worth 21 kilograms of rice, while in 1891 the same sheep was worth only 10 kilograms. Again, in 1847, 1 kilogram of gum arabic had the exchange value of 2.5 kilograms of rice, while in 1891 the price ratio was 1 kilogram of gum arabic for 1 kilogram of rice.[32] Swift seems to argue that this unequal exchange was partly due to the unorganized nature of the pastoralists in the face of an organized merchant "class." In doing so, Swift overlooks the capacity of the unorganized pastoral society to partially withdraw from this unequal exchange situation when conditions in the pastoral economy permitted. Later on in this chapter I will show that the pastoralists indeed had the "exit" option; they could partially withdraw from trade when they deemed the exchange unfavorable.

In summary, the precolonial pastoral economy and society had six salient features. First, there was a family-centered subsistence economy. Second, it was not a self-sufficient economy and therefore traded with the outside world to procure that part of its necessities which was not domestically produced. In other words, it was peripherally and organically articulated to the regional merchant economy. Third, it was an economy and society dominated by the cycles of the climate. The Somali herding family is renowned for its skillful herd management, and the poverty and deprivation present in this society were largely a consequence of the harsh environment. Fourth, the dia-paying group was the anchor in a sea of continually shifting political loyalties. These loyalties were principally determined by the material needs of the unit of production. Fifth, this society had no chiefs, no state authorities, and no precapitalist landlords (or stocklords). All members of this society had access to the means of production (land and livestock), although this does not mean that there was equal distribution of livestock among pastoral households. Finally, economic growth and accumulation were equated with herd growth. Owing to the lack of internal or external markets for livestock and consequently the absence of any means of transforming livestock into other forms of productive capital, the pastoral economy was incapable of internal self-transformation.[33] Such internal self-transformation was essential in order to ameliorate the dominance of the cycles of the climate.

The Colonial Administration and the Pastoral Society

During the 1870s a new era was dawning in the world, that of colonial imperialism, but the Somali coast had long before attracted the attention of world powers. British involvement here began in 1825, when the British brig *Mary Anne* was plundered off the coast of Berbera and two of its lascars were murdered.[34] The British government blockaded the coast using Indian troops. This blockade led to a treaty of friendship and commerce in 1827. But it was only after the British occupation of Aden in 1839 and the establishment of a military installation there that northern Somaliland attracted more intense British interest, and thereafter Aden became wholly dependent on the Somali coast for its meat and supplies. The opening of the Suez Canal in November 1869 further increased the strategic role of the British installations in Aden and consequently the usefulness of the Somali coast. Britain jealously guarded the Somali coast subsequent to the sudden emergence of the Red Sea as a major international trade route. During the middle decades of the nineteenth century, friendship and commercial treaties were signed with the Somali residents along the coast, ensuring the flow of trade to Aden. During these decades Britain was the dominant industrial and commercial power in the world. This was the golden age of the era of free trade for Britain; she had an overwhelming competitive advantage over her rivals and therefore little need for colonies (except in some cases such as India).

With the second wave of the industrial revolution came other industrial and commercial powers such as France and Germany, and their arrival altered the balance of power in the world arena.[35] The ensuing competition for resources and markets heightened the strategic importance of economically marginal territories like northern Somaliland.[36] In this intensified international competitive environment, Egypt, under the leadership of Khedieve Ismail I, sent its fleet to the Somali coast and by 1875 had established itself in northern Somaliland, including the city of Harar. Although the British government protested this "intrusion," it nevertheless accepted Egyptian occupation of the coast, since its effect on British interests in the coast was negligible. The primary British interests in the area were to maintain the uninterrupted flow of trade between the Somali coast and Aden with a minimum cost. Egyptian occupation of the coast kept the trade routes open and also preempted other European powers who had their eyes on the coast, therefore saving Britain the cost of occupation.

The rise of the Mahdi-led resistance in the Sudan in 1870s and 1880s forced Egyptian evacuation of Eritrea and Somaliland, as Egypt did not have the financial and military resources to simultaneously meet the requirements of war and the cost of its empire.[37] Italy, with British consent, took over Eritrea after Egyptian departure from Somaliland; the concern in Aden was to safeguard the trade routes and to ward off French ambitions. The Gladstone administration, under pressure from the India and Foreign Offices, reluctantly accepted the occupation of Somaliland.[38] These officials decided that matters concerning Somaliland administration should be the affair of the Indian government, since the coast was of extreme importance to India. Lord Dufferin, the viceroy of India, suggested to the British government in London that his government would administer the Somali coast at British expense.[39] The Treasury rejected this offer, and the Indian government unenthusiastically agreed to take over the administration of Somaliland.

Within two years after Egyptian withdrawal in 1884, the British government signed treaties with elders of individual clans along the Somali coast.[40] In these treaties the British government accepted the responsibility to maintain the "independence" of "tribes" and to preserve order. In return, the Somali elders agreed "never to cede, sell, mortgage, or otherwise give for occupation, save to the British Government, any portion of the territory presently inhabited by them or being under their control." Once these formalities were taken care of, the process of colonial administration was under way. The government of India made it clear that Somaliland was to be a coast colony, and in that fateful year three British vice-consuls and forty members of the Aden police were dispatched to establish the rudimentary structures of the colonial administration. These vice-consuls were posted in the major ports in the colony, Berbera, Bulhar, and Zeila. The peripheral nature of this colonial acquisition was clearly restated by the government of India: "The primary objectives of Government are to secure a supply market, to check the traffic in slaves, and to exclude the interference of foreign powers. It is consistent with these objectives, and with the protectorate which the India Government has assumed to interfere as little as possible with the customs of the people, and to have them to administer their own internal affairs."[41] Somaliland did not offer the kind of resources that would have necessitated vigorous colonial state intervention. Its marginality determined the function and form of the colonial administration that was to take root.

The British government of India was not inclined to provide grants-in-aid to the protectorate, so the protectorate's administrative cost had to come from local resources. Among the ways that the administration could have raised revenues from local sources was by levying hut and poll taxes, as was done in many British colonies in Africa. Alternatively, the administration could have required the establishment by the colonial power of state organs such as chiefs and headmen to collect taxes from their clansmen, since this pastoral society lacked sufficient centralized authority structure for this levy. The creation of such chiefdoms would have tremendously altered the structure of this stateless society and would also have required an enormous military establishment to ground the new authority structure. There were no colonial economic groups who had an interest in Somaliland which might have required the establishment of a modern colonial state and hence made a large tax base a prerequisite.[42] Aden's meat requirement was the principal reason that neighboring Somaliland was acquired as a colony. The maintenance of the meat supply could be secured by a simple administration of the coast, which could be met without resorting to radical taxation methods.[43] Consequently, the colonial administration in the Somali coast was to be small in scale and inexpensive to run. Taxes on exports and imports constituted the chief source of state revenue.

The cost of colonial administration was provided from local revenues very early in the colonial period. Customs duties were the principal source of revenue. There was a 5 percent import duty and 1 percent duty on all exports except livestock, which remained duty-free until 1889, when the protectorate was taken over by the Foreign Office. The customs duties accounted for approximately 90 percent of all revenues, yet the total sums of money involved were very small. For example, in the years 1886–87 and 1896–97, total protectorate revenues were £8,961 and £21,263 respectively.[44]

Although this was supposed to be a coast colony, the livestock resources which brought about the colonization of Somaliland lay beyond the coast. The primary internal functions of the Somaliland administration were to keep peace and order (particularly on the coast) and to ensure that caravan routes remained open. As a result of fiscal and manpower constraints, the colonial administration had limited instruments at its disposal to accomplish its tasks. The police were sufficient to keep "peace and order" in the vicinity of the ports, and with the help of periodic reinforcements from Aden, punitive expeditions were dispatched into the interior to clear caravan routes and occasionally punish those who disrupted the trade.[45] In its desire to exercise some authority over territorial clans, the administration also resuscitated the Alkils, clan elders who were paid agents of the administration. They nevertheless had no authority over their clansmen. At best they functioned as communication links between the administration and their respective clans.[46]

In spite of its frailty, the colonial administration was generally able to ensure the safety of the caravan routes and maintain peace and order in the ports. During the first fifteen years of colonial rule there were no major trade or economic changes in the protectorate, although livestock began to account for a larger share of the value of this trade. As Table 2 suggests, the trade link between the pastoral and the world economy was stable. The data indicate a slow increase in the values of this trade despite significant year-to-year fluctuations.[47] These fluctuations were due mainly to epidemics, climatic changes, and wars within the region. The figures in Table 2 include the value of commodites whose origins or destinations were outside Somali territory but do not include the value of commodities that were exported or imported through Somali ports other than Berbera and Bulhar, such as Zeila, Hais and Karam. According to one estimate, the Somali coast as a whole exported to Aden over 4,000 camels, 500,000 sheep and goats, and 6,000 horses and mules a year before the end of the century.[48] Although Alamanni's estimates of the annual exports are exaggerated, they demonstrate that livestock had unquestionably become the most important commodity in the Somali trade with the outside world.[49]

Table 2. Value of Berbera and Bulhar Trade, 1887–88 to 1899–1900

Year	Exports	Imports
	Pounds sterling	
1887–88	167,825	196,801
1888–89	207,373	213,401
1889–90	162,266	157,239
1890–91	141,279	191,712
1891–92	119,553	161,112
1892–93	182,139	218,145
1893–94	200,139	219,075
	Indian rupees	
1896–97	2,142,660	2,355,172
1897–98	2,447,765	2,795,750
1898–99	2,902,793	3,039,750
1899–1900	2,871,962	3,039,465

Source: See Table 1.

Despite the changing composition of pastoral exports, the slight increase in trade, and the fact that the colonial administration was able to keep the caravan routes open, the administration gained little control over the pastoralists. The Somaliland administration, in sharp contrast to its East African counterparts, had no immediate need to subjugate the precapitalist society.[50] The primary responsibility of the Somaliland administration was to ensure the reproduction of the organic linkage that had developed between the pastoral society and merchants' capital. Its task was further facilitated by the absence of industrial capital, which would have required more vigorous intervention into the precapitalist pastoral economy.[51] Therefore, the colonial administration did not have to engage in the double task of destruction and regeneration.[52]

We have seen that British colonial policy in Somaliland was largely the outcome of British imperial interests elsewhere. Earlier, the suggestion was made that the form and function of the Somaliland administration was dictated by the security needs of colonial India. This Indian factor had very important implications for the future development of the pastoral society; that is, the locus of the pastoral economy was only marginally affected by colonialism. The Indian factor, moreover, had severely curtailed the ability of the Somaliland administration to intervene in the affairs of the pastoral society beyond the confines of the coast. As a recent commentator has pointed out, the Somali pastoral society escaped most of the European colonial oppression that had been so characteristic of colonial rule in Africa.[53] This commentator fails to realize, however, that the nature of colonial oppression depended significantly on each colony's particular resources that the imperial country wanted to exploit.

In spite of the reported lack of colonial oppression in Somaliland, the pastoral society did not escape the consequence of British colonial policy elsewhere. It will be recalled that Egyptian withdrawal from the Somali coast and its subsequent British occupation was, in fact, brought about by the rise of the Mahdi in the Sudan. Italy, which replaced Egypt in Eritrea, had also claimed nominal overlordship in Ethiopia. The British government reluctantly accepted these claims until the forces of Menelik (the Ethiopian monarch) destroyed Italian illusions at the battle of Adowa in 1896.[54] Menelik, conscious of the implications of his victory, is said to have advanced an alliance with the Khalifa of the Sudan, the Mahdi's successor.[55] The British government, concerned about the possibility of another Mahdist resurrection in the Sudan, was very eager to negotiate with Menelik. Their objective was not only to preempt a possible alliance between the Khalifa and the new "African master," but also to prevent Menelik's support for the French in the Upper Nile region. Consequently, the British government dispatched its first secretary in Cairo to Addis Ababa to negotiate with the emperor in 1897. The ensuing negotiations finally led to the 1897 Anglo-Ethiopian treaty. Negotiating from a position of strength, Menelik made very few concessions to the British. He accorded Britain the most-favored-nation status in commerce and trade and assured the British that his kingdom would not allow arms shipments to the Sudan through its territory. Conversely, Menelik was able to exact virtually all his demands from the British. These concessions included the agreement of the British government to allow shipments of arms for the Ethiopian emperor through its Somali ports. Britain also waived customs duties on imports that were for the emperor's use. Lastly, and most critically, western Somaliland (the Ogaden) was ceded to Ethiopia, although provisions were made for the grazing and watering "rights" of the pastoralists.[56] The ceding of pastoral territory to Ethiopia did not directly affect the purpose for which Somaliland was colonized. What remained of the Somali territory under the British administration, in conjunction with the grazing rights in "Ethiopia," could still furnish the meat supply for Aden.

The Somali clan elders who had entered into treaties of friendship and protection with the British crown in the 1880s were not advised about these new developments regarding Somali lands. The British India government still administering Somaliland was concerned about trouble with the clans once they realized what had happened and about the financial burden that would result not only from trouble with Somaliland, but also from what seemed like an imminent clash with the expansionist Menelik.[57]

The Foreign Office, which was responsible for the Anglo-Ethiopian treaty, finally took over the administration of Somaliland in 1898.

The Somalis inhabiting the western fringes of the Somali peninsula felt the pressure of an expansionist Ethiopia long before the Anglo-Ethiopian treaty of 1897. In fact, two years prior to the signing of this treaty, Menelik marched his troops into the old city of Harar. He turned this ancient Islamic citadel into a bastion from which his forays into the western Somalilands originated.[58] This Ethiopian expansion into Oromo and Somali lands was a product of political, social, and natural events occurring in the highlands. The recent unification and centralization of the kingdom in the Ethiopian highlands entailed the development of a large, centrally controlled army. The newly unified feudal Ethiopian state was not able to support such an army and consequently found the resources of the surrounding lowlands to be a source from which it could draw tribute. The internal politico-economic pressures which necessitated this expansionist strategy were further accentuated by the devastating drought and famine in the heart of the highlands in the 1880s.[59]

Unable to feed his growing army, Menelik had no practical political alternative but to let them live off the land. The annual tribute-extracting expeditions brought Menelik's troops to the banks of the Shabelle River in the southeast and within a little over a hundred miles from the British- "protected" port of Berbera. The devastation caused by these expeditions was widespread. In the southern reaches of the Shabelle River, the calamity brought about by one of these ruinous expeditions was recorded in a poem:

> When I was still a young man
> Into the World I loved the Amhara came
> They came from Jigjiga and the confines of Awdal
> Crossing the Ogaadeen, they killed many from
>   the Karanle. . . .[60]

The pastoral resources taken in some of these raids were vast. Oral tradition has it that between 1890 and 1897 Menelik's army seized 100,000 cattle, 200,000 camels, and 600,000 sheep and goats from western Somalis.[61] Although these estimates may be exaggerated, they underline the far-reaching social, economic, and political impact these expeditions had on Somali pastoralists. The ravaging tribute-exacting incursions of Menelik's marauding armies into western Somaliland, reminiscent of precapitalist modes of extraction, contrasted sharply with British colonial involvement in Somaliland.

The "feudal" Ethiopian state was primarily interested in tribute collection rather than developing an administrative and government structure in western Somaliland. Although little is known about the frequency of these tribute-collecting forays, some of them must have taken place in years when the pastoralists were experiencing difficulties due to natural calamities such as droughts. Droughts would have facilitated the task of Menelik's army, since the pastoralists necessarily congregated around water sources. Imperial tribute during such difficult times must have significantly reduced the likelihood that some pastoral groups could weather the calamity. These expeditions struck two sensitive chords central to the subsistence and the ideology of the pastoralists. First, the tribute must have undermined mechanisms developed by the pastoralists over the years to keep them from perishing during hard times. As these expeditions took place at least once every few years, the tribute must have reduced the herds of the pastoralists. This reduction in the herd size would have affected even those groups who did not directly fall victim to the raiding army, since they were party to reciprocal social arrangements which mandated help for those afflicted. If such forays by the Ethiopian army took place when the pastoralists were recovering from drought and rebuilding their herd, this again would have destabilized their time-tested crisis-management strategy. Second, the pastoral society was essentially stateless. Until this time pastoralists had known no authorities that forcibly appropriated part of their herds. Prior to this time each clan ensured the security of a member's life and livestock. Occasionally when a group raided the livestock of another, the lineage or clan of the deprived group demanded restitution. These intra-Somali conflicts were resolved either through negotiation or at spearpoint. Consequently, no specific pastoral group was historically able to dominate others through the use of force and hence exact tribute.

While the concessions made to Menelik saved Britain from entanglement in another costly African war, the pastoralists who formally came under the "protective" wings of the Ethiopian emperor were not so fortunate. Individually, each clan was defenseless in the face of the large and well-armed Ethiopian army, as some western Somalis expressed the sentiments of the time to Captain Swayne in 1891: "We ask you now to rid us of these Ethiopian intruders. They wish to treat us as they treated [another Somali clan], to seize our flocks, kill our people and burn our Karias (villages). They wish to settle in our country and oust us. We will not have it."[62] Despite the political cleavages within the pastoral society, the crisis of subsistence brought about by the marauding Ethiopian army heightened the need for a supraclan response.

The crisis of the pastoral society found expression in the leadership of Mohamed Abdille Hassan (known as Sayyid Mohamed). Sayyid Mohamed travelled to all centers of Islamic learning in the Horn of Africa and, after

having exhausted their theological resources, spent some time teaching.[63]
In 1894 he set out on a pilgrimage to Mecca. During this time there were
resurgent theological currents in centers of Islamic learning. Martin gives
two reasons for this resurgency.[64] First, he suggests that some Muslim
thinkers of the nineteenth century believed that many Muslims had
strayed away from the dictates of the Sharia because of the significant influence of Sufism in the Late Middle Ages. Second, most Muslim societies had fallen victim to European colonialism and Western capitalism.
Europe, which was once the periphery of the Muslim world, was now on
the verge of controlling and dominating the entirety of Islamic world. To
many Muslim intellectuals the solution to both of these menaces was to be
found in a return to the basic teachings of Islam. One school of thought
argued that Muslims must borrow scientific developments from the West
and integrate them into the Islam way. They suggested that this was crucial if Muslims were to keep Europe at bay. Other schools were more or-
thodox in their views. It was during his pilgrimage to the holy city of
Mecca that Sayyid Mohamed came under the tutelage of one of the re-
vivalist teachers. Sheikh Mohamed Salih was the teacher of a new order in
Islam, namely Salihiya.

Sayyid Mohamed returned to Berbera and settled there to proselytize
the Islamic interpretations of his teacher. He was not very successful in
attracting a large following, as his message called for a stricter devotion to
Islam and a return to a more austere life. Moreover, his caustic critique of
the "degenerative" lifestyle in Berbera earned him not only the distaste of
those attached to commerce but, more importantly, the suspicion of the
leaders of more established Islamic orders. After some engagements with
the more conservative religious leaders, the Sayyid decided to move back
to his maternal home, in the eastern Haud, in 1899. There, pastoral life
was still untouched by the coastal culture. While inland he travelled far
and wide among his maternal and paternal kinsmen preaching the ways of
the new order and increasingly asking his fellow Muslims to rebel against
Christian domination. At the same time, he used his religious zeal and
political skills to restore peace among warring clans, efforts that were
commended by the colonial administration on the coast.[65] In the meantime the Ethiopian army launched one of its vicious expeditions far into
the Ogaden. The spoils were large and the devastation unimaginably so.
The Sayyid was quick to respond to this catastrophic Ethiopian intrusion
and skillfully seized the moment. His message, couched in Islamic language, was simple:

In the name of God the Beneficent, the Merciful, my brothers I come to you in
the name of God, who is strong, all wise, and everlasting. It is He who is with me

and guides my steps. Infidel invaders have come to surround us. They have come to corrupt our ancient religion, to settle our land, to seize our herds, to burn our *qaryas* . . . and to make our children their children. . . . Are there any among [you] who have not felt the scourge of the Amhaar? [They] carried off many of [your] camels as loot. If you follow me, with the help of God, I will deliver you from the Amhaar.[66]

Soon after he delivered this epic speech, the Sayyid started collecting arms and accepting contributions. In 1899, at a large assembly in his maternal country, he called on young men from all clans to come and join him in the struggle to save their land and faith.[67] Before the end of the year, the Sayyid had raised an army of 5,000 men. He then declared his holy war against the Christian colonizers.[68] Rumors of the Sayyid's intentions to march to the coast spread quickly, and the reported exchange between the Sayyid and the British consul led the nervous and callous Col. Hayes Sadler to declare the Sayyid a rebel and request his government to prepare an expedition to tame him.[69] The twenty-year Somali saga had begun in earnest. The cost-conscious and war-weary British colonial government became entangled in a resistance movement that was aimed principally at countering Ethiopian expeditions in the Somali lands. The year ended without any clashes between the Dervishes (as the Sayyid's troops were known) and the Christian colonizers. Realizing the might of his enemies, the Sayyid began importing guns and ammunition through Djibouti (French Somaliland) and the northern ports of Italian Somaliland. By early 1900, the Dervishes numbered 6,000, and the Sayyid led them into their first field test. Jigjiga, where the Ethiopian army was holding the booty of the previous year, was the target of this Dervish expedition. The Dervishes reclaimed the herds but at a high human cost.

Though this was principally a campaign against the Ethiopian army, after this first successful engagement the foci of the war shifted toward the British colony.[70] The history of the Dervish struggle has been recorded elsewhere and does not require detailed treatment here.[71] Heady from the success of the Jigjiga episode, a segment of the Dervishes raided some of the British-protected clans. The swift raid forced many of these clans to move early to their winter wells. The resultant overcrowding had a severe environmental impact which alarmed the colonial authorities. In collaboration with Menelik they set out to uproot the Dervish movement. Some of the British attempts were more successful than others, but the Dervishes were always able to recover quickly from their defeats. After their first engagement with the superior colonial troops, the Dervishes resorted to guerrilla tactics. The stunning defeats of 1903 depleted the ranks of the Dervishes and forced the Sayyid to agree to peace in 1905. This agreement lasted for three years, and during the lull, the Dervishes rebuilt their strength and made attempts to wean many clans from their supposed loyalty to the British. In 1910 the colonial government, in order to avoid another costly engagement with the Sayyid, decided to pull back all its forces to the coast. In the wake of its retreat to the coast, the colonial administration armed the "friendly" clans. It was the hope of the administration that, in self-defense, these clans would set up a counter-Dervish leader.[72]

Instead, the clans used their newly acquired firepower to settle old scores among themselves. The ensuing strife and the consequent famine reduced the population of the colony by about one-third. The famine of 1911–12 was the worst one in the recent history of this society. It became known as the *Xaarama Cunkee*—the time of filth eating.[73] In 1912 the British government decided to raise troops and restore "peace" inland without engaging the Sayyid. Not engaging the Sayyid was of course impossible, and consequently the struggle between the Dervishes and the administration continued for nine more years. It was not until the end of the First World War that Britain was able to commit a significant force and resources to the "Somali Problem." In 1920 a coordinated sea, land, and air attack was launched against the Dervish forts. They had very little defense against this massive onslaught. As on so many past occasions, the administration failed to capture the desert warrior: with a handful of his surviving followers, the Sayyid crossed to the Ogaden, where he died of malaria in 1921.

The twenty-year-long Dervish struggle against the colonial administration seems to have had no significant impact on the pastoral products traded to the outside world. There is no detailed information available (to this author) to indicate the quantity of products involved in such trade over this period. If, however, the monetary value of exports can be used as a proxy to estimate the quantities involved, then it is clear that the war had a tremendous negative impact on exports, particularly between 1900–1901 and 1906.[74] As Figure 4 indicates, the value of pastoral products declined by more than 50 percent between 1900 and 1906. After this sharp decline, the value of export commodities stabilized at low levels for the rest of the resistance period. The decline in the value of exports in the years 1914–16 was due principally to the interruption of the skins trade during World War I. Furthermore, the good rains and pastures of 1914–15 allowed the pastoralists to rely more on their own products, and they therefore needed fewer imports, which in turn depressed exports.[75] The increase in the value of exports in 1917–19 was due mainly to increases in the prices of skins and livestock. For instance in 1917–18, 104,768 head of sheep and goats were exported at a value of £45,031. In 1919–20, 64,483 head were exported at a value of £44,258. The trade in skins shows an

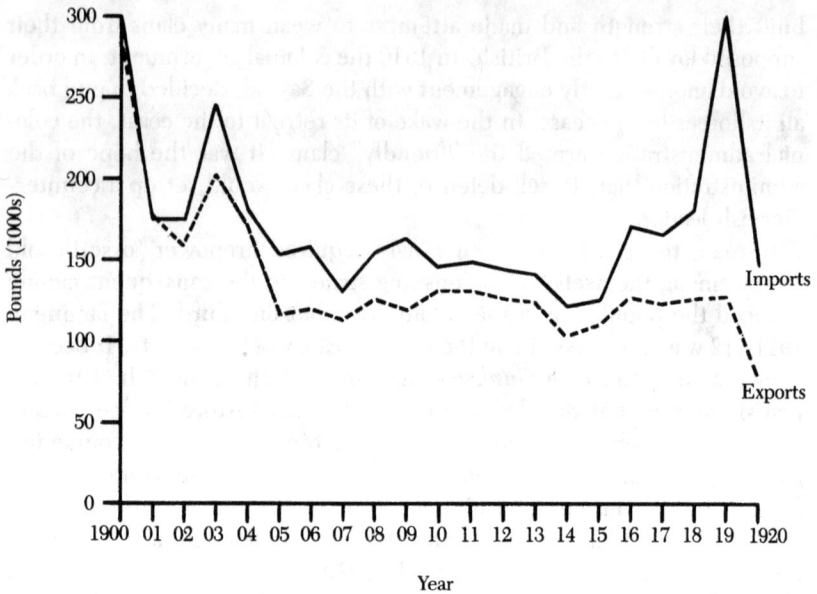

Figure 4. Value of Imports and Exports, 1900–1920
          Source: Colonial Office, Annual Reports, 1900–1920

even higher price increase. In 1919–20, the 1,238,821 skins exported fetched £134,011, while two years earlier 1,498,365 skins were exported at a value of £68,195.[76] Two factors may have been responsible for the price increases of sheep and goats. First, there was a high demand for meat due to the high concentration of British field forces in Aden during this period. Second, since 1919–20 was the year of the coordinated raid against the Dervishes, this may have interrupted the supply of livestock exports and consequently raised the price of these products. The resumption of the skins trade after World War I and the high demand for them in Europe and America were responsible for the high prices for skins of the period. The sharp decline in 1920 was the outcome of a slump in skin trade, good rains and grazing, and a restriction of imported foodstuffs (due to conditions in India) by the Indian government.[77]

The difficulty in using the value of exports as a proxy for the actual export quantities is quite apparent. These aggregate figures do not tell us much about the mix or composition of exports. Moreover, the lack of detail in these values makes it impossible to gauge the barter terms of trade between the pastoral sector and the outside world except in the most aggregate form.

Although Dervish resistance merely slowed down the flow of pastoral

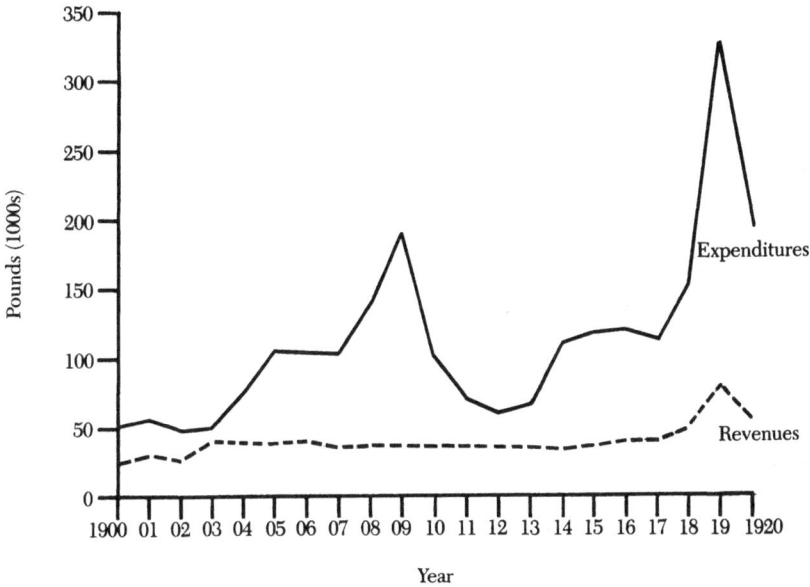

Figure 5. Revenues and Expenditures, 1900–1920
    Source: Colonial Office, Annual Reports, 1900–1920

exports, other sectors of the colonial society did not fare as well. The Somaliland administration, which had had every intention of being "small and cheap," had at the end of the Dervish war cost the Exchequer hundreds of thousands of pounds (as shown in Fig. 5). The sharp increases in government expenditures correlate perfectly with imperial expeditions against the Dervishes. The precipitous decline in expenditures from 1910 to 1913 coincided with the withdrawal of colonial troops from the interior (the so-called coastal concentration). Expenditures again skyrocketted as the pace of the war increased.

Regardless of the increasing war costs, the colonial administration was not in a position to increase local sources of revenue. If it had attempted to significantly raise customs duties, which constituted three-quarters of the local revenues, the pastoralists would have partially withdrawn from trade. In fact, during good rains and grazing years, the pastoralists did export less of their products. In addition to the withdrawals induced by a generous climate, the pastoralists also refrained from trading their products when import prices were too high, and as a result the colonial treasure suffered.[78] Imposing new taxes was also politically inexpedient, as this would have given the Sayyid an additional propaganda tool to use against the administration, and the collection of such new taxes would have been militarily unenforceable. Trapped in this dilemma, the colonial administration had to absorb the financial burden of the war. For example, the administration received an imperial grant-in-aid of £1,369,000 between 1901 and 1920. This entire amount went to the war effort. In contrast, all locally generated revenues for the same duration amounted to only £679,004.

Since the colony's creation in 1884, livestock had increasingly dominated pastoral exports. By the end of the Dervish war, livestock and livestock products such as skins had become the most important pastoral trade items. It will be recalled that before the opening of the Suez Canal, exports from the Somali coast were mostly nonlivestock pastoral commodities such as gum arabic, myrrh, ivory, ostrich feathers, and wax. At the end of the war these commodities had almost vanished from the trade register. Little is known about the impact increased trade in livestock had on the social and economic logic of the pastoral society. It is safe to assume that during this period livestock trade had a marginal effect on the individual pastoralists, since the number of sheep and goats involved in this trade in any given year was rather small,[79] although livestock rather than other pastoral products became the main items of trade. In spite of this marginal quantitative impact on pastoralists, the process of pastoral commoditization was clearly under way.

As the preceding paragraphs indicate, the colonial administration focused its entire effort on the containment of the resistance movement. Although the "coastal-colony" mentality was abandoned in 1905, when the Colonial Office took over Somaliland from the Foreign Office, there was little administrative infrastructure visible beyond the coast. In fact, in 1911 there was only one municipality in the entire colony, the port town of Berbera. During the war years there were three government "schools" in the three main port towns, where the sons of Indian and Arab merchants were taught Arabic and the Koran with an occasional sprinkling of basic arithmetic. The total cost of these schools to the government was on the average less than £100 annually. This apparent neglect of the development of native clerical and supportive administrative cadres was in keeping with the original purpose of the colony. In addition to this, the European resident population was only 36 in 1918–19.[80] In spite of the absence of much colonial administration, the resistance brought most parts of the colony under increased colonial scrutiny.

While the colonial administration and the Dervishes were locked in the war, some of the pastoral clans in what is today the northwest region turned to cultivation in order to supplement their pastoral diet. It will be recalled that in the nineteenth century there was an Islamic revival throughout the Muslim world which affected Somali society. Those who were preoccupied with the management of their herds in the pastoral environment had very little time to spare for nonpastoral endeavors. The holy men who were interested in deepening the roots of Islam in Somaliland were very much aware of the contradictions between devotion to Islam and the demands of pastoralism. These holy men had spent some years in Harar, the center of Islamic learning in the Horn of Africa, during which time they were exposed to farming and cultivation. It became clear to them that some form of sedentarization was a necessary prerequisite for keeping their students together for extended periods. Fortunately for some of them, the climate of parts of the country was suitable for rain-fed farming. Out of these ideas and experiences emerged the *jamaca*, or the sedentary community. Residents of these small communities such as Hargesia were among the first cultivators in what was to become British Somaliland, in the last few decades of the nineteenth century.[81] Over the following few decades a growing proportion of the pastoral population in the western part of the colony followed in the footsteps of these communities and turned to cultivation.

This "voluntary" sedentarization of some Somali pastoralists is in sharp contrast to the many state-sponsored schemes that have been imposed upon many modern-day pastoralists.[82] Many contemporary analysts of pastoralism indicate that cultivation and sedentarization is an option which pastoralists resort to under specific crisis conditions. Pastoralists turn to cultivation when their herds have been decimated by drought or disease. Moreover, when the barter terms of trade (price ratio of livestock and grain) are not in their favor, pastoralists turn to cultivation to grow their grain requirements.[83] Most of this literature focuses on what is called "temporary sedentarization." Temporary sedentarization simply means that pastoralists move in and out of cultivation depending on the dictates of current economic or ecological conditions.[84] In other words, once the crisis that resulted in this temporary sedentarization is over and the pastoralists have rebuilt their herds, cultivation is abandoned. Despite the desire of many afflicted pastoralists to return to their old mode of life, many of these people have not been able to do so and have had to continue as cultivators. Cisse points out that this conversion is due mainly to the development of particular economic, social, and historical conditions that are not favorable to the preservation of pastoralism. Furthermore, he notes that "the major socioeconomic factor encouraging sedentarization of pastoralists in . . . Mali is the imbalance between population and available resources, the most important of which is land."[85]

What conditions in northwest Somaliland forced the pastoralists to turn to cultivation? Some commentators of the Somali pastoral scene seem to equate the emergence of the cultivating religious communities with the spread of cultivation in the northwest. If that were sufficient to persuade the pastoralists to turn to cultivation, then why had these same pastoralists (now peasants), who had traded with the cultivating societies of eastern Ethiopia, not adopted cultivation earlier? Although the example of these religious communities played a role in facilitating the adoption of cultivation by pastoralists, it was certainly not the cause of cultivation. Little is known about many of the demographic and other critical natural and social factors which may have played an important part in this permanent transition.

Certain important changes in the political structure of the pastoral society took place during the first three and a half decades of colonial rule. The resistance movement led by Sayyid Mohamed Abdille Hassan had far-reaching implications for the future leadership in the pastoral society, especially in terms of the changing power relationships among clan elders, colonial administrators, and Islamic holy men. In the stateless society, each clan had an elder as its figurehead, whereas religious men were spiritual leaders and did not often indulge in the secular affairs of the clan. At the time of colonization, the elders of the coastal clans signed treaties of friendship and protection with the British, and later on, some of these elders were incorporated further into the colonial administration by being appointed *akils,* or chiefs. Furthermore, the leaders of the established Islamic orders had shown very little antagonism towards the colonizing "infidels." Though these religious authorities were not incorporated into the administration, as the elders were, nonetheless there existed an uneasy but benign relationship between the administration and the holy men. It was their lack of opposition to Christian colonization that had enraged the more militant Sayyid while he was in Berbera. Despite the Sayyid's acidic criticism of these complacent holy men, the resistance movement that he inspired and led against the infidels had upstaged clan elders and propelled the *ulema* (holy men) into a position of political leadership that was hitherto foreign to them.

By coaxing clan elders to help them in the war, the colonial administration inadvertently enhanced the future leadership role of the clergy. As the state became more involved in pastoral politics, each clan elder "represented" its segment in a new political spectrum in which the state had "ultimate" sanctions. The growing centrality of the colonial state and the subsequent competition between various clan elders for state favors further undermined the potential of these elders to develop into supraclan leaders in the future. This is not to suggest that the colonial administration was able to control these elders completely. On the contrary, the elders opposed the introduction of important state instruments such as taxation into the pastoral society. These elders had no Somali-wide moral or ideological tools at their disposal in the event that these occasional clashes with the colonial authorities turned into major confrontations. In contrast to the elders, the charismatic holy men possessed the qualities of supraclan moral and ideological virtue, and consequently were able to circumscribe the degree of postresistance colonial intervention into the pastoral society.

Postresistance Colonial Society

As a result of the experience of the preceding twenty years, British administrators ranked two goals high in colonial policy in Somaliland: (1) ensuring political stability in the colony to prevent the rise of any more Sayyids, and (2) making the colony financially self-supporting. These two priorities shaped policy in the years between 1920 and the Italian invasion of British Somaliland in 1940. It is difficult to comprehend British colonial policy in Somaliland during this period without bearing in mind these fundamental administrative guidelines. The contradictions inherent in these two policy priorities, however, dampened the initial euphoria that prevailed in the hallways of the colonial administration after the successful suppression of the Dervishes.

Confident because of the success against the Dervishes, the colonial governor immediately began searching for ways to boost state revenues. Both an increase in custom duties and some form of taxation (preferably stock) on the pastoralists were considered. The second means, which the governor seems to have preferred, was "to bring Somaliland into direct line with [Britain's] East African Protectorates."[86] The tribute that the governor preferred was an old proposition that had been turned down by the Colonial Office during 1916–17 because of its obviously deleterious political ramifications. Geoffrey F. Archer, the governor, was adamant about the feasibility of such taxes despite a nervous Colonial Office and was willing to impose and collect them in spite of their unpopularity among the "tribesmen." In a telegram to the reluctant Colonial Office, Archer informed them that he could collect the "necessary" taxes while at the same time bringing the opposition in line:

Direct tribal payments can be enforced in full without any chances of failure or opposition by proceeding at once with the formation of a small air-force. . . . Aerial demonstration alone in my opinion could induce compliance without punitive action, and rifle questions could be dealt with simultaneously and satisfactorily. . . . But as an addition . . . company British battalion in Aden be stationed at Sheikh temporarily . . . assuming that company would remain charged against Imperial funds.[87]

The Colonial Office, wary of another uprising in Somaliland, was not in a mood to commit itself to the governor's proposal.

In pursuit of the governor's desire to raise taxes, Henry Rayne, the district commissioner of Hargeisa, convened a large assembly in Hargeisa which two thousand "men and boys" attended. In what turned out to be a wrangle with the mullahs, the commissioner's argument did not convince even all the akils (chiefs). The mullahs' response to Rayne's argument was "that the tax was 'haram' [forbidden by Islam], that the Government was in no need of money; that it wished money to pay Akils and police, who were of no use to the people."[88]

According to government reports the resistance against these taxes was stronger in Burao, where it ultimately led to the killing of the commissioner. This incident terminated any further discussion of tax hikes or tribute. Interestingly enough, the Colonial Office had preferred increased imperial grants to the governor's proposals all along.[89] Despite the failure of Governor Archer to levy the taxes he desired so much, the fact that his policy resulted in the killing of the officer gave more courage to the pastoralists, and this consequently necessitated the transfer of that aerial and military support that he wanted. Although minor increases were effected on custom duties in the following year, a large part of the state expenditure had to be met by either imperial grants-in-aid or loans from the Treasury. Table 3 shows the amount of imperial grants and loans that the administration received between 1921 and 1937.

Table 3. Imperial Grants and Loans to Somaliland Protectorate, 1921–1937 (pounds sterling)

Year	Grants-in-aid	Loans-in-aid
1921	0	100,000
1922	82,862	75,000
1923	60,000	29,000
1924	47,000	23,000
1925	60,000	0
1926	45,000	0
1927	43,000	15,750
1928	45,500	5,250
1929	95,000	0
1930	50,000	0
1931	59,000	32,250
1932	42,000	16,000
1933	29,000	2,750
1934	36,000	16,000
1935	71,000	0
1936	52,000	0
1937	44,000	0

Source: Somaliland Reports, 1921–1937.

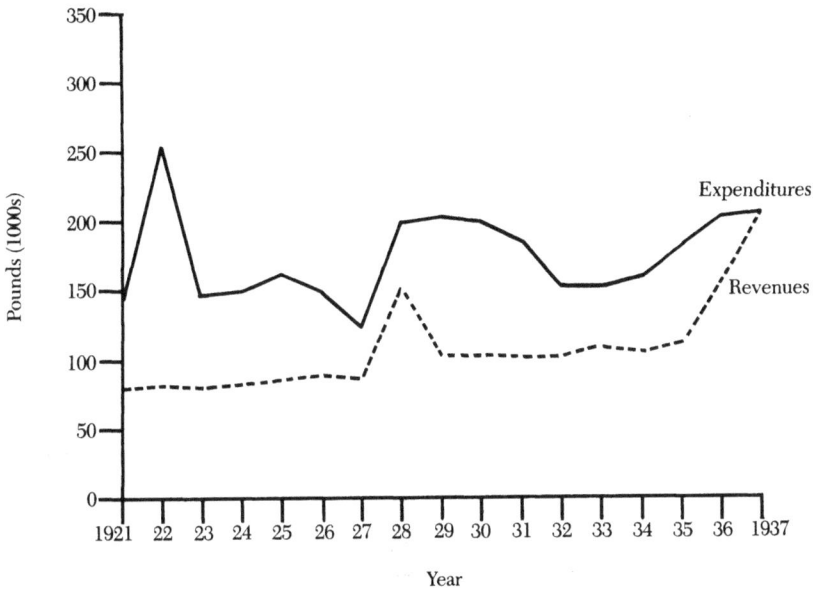

Figure 6. Revenues and Expenditures, 1921–1937
Source: Colonial Office, Annual Reports, 1921–1937

The grants-in-aid were used to cover military expenditures, while the loans-in-aid were meant for civilian expenditures. The loans were repayable to the Imperial Treasury upon the improvement of financial conditions in the colony. Far from being self-supporting, at this point the Somaliland administration depended upon the Imperial Treasury for its fiscal health. The powerlessness of the administration to increase its revenues is further indicated by the fact that the only year after the end of the Dervish war that revenues exceeded expenditures was 1937, as is shown in Figure 6. This phenomenal increase in revenues was due to the Italian occupation of Ethiopia, which opened a vast market for imports entering through the Somaliland port. In fact, the value of the transit trade bound for Ethiopia increased from £86,554 in 1933 to £154,109 in 1937.[90]

The administration's inability to levy taxes and raise local revenues did not affect its intention to occupy the colony and maintain stability. Soon after the war the administration began laying the foundation for its administrative infrastructure, and by the late 1920s, there were five administrative districts in Somaliland—Berbera, Hargeisa, Zeila, Burao, and Erigavo (Map 2). These administrative centers were linked by dirt roads. The government's sole agent in each district was a district commissioner, who was accountable to the governor. The main function of these commis-

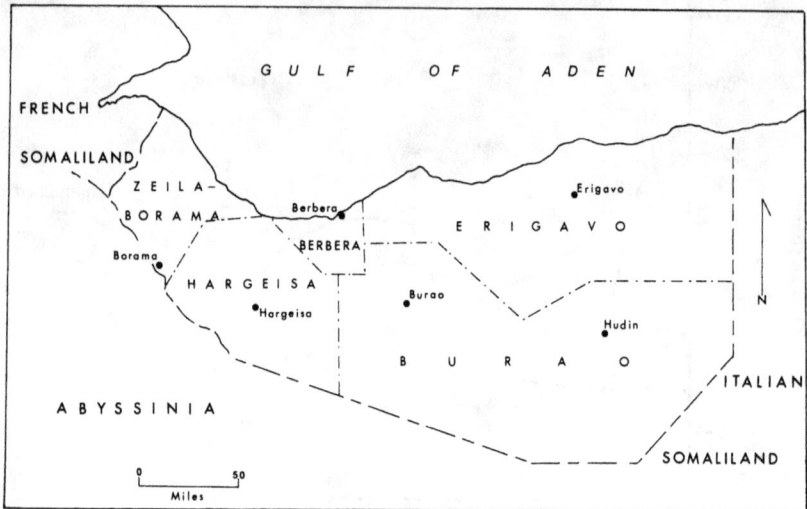

Map 2. Districts in British Somaliland in the 1920s
Source: Colonial Office, *Somaliland: Report for 1928*

sioners was to monitor "political activity" and maintain peace. It was also part of their job to administer justice.

As the administration began to take root in these remote centers, more natives began to take their grievances to the courts rather than resolving them through traditional means. The flood of court cases soon overwhelmed the commissioners. In order to relieve the commissioners of their unrewarding task, the governor enacted an ordinance in 1921 which created a subordinate court system called Akil's Courts.[91] These courts were accountable to the commissioner.

In spite of the extension of colonial government to all corners of the colony, the Somaliland government did not have the financial resources to train even a small administrative cadre. The commissioners and their administrators were assisted by a small number of Indian and Pakistani clerks. The British in Somaliland, unlike those in other African colonies, made no significant effort to cultivate a small segment of the local population to take over part of the business of administration. This, of course, was in line with the peripheral nature of the Somali colony. When the administration finally came around to the idea of establishing some form of educational system, the mullahs, who were now firmly established as influential public figures, frustrated whatever schemes the administration had. The administration did not help its educational effort by appointing a Christian to supervise Koranic schools receiving government assistance.

This move played into the hands of the mullahs, who were interested in preserving their power base through maintaining their monopoly on literacy.

By the mid-1930s, a handful of Somalis in Aden who were more exposed to world affairs and were relatively well-educated began to petition the Colonial Office concerning what they termed "neglect and abuse" of the Somali colony by Britain.[92] The most prominent of these individuals was Haji Farah Omar, whose activities in Somaliland and direct petitions to the colonial secretary were a thorn in the side of the administration. In a petition supposedly signed by many elders of the colony, Haji Omar enunciated those things that most grieved the Somali population: heavy customs duties, absence of educational services, lack of Somali employment in government, lack of facilities for agricultural development, and harsh treatment of the natives by the militarized administration. As Haji Omar put it in one such petition, "Therefore the British Somaliland loyal subjects, appeal to Great Britain against this blood thirsty Irish Commissioner."[93]

Although Haji Omar sought to champion the "Somali cause," he vigorously opposed the "new" educational policy of 1930s. This policy sought to establish a number of elementary schools, and the director of education, a Mr. Ellison, decided to make instruction in the Somali language a central feature of the curriculum of these schools. Haji Omar and his Islamic and pro-Arab sympathizers used all their influence to discredit the program as un-Islamic. The reasons given against this policy by the influential Somalis of the time (in an assembly in Burao) are revealing.[94] First, they argued that the teaching of Somali would tend to lessen the importance of Arabic in the eyes of the children and consequently weaken religious teachings. Second, the teaching of Somali would mar Somali prestige by reducing the people to the status of other East African tribes. Third, those opposed to this policy argued that the administration had the intention of reserving government clerical jobs to Indians who had knowledge of English.

The administration contended that the majority of reasonable Somali elders were in favor of the educational policy, but they had to shelve it in order to avoid the political crisis that could have resulted from the issue. Although the "instinctive opposition" of Somalis to secular education gradually waned, there was only one elementary school in the country at the end of the decade, and a mere handful of Somali students were being educated in the Sudan, with the cost of their education being borne in part by their families.[95]

The Dervish war had the effect of expanding the colonial administration to all corners of Somaliland, but it had not changed the purpose for which

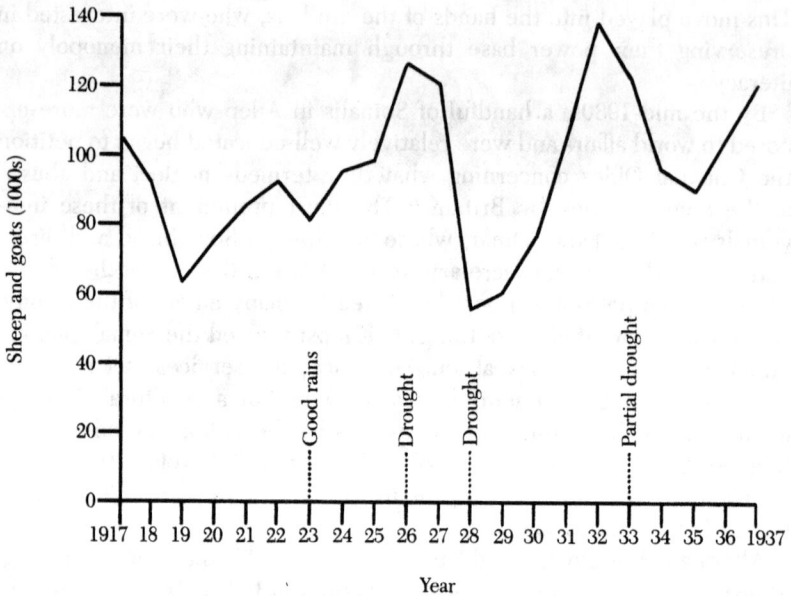

Figure 7. Sheep and Goat Exports, 1917–1937
         Source: Colonial Office, Annual Reports, 1917–1937

Britain had acquired Somaliland. In step with its policy of "cheap and small," the administration did not intervene into the pastoralists' world so long as the caravan routes and the general peace went undisturbed. In fact, the colonial state had built enough strength to ensure the operation of this trade. As was indicated earlier, the administration failed to levy tribute or taxes on the pastoralists. Elsewhere in Africa, the British colonial administration had used taxes to force local populations to partake in the colonial economy. In Somaliland this old colonial practice was rendered worthless by the recalcitrant forces of precapitalism. As can be seen in Figure 7, it was the forces of nature that had determined how much of the pastoral herds were turned into export commodities. The cycles in Figure 7 perfectly illustrate the time-tested pastoral strategy of crisis management at work. The two peaks in the graph coincide with the droughts of 1926–28 and 1932–33. The 1926–28 drought brought utter devastation to the pastoralists. It was estimated that 80 percent of the stock perished. The Somalis called it *Qorkii*, referring to the time when they had to *register* in relief camps. The increase in exports of sheep and goats during these two periods was a result of pastoralists' attempts to get rid of as much of their herds as possible despite declining prices. The troughs in the graph represent low exports as the pastoralists were en-

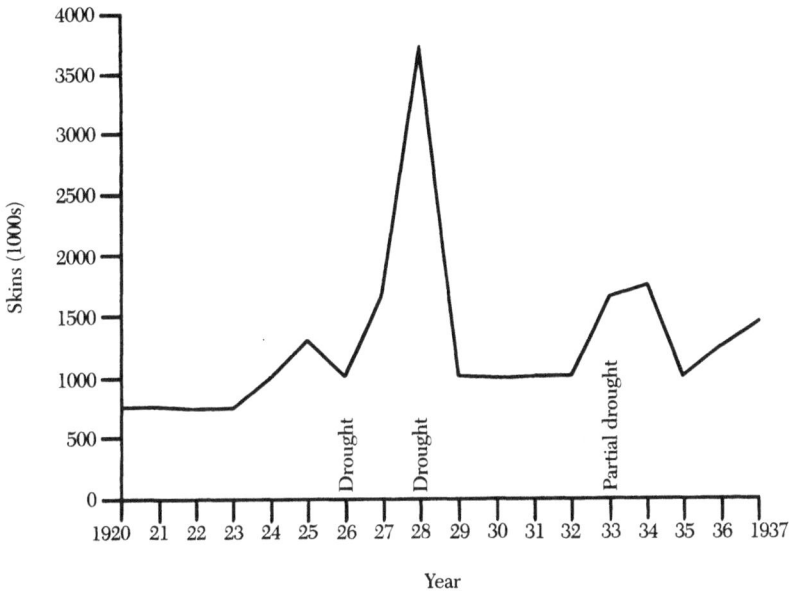

Figure 8. Skins Trade, 1920–1937
    Source: Colonial Office, Annual Reports, 1920–1937

gaged in rebuilding their herds. Similarly, the increases in export figures for sheep and goat skins (shown in Fig. 8) more dramatically illustrate the same point. In short, massive slaughter and sale of livestock went hand in hand in times of crisis. However, the irony of the story is that while the pastoralists were being devastated, the state's revenues (shown in Fig. 9) improved markedly as a result of the increase in trade of skins, sheep and goats, and food imports (illustrated in Figs. 8, 7, and 10, respectively).

In one of those rare moments in the history of British colonial policy, the Somaliland administration, with the approval of the Colonial Office, broke with its tradition of "small and cheap" by creating a veterinary department in 1924. The reason for this break with tradition—stated by the governor in a letter to the colonial secretary—is revealing:

It has recently been brought to my knowledge by the merchants trading in skins at Aden and on this coast that the Government of the United States of America threatens to place an embargo on the imports in the USA of skins from this and neighboring countries unless provided with certificates signed by competent veterinary authorities to the effect that . . . the country of origin is free from anthrax. . . . The sheep skins exported here are in considerable demand in the USA and the UK for the purpose of the glove trade . . . I estimate annual expenditure involved in the establishment of a veterinary department will amount to £1,500

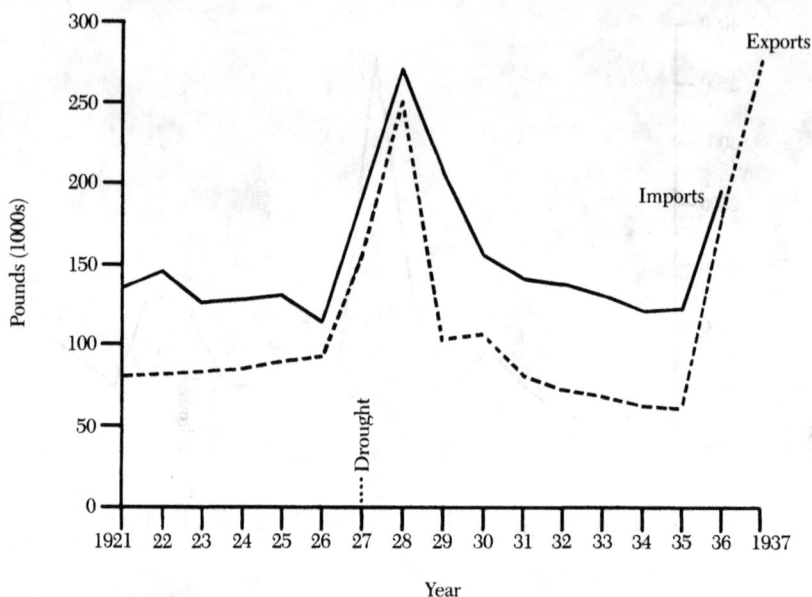

Figure 9. Value of Imports and Exports, 1921–1937
         Source: Colonial Office, Annual Reports, 1921–1937

and I am convinced that if we neglect to take the necessary steps the loss to Customs Revenue will be very greatly in excess of this amount.[96]

Skins were the principal export commodity of the colony, sometimes accounting for approximately 60 percent of total value of exports. Following these communications a veterinary department was established in 1924. Fortunately for many pastoralists, the arrival of the veterinary officer coincided with "one of the worst outbreaks of rinderpest in many years."[97] As the annual reports from 1924 to 1937 show, the services of the veterinary department were put to a worthy use. Many of the livestock epidemics that had ruined pastoralists' flocks in the past were brought under control. In additon to veterinary services, the colonial administration, with the help of a grant from the Colonial Development Fund, began in 1930 a program of water boring and conservation in the colony. The grant from this fund amounted to £42,265 for the period 1930–36.[98]

   In spite of its weakness and its inability to levy taxes on the pastoralists, the colonial state had a far-reaching effect on pastoralism. It will be remembered that in the early years of colonialism, *abaan*, or guides, were the main links between the pastoralists in the interior and coastal merchants. In that insecure environment abaans owed their safety and the security of the caravan routes to the leverage of their clans. As the colonial state gained strength and "opened up" new areas, the abaan system began to lose ground. Trade expanded with improvements in communication. Increased security, improved communication, and the slow but steady spread of trade had the combined effect of gradually rendering the abaan system obsolete. In place of the declining system rose a new organization; the *dilaal-sawaaqui*-merchant chain (*dilaal* means "broker," *sawaaqui* means "drover").[99] The dilaals conducted livestock transactions near the main wells close to the new administrative centers of Hargeisa, Burao, and other villages. The sawaaqui collected the purchased herds and drove them to the coast. The new administrative centers provided a small number of emerging traders with bases close to their pastoral clients.

During the earlier decades of the century, coastal trade was monopolized by merchant houses owned by South Asians—including Cowasji Dinshaw, Premji Brothers and K. P. Tamber—and a few European firms, such as M. A. Besse Company.[100] These coastal merchants had not penetrated the interior of the colony. The abaan and later on the dilaals provided the necessary link. As more of the colony was "opened up," a handful of Somalis (abaans, dilaals, and ex-sailors) who had accumulated some wealth began to take a more significant role in local trade. The Italian invasion of Ethiopia further enhanced their fortunes by expanding the internal market overnight, as is shown by expanded imports in the late 1930s in Figure 9. Some of these aspiring merchants sold their entire herds to take advantage of the spoils of the war. The administration was delighted: "The possibilities of profit from the trans-frontier traffic appears to be weaning Somalis from their traditional belief that livestock is the only satisfactory form of wealth. There are many instances of stock owners having sold the bulk of their livestock to invest in motor vehicles, and by the autumn more than a hundred Somali motor owners were in contract with the Italian transit traffic authorities."[101] Apart from the satisfaction expressed by the administration, there is little known about the impact this "weaning" had on the production and distribution of pastoral assets.

What is known, however, is that apart from the small number of Somalis who lived in the coastal ports such as Berbera, Zeila, and Karam, most natives had pursued a pastoral existence. This began to change as new administrative centers were established. The most important catalyst of this change was the development of trade. As trade grew, what had been seasonal and temporary markets gradually became permanent market villages. The markets created by the Italian occupation of Ethiopia gave a spectacular boost to the development of this trade and consequently to the growth of towns. Although there were some estimates of Somaliland population of the time, there existed no similar population estimates for these important nodes of trade. The paucity of such data notwithstanding, and with the benefit of hindsight, it is tempting to suggest

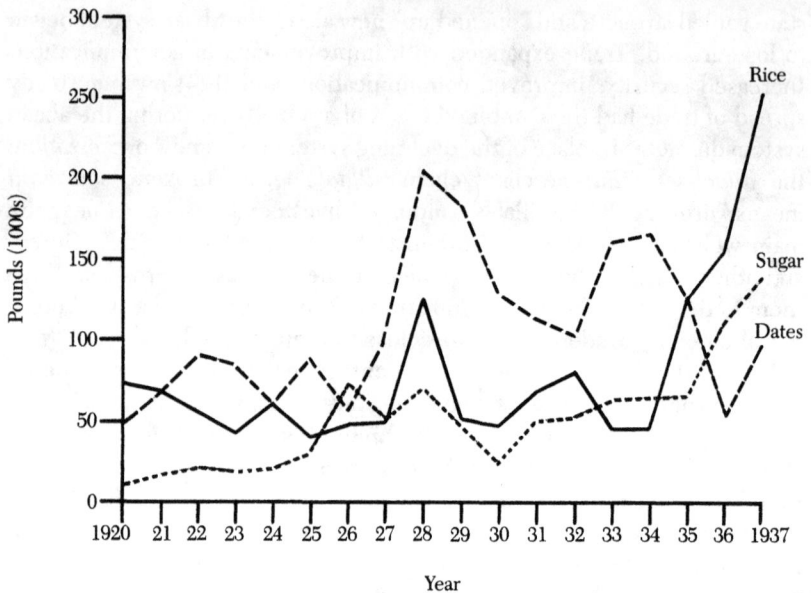

Figure 10. Food Imports, 1920–1937
        Source: Colonial Office, Annual Reports, 1920–1937

that embryonic urbanization had begun in Somaliland in the late 1920s and early 1930s.

Available data on food imports strongly suggest that the pastoral-colonial economy was undergoing important changes. The pastoralists depended on trade (barter) to secure that part of their food needs which they did not produce. Figure 10 illustrates the quantities of rice, dates, and sugar imported between 1920 and 1937. As the graph demonstrates, increasing amounts of rice and sugar were imported; the downward breaks in the otherwise upward trend in these two imports were due to the terrible drought of 1926–28. Merchants imported vast quantities of all the commodities at the beginning of the drought but were left with excess amounts as the drought waned. These excess stocks necessitated curtailment of imports in the following years.[102] The import data for 1920–34 graphed in Figure 10 include goods that were in transit to Ethopia. These transit shipments exaggerated the quantities of food imported to the colony. However, the data for 1934–37 in Figure 10 exclude food imports that were destined for areas outside the colony. In spite of the exclusion of these transit commodities, the data show that food imports to Somaliland continued to increase sharply. There are three possible scenarios under which such increases could have occurred. First, the pastoral population started to consume more of these commodities. Second, the larger imports were necessitated by population growth. Third, the increases in food imports were necessary because of the emergence of population centers "outside" the pastoral sector which significantly depended on food imports. Though each of these propositions seems reasonable, it is more likely that their combined effect produced the increase in imports. Moreover, it is most probably the final condition—that is, the development of population centers—that was most responsible for the increase. This seems all the more likely considering that the quantities displayed in the figure prior to 1934 include transit commodities.

Although the pastoralists in the western part of the colony had begun their transition to agriculture in the early years of the century, nevertheless, this very important social and economic event was not greeted with the same urgency as the one that resulted in the creation of the veterinary department. The governor, in a long letter to then colonial secretary Winston Churchill discussing the resources of Somaliland, impressed upon the secretary the need for an agricultural officer in the colony.[103] The governor argued that although agriculture in the colony would not prove to be of any real value to the empire, it might enhance the financial position of the protectorate and of the inhabitants of the colony. Four years later, in 1925, the colony's government geologist was given an additional appointment as director of agriculture.[104] The responsibility of the director and his staff was "to improve native methods of growing the local crops and introduce plants which will be of more value to the natives and to the revenue of the Protectorate." One of the first acts of the department was to import two light ploughs from Canada in 1925 and to begin to form a small experimental farm.

In the succeeding years the administration and the department of agriculture reported the unrestrained willingness of the peasants to use new methods and instruments. Many of the experiments on new crops such as Ethiopian barley, peanuts, and grain were very successful, and the peasants expressed interest in growing these crops. Other experiments in fruit-growing were also generally successful, and in similar fashion there was enthusiasm for their adoption by the peasants. In spite of these successes in experimentation and the eagerness of the peasants, the Department of Agriculture was abolished in 1934 for unexplained reasons.[105] Agriculture was annexed to the veterinary officer stationed in Burao (far away from the farming districts). Although the area of the colony under cultivation was quite small (about 400 square miles), it had already made its contribution to a colony that had originally imported all cereals consumed locally. Rice imports to the colony decreased because of increased

Table 4. Maize and Sorghum Sold in Hargeisa Market,
          1931–1933 (lbs.)

Year	Sorghum	Maize
1931	130,012	26,182
1932	1,836,193	15,584
1933	733,171[a]	10,536

Source: Colonial Office, Annual Reports for 1931, 1932, and 1933.

[a]The falling-off in the sale of sorghum in 1933 compared to 1932 was due to the fact that much of the crop was not brought to Hargeisa but sold elsewhere.

sorghum production. Peasants' grain production not only met their household needs but also generated a small surplus that contributed to the development of grain markets, as shown in Table 4.

Though grain markets became a permanent economic feature in the western part of the colony towards the end of the 1930s, the Italian invasion of Ethiopia, which had such an important impact on trade and pastoralism, had had no direct effect, up to this point, on subsistence agriculture. A by-product of the Italian invasion of Ethiopia was the appearance of a few Somali traders (former dilaals, seamen, and abaans), who liquidated their livestock holdings and invested in trade and trucks. Peasant agriculture was far less involved in the market and was therefore less attractive to investment. These budding traders had their eyes elsewhere during the boom times of the late 1930s.

Conclusion

Despite its initial parsimonious policy predisposition, towards the end of the 1930s the colonial administration had sunk its roots far and wide in Somaliland. In sharp contrast to the colonial administrations in other East African colonies—Kenya, Uganda, and Tanzania—the Somaliland administration did not have to mediate between various imperial economic interests and the precapitalist African society. As there existed no settler society, nor industrial and strong merchant capitals, there was no need for the administration to open up the precapitalist society for capitalist exploitation.

In spite of the absence of such "destructive-conservation" state policy, the Somali society nonetheless underwent important economic, political, and social changes after the dawn of the colonial era. The colonial state played an important role, directly or indirectly, in these processes. Among the most critical of these changes were the following:

First, there was a strengthening of trade relationships between the pre-colonial subsistence pastoral economy and outside markets. Since the local economy did not produce all the food and other necessities of the population, some pastoral products were traded or bartered to gain access to such essential commodities as grain and cloth. This articulation between the pastoral economy and the regional economy was strengthened and expanded during the period under study. This relationship was a difficult one, since the amount of pastoral products traded and consequently commodities imported was subject to the vagaries of the climate and other precapitalist social constraints. However, increasing commoditization of livestock (the staple of pastoralists), the changing consumption habits of the pastoral population, and that population's consequent integration into the regional mercantile trade gradually but certainly assured the permanancy of pastoralist participation in the colonial economy and the demise of the "exit" option. Despite these obstacles, trade between these two economies had expanded so much by the end of the 1930s that a small but growing commercial sector had become a very important and novel economic feature in Somaliland.

Second, there emerged in the northwestern part of the colony a peasant economy. It is clear that the colonial state did not play any direct role in the establishment of this sector; however, the growing involvement of the pastoral economy in the world market, the crisis precipitated by the Dervish war, and the expansion of the marauding forces of Imperial Ethiopia all contributed to this shift. Apart from minor agricultural experiments, distribution of new seeds, and the marking out and surveying of agricultural land, the colonial administration had very little contact with the peasant.

Third, the emerging "urban" economy and urban traders had begun to challenge the supraclan leadership role of the mullahs, who had gained eminence as a result of the Sayyid. The dominance of the mullah leadership was still beyond dispute, however.

Fourth, rather than displacing or destroying the precapitalist political structures, the colonial administration had instead used them selectively as a basis of their administration—that is, they had used clan heads as akils and had marked off political boundaries or districts to conform to particular clan "territories."

3

Somali Colonial Political
Economy, 1940–1960

Abundance and scarcity are never far apart; the rich and the poor frequent the
same houses.

> Somali proverb
> cited in I. M. Lewis's
> *A Pastoral Democracy*

The emphasis on Somali homogeneity and egalitarianism, while valid and indis-
pensable, may obscure a process of class development underway in British Somaliland during the interwar years that eventually produced the political groups
which articulated the determination to reunite the Somalilands.

> Charles Geshekter
> "Entrepreneurs, Livestock, and Politics"

In African colonial history, 1940–60 is usually considered to be the period
when the second wave of African resistance to colonial rule "matured."
While this chapter will pay due attention to the historic process, it will
attempt to lay bare the evolution of the economic and political forces
which shaped the Somaliland Protectorate's underdevelopment at this
time. Underdevelopment, in this context, has three intricately linked features: first, the absence of the development of productive forces in the
rural sector and the rise of an unproductive urban economy; second, the
intensification of the interaction between the rural economy and the mercantile world; and third, the development of merchant and bureaucratic
classes that have a claim on rural production. The first part of this chapter
will look into the triangular relationship and interaction between the colonial state, the rural sector (pastoral and peasant), and the urban sector,
and how this led to ecological deterioration and partial commoditization of
pastoral production without concurrent development of productive force.

It is usually assumed that the politico-economic frustrations of the nascent local petite bourgeoisie, caused by the incapacity of the colonial
economy to accommodate this class's growing aspirations, led to the emergence of nationalist movements. The second section of this chapter will
suggest that it was not the thwarted economic ambitions of the petite
bourgeoisie which led to the "struggle" for independence but, rather,

58

extraeconomic and extraterritorial factors. It will be pointed out that the acute degree of economic underdevelopment in the protectorate militated against the development of such contradictions. At early stages of underdevelopment, the petite bourgeoisie is very dependent on the colonial state, and such was the case in British Somaliland after the Second World War.

The State, Trade, and the Rural Economy

On April 4, 1940, the Fascist troops of Italy launched an attack on British Somaliland from their Ethiopian bases. Within a matter of days they had complete control over the protectorate, and the colonial administration, under heavy gunfire, fled to Aden. Italian occupation did not last for long, however; the imperial troops drove the Fascists out of Berbera and the territory by March 16, 1941. The British did not stop at the former Somali-Ethiopian boundaries but pushed the Italians back until the whole of the Italian East Africa empire came under British control. In addition to the destruction of some of the physical infrastructure such as government buildings, the brief Italian occupation of Somaliland also disrupted trade with the colony. The British blockade of the Somali ports brought export and import trade to a halt, and the pastoralists who depended on trade for an important part of their daily necessities had to do without such commodities for at least the winter of 1940–41. The duty of the victorious British was to reestablish the colonial economy.

The first task of the returning British administration was to resuscitate the administrative infrastructure of the colony. To the surprise of the administration, the Somalis were more than delighted to have the British back. This was confirmed by the immediate and voluntary reporting of the majority of the pre-occupation police force for duty within a matter of days: 540 out of 551 policemen reported to work within less than a month after reoccupation.[1] In April 1941 the military governor took up residence in the new capital of Hargeisa, since many of the state buildings in Berbera had been destroyed.

Because Britain was still at war, an unusually large number of Somalis were employed by the colonial government, and British expenditure on wages and distribution of rations gave an instant stimulus to trade. Many of the traders who had been in hiding during the Italian occupation surfaced and took to their enterprises with renewed and unprecedented vigor. The British occupation of Ethiopia recaptured that larger market for the Somali traders. By the end of 1941, significant progress had been made in restoring the protectorate's prewar economic "foundation." The recovery was further assisted by the failure of the rains in 1942–43, which forced the pastoralists to sell off their herds in large numbers. In 1941, for example, 44,000 head of sheep and goats were exported, but in the following year the number rose to 112,000. The skins trade recovered rapidly, because of the drought as well as because skins had accumulated over the occupation period.[2]

Aside from the restoration of administrative functions and trade, another immediate preoccupation of the government was to address the supposedly deteriorating conditions of the pastoral range, an essential step since pastoralism was the productive sector of the colonial economy. The severe drought of 1942–43 brought the "crisis" home to the administration. Prior to the Italian invasion, the governor had asked Mr. Edwards, a member of the colonial administration, to look into the problem of the pasturelands.[3] Soon after the military administration regained its footing, it carried out another survey of the range.[4] These were the first systematic studies of the problem of range deterioration, and there were important disagreements among the researchers as to its magnitude. Edwards, Gilliland, and others suggested that although range deterioration due to overstocking was becoming a serious problem, it was confined to only a few localities. In contrast, Glover emphatically insisted that the range deterioration due to overstocking was more widespread and that overstocking was "the crux of the problem."[5] The difference in the conclusions of these studies was in large measure a result of the varying assumptions and methods they used in estimating the livestock population of the protectorate. While Gilliland and others accepted livestock estimates of the prewar general survey, Glover rejected them as extremely low and consequently offered his own. Table 5 shows the contrast between the two estimates. Calibrating from his own estimate of livestock population and livestock and skins exports, Glover suggested that in any

Table 5. Estimates of Livestock in Somaliland, 1947

	General Survey estimate	Glover's estimate
Sheep	1,799,000	10,000,000
Goats	1,391,000	3,000,000
Camels	1,240,000	2,500,000
Cattle	NA	500,000
Donkeys	6,200	6,200
Horses	450	450
Total Stock	NA	16,006,650

Source: *The Pastures of British Somaliland with Special Reference to the Glover Report and Future Policy* (Hargeisa, 1947), p. 20.

one year 20 percent of the protectorate's livestock were either slaughtered or sold (20 percent off-take rate).[6]

Despite the substantive difference of opinion among these researchers as to the degree of range deterioration and the livestock population, their policy recommendations were surprisingly similar. Both groups indicated that grazing controls were necessary in order to slow down and ultimately reverse the deterioration of the range. Gilliland and his associates suggested that a more even distribution of livestock over the range would ameliorate the localized range devastation. Glover argued for a more drastic approach. He indicated that herd population would have to be reduced by 70 percent in the long run and 50 percent in the short term.

In spite of the failure of the prewar grazing controls, the military administration decided to give them another try. In the meantime, the authorities also considered the idea of introducing direct stock taxation in order to provide an incentive for the pastoralists to dispose of some more of their surplus herds. From past experience, the administration was aware that it needed more information about tribal pastoral movements in order to plan and effectively implement its grazing controls. With this idea in mind, the administration commissioned a geologist, J. A. Hunt, to carry out his general survey. When the decision was made to enclose shifting portions of the range throughout the year, the problem of how to enforce the controls emerged. The administration, conscious of the fact that it did not have enough resources and manpower to make the controls effective, attempted to make the "tribes" responsible for the administration of the reserves of "their" respective territories. As we have already seen, the tribes had no formal authority structure, the presence of the colonial administration in the past sixty years had not altered that fact, and the commoditization of livestock and rural life had progressively undermined precapitalist control systems. The unenviable task of the administration was to create some form of tribal authority. This attempt was, of course, unsuccessful. Once again the colonial administration was rendered powerless in laying the basis for indirect rule and intervention into pastoral production. Despite some trials in grazing controls in 1943 and thereafter, it became increasingly apparent to the administration that this policy was doomed to failure. This realization was enunciated by the director of agriculture and veterinary services in 1953:

The approved policy of the Department was fully set out . . . in 1952. However, it is possibly of some interest to point out that there has been, in the last year or two, a perceptible shift of emphasis from stock husbandry and pasture improvement to crop husbandry. . . . This change in priorities in a country which is entirely dependent on stock and stock products for its national income may well be deplored,

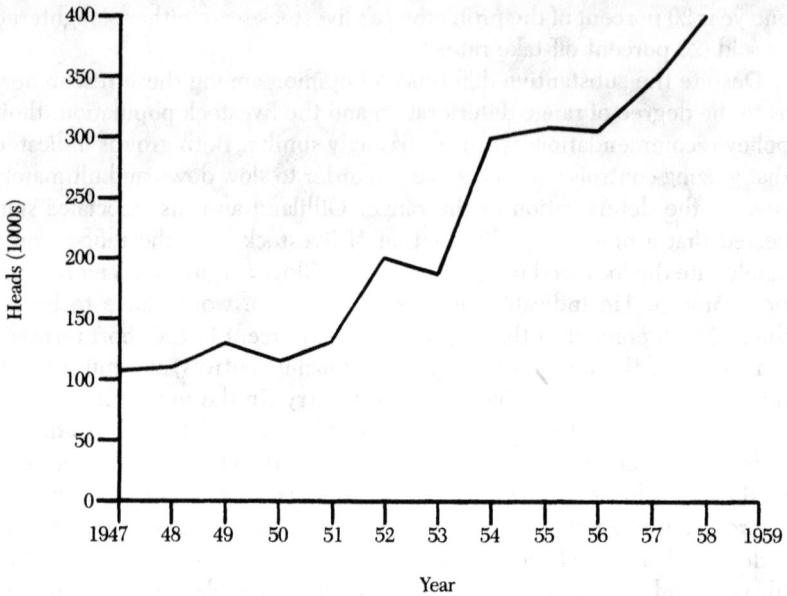

Figure 11. Somaliland Livestock Exports, 1947–1959
          Source: Colonial Office, Annual Reports, 1947–1959

nevertheless, without the cooperation of the Somali grazier little progress can be
made in implementing schemes designed to improve his stock and grazing. This
cooperation is not forthcoming and it is considered prudent and desirable to concentrate on crop husbandry.[7]

The pastoralists' successful evasion of the state's attempt to bring pastoral production within its grasp notwithstanding, the pastoral sector increased its involvement in the market, which benefitted the state in terms
of increased revenues. Immediately after the reoccupation, trade in livestock was revived, and in 1941, 44,000 head were exported. Eighteen
years later, and without the "benefit" of stock tax incentives, the pastoralists marketed a larger portion of their herds, almost half a million
head. As indicated in Figure 11, the increasing involvement of the pastoral sector in trade was uninterrupted and unprecedented in scale. The
figure illustrates the absence of the familiar cycles that had been endemic
to pastoral exports in the past (1920–37). These cycles were a product of
droughts, good rains and grazing, and occasionally high prices of imported
goods unmatched by price mark-ups of livestock. Although there were no
droughts between 1942 and 1960 as damaging as that of 1927–28, which

destroyed 80 percent of the stock, the protectorate witnessed at least four droughts of differing magnitudes in 1950, 1955, 1956, and 1959. None of these droughts seem to have had any detectable impact on the livestock traded or kept in the pastoral sector. The drastic declines in livestock exported after fantastic increases in stock sales during the drought do not appear in Figure 11.

In the absence of direct state involvement in pastoral production, what had happened in the pastoral sector that gave impetus to these tremendous increases in the number of livestock traded? And why are the usual effects of droughts on trade not reflected in these figures? There is little information available pertaining to these issues, but one can surmise from the fragmented data available some of the factors that may account for the heightened pastoral trade. It is likely that in the absence of major disease epidemics and devastating droughts, livestock population grew. This must have enabled the pastoralists to sell a large number of animals without jeopardizing the subsistence herd. The increases in livestock sales must have been necessitated by the sharp price increases in importing commodities, particularly during and immediately after World War II, as shown in Table 6. For example, the price of millet increased fourfold, that of sugar fivefold, and that of dates more than fourfold. The price of livestock did not increase as much.[8] Later on, in the 1950s, the oil boom and the growth in the number of foreign pilgrims in Saudi Arabia, with the subsequent increase in demand for meat (Table 7), which drove livestock prices upwards, generally improved the terms of trade of the pastoral sector.[9]

Table 6. Prewar and Postwar Prices of Selected Commodities (rupees)

Commodity	Unit	Price				% increase[a]
		1939	1947	1948	1949	
Rice	1 bag	15	112	110	100	633.3
Millet	1 bag	8	32	35	32	337.5
Meat	1 lb.	−/2[b]	−/5	−/4	−/6	264.0
Dates	168 lbs.	11	48	40	50	263.6
Sugar	1 bag	22	115	110	110	400.0
Tea	1 lb.	−/14	2/8	2/4	2/6	271
White long cloth	40 yds.	23	85	70	46	204.3
Grey sheeting	30 yds.	12	70	64	27	433.3

Source: Colonial Office, *Annual Report on the Somaliland Protectorate for the Year 1949* (London: H.M. Stationery Office, 1950).

[a] Computed from figures for 1939 and 1948.

[b] −/2 means 0 rupees and 6 annas.

Table 7. Value (in British pounds) and Percentage of Somaliland Exports to Countries of
Destination, 1952–1959

Year	British Arabia[a] Value	%	U.K. Value	%	Other British countries Value	%	Other countries Value	%
1952	849,173	82.6					75,146	7.2
1953	990,174	93.1					73,824	6.9
1954	1,081,756	89.5	—	1.0	1,440	0.1	125,447	10.4
1955	977,884	71.1	26,490	1.9	3,515	0.3	367,352	26.7[b]
1956	881,412	68.2	53,590	4.2			357,145	27.6[b]
1957	706,477	52.1	59,493	4.4			589,925	43.5[b]
1959	911,252	45.4	73,195	3.7			1,020,088	50.9[b]

Source: Somaliland Protectorate, Annual Trade Reports, 1952–57, 1959.
[a] Mainly Aden.
[b] Increasing percentages reflect the livestock export trade boom to Saudi Arabia.

Although some analysts of the Somali pastoral sector indicate that significant structural changes had begun to result from the increased commercialization of livestock,[10] the available evidence is not sufficient to warrant such a conclusion. Despite a lack of such evidence, one can argue
that a critical beginning was made by a handful of merchants who began to
grow livestock for purposes of trade only, although the overwhelming
number of stock traded still came from pastoralists' herds. Furthermore,
it is reasonable to assume that pastoral families were differentially involved in this trade. In sharp contrast to the prewar period, there were no
complaints on the part of the colonial authorities that the pastoralists were
living off the herds (in good grazing years) and significantly abandoning
trade. This critical change was brought about by two factors. First, the
Somaliland administration was heavily subsidized by the Imperial Treasury through the Colonial Development and Welfare funds and other
grants-in-aid. Consequently, the era of "spend no money and have no
ideas"[11] was gone forever. Second, because of the development of trade,
communication, and towns, imports such as sugar, grains, and clothes became a normal part of pastoral livelihood. As a result, the consumption of
these commodities did not depend on the quality of grazing and rain in
any one year.

The increasing involvement of traders in livestock (a few of them emerging from among the pastoralists) was an important factor in the ameliora-
tion of drought impact on pastoral trade. As transport and communication
developed, it became easier for many merchants and some pastoralists to
hire trucks to transport water and grass to the drought-afflicted flocks
from afar; indeed, some merchants had their own trucks.[12] Others owned

burkads (cement water tanks) and water reservoirs which greatly mitigated the impact of the localized droughts of the 1950s.[13] In fact, the re-
moval and transportation of grass on lorries began to seriously affect many
pastoralists, so that the colonial administration had to legislate against
such activity: "Legislation has been enacted prohibiting the transport
of grass on lorries [ordinance 14 of 1950]. So great had the trade become
that graziers were moved to protest that their essential dry-season grazing
was materially damaged."[14] Access to transport, grass, or water during
droughts must have had a differential impact on the pastoralist's ability to
cope with drought and certainly exacerbated already-existing inequalities
in herd ownership. The leveling effect that such calamities had in the past
was finally punctured.

During and after World War II the northwest region of the protectorate
was also going through important structural changes. In spite of the recent origins of farming, the small cultivated area significantly increased.
In 1949 the estimated area under cultivation was 50,850 acres; by 1954–55
it was 140,000 acres.[15] This expansion was triggered initially by the shortage of imported foodstuffs during the Italian invasion, when the protectorate was cut off from world trade and had to rely on its own food resources. This stimulus was further bolstered by the tremendous price
increases of imported consumer goods and locally grown sorghum (as
shown in Table 6). These price increases affected peasants and pastoralists
in different ways, but the consequences were similar for both groups. For
peasants who already grew the grains they consumed, price increases for
clothing, dates, sugar, and tea could be neutralized by increasing grain
production for sale. This was possible only through horizontal expansion
of production. Moreover, some pastoralists in the northwest responded to
the price pressure by turning to cultivation in order to produce their grain
requirements. The result of the expansion of cultivated area was to foster
an emerging competition for land.

The fear of being closed out of what was a common grazing land must
have pushed many who still preferred pastoralism to enclose their own
farms. This enclosure movement did not mean that pastoralists moved
to cultivation en masse overnight. The process took some years to mature and continues to the present day. The increases in sedentarization
pitted pastoralists against peasants. J. M. Watson, the director of the Agricultural and Veterinary Department, took note of the genesis of the conflict; it was

the incessant demand by members of all tribes for allocation for cultivation of
areas which have in the past been primarily regarded as range land. This is . . . an
indication of the slow decline in the production of milk and meat from the onetime
excellent grazing grounds and the subsequent necessity of increasing home grown

food supplies. The need is now of some . . . urgency not only to off-set this loss, but also to replace the importation of foodstuffs which once, before the World War, were obtainable at low cost, are now almost an expensive luxury.[16]

The sociopolitical consequences of this process, he continued, "are legion, the growing conflict between grazier and farmers are of the more apparent, but fortunately it is not the direct function of this department to provide a solution to the many socio-political problems which are springing up in its wake."[17] The administration's policy was to encourage any Somali wishing to leave the Reserved Areas (part of Somali territory under Anglo-Ethiopian rule) and to accommodate resettlers by giving them farmland in the Tugwajaleh plain. This may have further contributed to the conflict between pastoralists and peasants and to the deterioration of the environment.[18]

Among the "nonpolitical" consequences of this conflict was the ecological deterioration which became the primary concern of the protectorate's agricultural department. The incessant competition for agricultural land and the resulting privatization of land required physical enclosure of the private farms. Such enclosure was necessary not only for the purpose of identifying the property but also for protecting crops from man and beast alike. Consequently, sedentarization and privatization were accompanied by the destruction of vegetation used for making the enclosing hedge. The destruction of the bush, the deterioration of the pasture, and the bringing of more land under the plough exposed large tracts of land to erosion and denudation.[19]

Neither the agricultural department nor the colonial administration could alter the external forces that played an important role in the emergence and evolution of the pastoral and agricultural problem. The most the administration could do was to carry out a few projects intended to curb the "destruction" of agricultural land. In contrast to its failure to halt the deterioration of the pastoral range, the administration was relatively more successful in agriculture, despite the meekness of its efforts and its poor timing. Once the agricultural problems were identified, the solutions seemed straightforward and simple. The protectorate's agricultural problems were, according to the department, acute soil erosion, poor farming practices, low farm productivity, and unfavorable public opinion towards farming. A number of development schemes were undertaken to rectify these problems with the assistance of the Colonial Development and Welfare funds. Among these schemes were a number of experimental plots and farms which were established immediately for studying the problems. Bunds (earth banks erected along contours) were found to be effective means of water and soil conservation. Water shortage was one of the critical constraints on production, and bunding was an effective way of retaining as much rainwater on the farm as possible. These bunds proved their worth particularly when sufficient rain had not fallen or had fallen at an inappropriate time. The yield per acre in the experimental plots was five times that of the peasant's farm (2,000 lbs. versus 400 lbs).[20]

Transferring these research findings from the controlled environment of the demonstration farm to the risky world of the peasant meant that ways had to be found to encourage peasants to make use of these advances. The department of agriculture was skeptical about the willingness of the Somali peasant to voluntarily adopt these innovations: "At the present time in order to carry improved methods of agriculture into effect the only means appear to be persuasion, demonstration, and confiscation of farmland. The Somali is largely immune to the first two and the last is too severe. The difficulty of enforcing the rules in isolated places without the assistance of a Local Authority of chieftain system is the stumbling block."[21] The reluctance of the Somali peasant to adopt improved farming methods was underscored by the conditions impinging on the peasant: the pressure to enclose the land and cut bushes, which led to soil erosion; the general skepticism about foreign intrusion which also worked against change; and finally the inability of the department employees to appreciate the material and social conditions which may have bred and nurtured peasant reluctance.

As there were no elite native progressive farmers and no white settlers who could have formed the "bastions of progress," the administration decided to search for alternative torch-bearers. The decision was made to import a few Yemani families (citizens of Aden) who were experienced in the methods which the department wanted to propagate. The request for the importation was made to the director of agriculture in Aden.[22] The inducements offered to these Yemani farmers were free grants of farmland in a suitable area of their choice, general subsidies, and guarantees of current prices for their crops. From this time onwards flood-irrigated farms carried the name "Yemani farms." Despite the label, I have no information indicating that the Yemani farmers were ever brought in (although money was allocated for farm colonization). Whatever the outcome of this strategy,[23] in the annual report of 1953 the director of agriculture pointedly downgraded the demonstrative value of Yemani farms. He noted that the peasants were already well aware of the value of extra water to their crops.[24] Three years later the same director, Mr. Watson, joyously expressed his satisfaction at the cooperation between the agricultural-division employees and the farming community.[25]

In the early days of the bunding program, most of the work was done by the few tractors in the protectorate, but as more peasants decided to bund their farms it became impossible to accommodate the growing demand (the cost of bunding was subsidized by the government at 40–50 shillings per acre). The department, with peasant consent, then decided to use the tractors to loosen the soil so that the peasants could then use scraper boards pulled by oxen to construct the bunds. In spite of these innovations only 150 miles of earth banks were made in 1959, which protected 1,500 acres.[26] The area protected from soil erosion and water loss by these improvements was only about 0.78 percent of the total arable land. Thus, only a few peasants benefitted from this program.

The agricultural department's main task after the war (in the 1950s in particular) was the soil and water conservation program. However, there were other minor programs in which the department was concurrently engaged. These can be lumped together under the general rubric of research and extension, and were funded by the Colonial Development and Welfare Fund. The research end of these schemes included a hydrological survey, the introduction of date palms, and an experimental farm. The extension half of the program, consisting of tractor hire and an agricultural credit plan, was of more direct and immediate benefit to the peasant.[27] The tractor hire program (distinct from the bunding scheme) was inaugurated in 1953. In that year the Massey Harris tractor available for hire worked 192 hours on 72 farms, in spite of unforseen difficulties. More popular than the tractor hire program was the agricultural credit plan, whose purpose was to encourage peasants to adopt better farming practices. Loans were made available for a variety of undertakings, such as the hire and the purchase of bullocks,[28] the construction of Yemani farms, the sinking and deepening of wells, the construction of walls and banks for irrigation, the purchase of pumps, and the hire of labor for improvement projects.[29] By the end of 1953, the total value of the loans since the initiation of the program amounted to £1,040, of which £943 was made in 1953 (72 loans). In the following years, the department encountered some difficulties in collecting the debts. By the end of the decade the credit program had amounted to almost nothing, and farming methods remained predominantly traditional.

The expressed hopes and policy declarations of the administration notwithstanding, the research and extension plans affected only a small minority of the peasants in the protectorate. Although the soil and water conservation schemes made an important start in combatting soil erosion, the administration's efforts were too little and too late. Unlike its attempts in the pastoral sector, the administration's attempt to levy some form of direct taxation on farming finally succeeded. In the closing years of the decade, an annual farm tax of six shillings was instituted, and there was no apparent resistance to it.[30]

The State, the Urban Sector, and Somali Nationalism

If, in the mind of the administration, the rural sector—and pastoralism in particular—was synonymous with recalcitrant precapitalism, the same accusation cannot be levelled against the emerging town and urban sector. In sharp contrast to the pastoralists, who were able selectively to accept and reject state intervention into pastoral production, the emerging urban groups seem to have demanded massive infusions of state resources and visible state leadership in the development of the urban economy. The demands of the urban sector were most explicit and had the greatest effectiveness in the field of education. It will be recalled that before World War II, the Muslim clergy, who were incessantly opposed to the development of secular education, dominated traditional political leadership, a source of frustration to the administration. At that time opposition to the educational policy of the Somaliland administration (with the introduction of written Somali to schools) brought together an uneasy coalition of forces—mullahs, petty traders, and religiously inclined literates— which virtually stymied colonial education policy. The colonial administration inadvertently lent further support to these forces by making the provision of secular education contingent upon the availability of locally generated revenues.

The constellation of forces that had successfully blocked the development of education in the prewar era were undermined by the socioeconomic conditions emerging during and after the war. These conditions arose from two factors, one of which evolved from within the protectorate and the other of external origin. The internal factor was in large measure a product of external forces. It will be remembered that the Italian occupation of Ethiopia gave fledgling Somali traders a new lease on life. This impetus toward occupations not tied to the land was later reinforced by the historical accident which made the Horn and East Africa a major battleground in World War II. During the East Africa campaigns, a large number of Somalis were employed by the administration, in military and other capacities. Most of these people were estranged from their pastoral and peasant roots and became part of the emerging town people.

The deteriorating conditions of the pastoral and peasant sectors in conjunction with their increasing involvement with the mercantile economy must have encouraged some of the rural populace to migrate to the growing towns. Those who migrated to the towns can be divided into two categories. The first was a small group that had been weaned from their attachment to the "camel" and had begun to take up trade. The second group, much larger, had become marginal in the rural economy owing to a complex web of factors including drought, a declining rural economy, the

Table 8. Business Establishments in Somaliland, 1945 (number of licenses)

	Coffee shops	Retail shops	Eating houses
District town			
Hargeisa	52	126	66
Main villages			
Gabileh	4	29	2
Arabsiyo	20	6	1
Dabollok	23	0	1
Bederwanak	19	6	0
Adadleh	9	9	3
Darburruk	8	10	0
Dubato	8	0	2
Interior	81 (38 places)	4 (1 place)	1 (1 place)
Entire district	224	190	76
District town			
Berbera	60	148	32
Main villages			
Sheikh	14	11	1
Mandera	13	2	1
Sheikh Abdul	5	1	1
Hudiso	5	0	1
Lafarug	8	0	0
Bulhar	5	1	0
Interior	36 (22 places)	0	0
Entire district	146	163	36
Subdistrict town			
Zeila	46	101	9
Main village			
Abdel Cader	11	0	0
Interior	19 (12 places)	0	0
Entire subdistrict	76	101	9
Subdistrict town			
Borama	20	73	6
Interior	21 (18 places)	0	0
Entire subdistrict	41	73	6
District town			
Burao	70	130	32
Main villages			
Odweina	13	33	8
Einabo	3	22	4
Ber	7	13	3
El Huma	12	4	0
Goriale	1	6	4
Interior	46 (23 places)	17 (12 places)	1 (1 place)
Entire district	152	225	52

Table 8. Business Establishments in Somaliland, 1945 (number of licenses) *(continued)*

	Coffee shops	Retail shops	Eating houses
District town			
Las Anod	12	27	4
Main villages			
Wad-Wad	5	4	1
Hudin	3	4	0
Interior	10 (7 places)	6 (6 places)	0
Entire district	30	41	5
District town			
Erigavo	12	39	4
Main villages			
El Afweina	1	2	0
Gerudduk	5	6	0
Heis	3	6	0
Elayu	0	7	0
Las Kureh	1	4	0
Interior	7 (5 places)	71	4
Entire district	29	135	8

Source: *Report of the Committee of Inquiry into Pauperism in British Somaliland* (Hargeisa, 1954), p. 20.

attraction of urban life, and a weakening of the precapitalist moral economic ties, and had sought relief and refuge in towns.[31] The movement to towns and the increased postwar involvement of the protectorate in the mercantile economy is indicated by the heightened commercial activity in towns and villages, which catered to both rural and urban populations. See Table 8, which is based on the first published record of business establishments in the protectorate.) By 1945 there were 478 coffeehouses, 830 retail shops, and 186 eating places in the towns and villages of the protectorate. Hargeisa, the capital of the protectorate, which had a population of about 30,000, had 52 coffeehouses, 126 retail shops, and 66 eating places. Another product of the war was the increased exposure of those employed in commerce and government to the advantages of education in a literate world and the promise of social mobility. The growing urban economy spawned a new social coalition composed of a small number of civil servants and merchants, which was finally able to situate itself in the political center stage and push the clergy to the wings.

The external factor had a great deal to do with the changing conditions in the colonial world and to the unique problem inside the protectorate. In spite of the absence of traditional authority, the Somaliland administration, for reasons referred to earlier, was unable to develop a local elite

which could have become the basis of native administration before World
War II. After the reoccupation of the protectorate, the military administration was faced with the same problem as its predecessors, that is, the
need for a collaborative class which could ease its administrative night-
mare. The hands of the prewar administration were tied by the lack of
Imperial and protectorate funds and also by the effective resistance of the
clergy-led movement. The funds made available to the colonies by the
Colonial Development and Welfare Act of 1940 partially removed the financial constraint.[32] During the postwar era—with the internal opposition
to secular education largely neutralized and the financial constraints mitigated—the politico-economic environment was now ripe for a new align-
ment of social forces. With both external and internal obstacles removed,
and an administration eager to expand education, the emerging petite
bourgeoisie feverishly took advantage of the situation and demanded
more expansion of schools than the administration was willing to provide.[33] The only conflict between the colonial administration and this
emerging social stratum was the rate of expansion of schools. This basic
accord marks the dawn of a new era.

Regardless of the new socioeconomic alliance (as indicated by the formation of the Protectorate Advisory Council, discussed below) and the
availability of funds, educational expansion between 1943 and 1959 was
modest, as the enrollment statistics in Table 9 reveal. The significant increases in school enrollment in the mid-1950s were made possible by the
larger amounts of Colonial Development and Welfare Funds, as shown in
Table 10, at the disposal of the protectorate in general and the education
department in particular. More specifically, only £13,119 out of the total
education expenditure came directly from the United Kingdom in 1956.
Two years later, United Kingdom subsidies to the department were more
than 50 percent of its expenditures. In 1956 only 1.40 percent of school-
age children were in school. In the same year there were 450 applicants
for the 60 places in the two existing elementary schools in the protectorate
capital.[34] In 1958, a year before the protectorate was granted independence, just a little over 2 percent of the children were enrolled in school.

The initial purpose of the educational policy, as enunciated in 1952, was
to produce a small group of "well-educated boys" who would fill government posts (as civil servants) and key positions in commerce and craft.[35]
Given the unlikelihood of any industrial and agricultural development in
the protectorate, the administration had no intention of providing "inappropriate" education which would undermine the kind of life which the
Somalis "could reasonably hope to maintain."[36] Despite its predisposition, the administration did not singlehandedly determine future educational policy. The growing town masses under the leadership of the in-

Table 9. School Enrollment in British Somaliland, 1943–1959

Year	Elementary	Intermediate	Secondary, tec., and voc.	Total
1943	99	0	0	99
1946	408	0	0	408
1949	469	0	0	469
1951	639	274	0	913
1953	1,050	345	49 [a]	1,444
1954	1,017	496	50	1,563
1955	—	—	33	1,686
1956	1,191	431	161 [b]	1,783
1958	1,967	914	81 [c]	—
1959	—	—	—	3,906 [d]

Sources: Colonial and education reports, 1943–59.

[a] First secondary school in the Protectorate was established in 1953 (16 out of the 49 boys constitute the first class).

[b] Includes 63 in secondary education, 25 in teacher training (after intermediate school), and 73 in technical or vocational training.

[c] Secondary education only; figures for teacher training and technical and vocational education unavailable.

[d] In addition, there were 133 students studying abroad.

Table 10. Expenditure on Education in Somaliland, Selected Years, 1935–1958 (pounds)

Year	Recurrent expenditures	Nonrecurrent expenditures	Total
1935–36	—	—	509
1943–44	—	—	2,386
1947–48	—	—	18,472
1949–50	—	—	33,315
1956	78,271	4,874	83,145
1958	133,754	134,361	268,115

Sources: Colonial and education reports, 1936–58.

cipient but vocal petite bourgeoisie in the Protectorate Advisory Council, a group of Somali opinion-makers selected by the colonial government to assist it in domestic policy formulation and administration, challenged and modified the views of the administration.[37] The expansion of schools in the middle and late 1950s was partly a product of increasing pressure by the leadership of the Advisory Council. In spite of these expansions in school capacity, the use of boarding facilities to accommodate more children, and the wider geographical distribution of schools (as shown in Map 3), the overwhelming majority of pastoral and peasant children were untouched

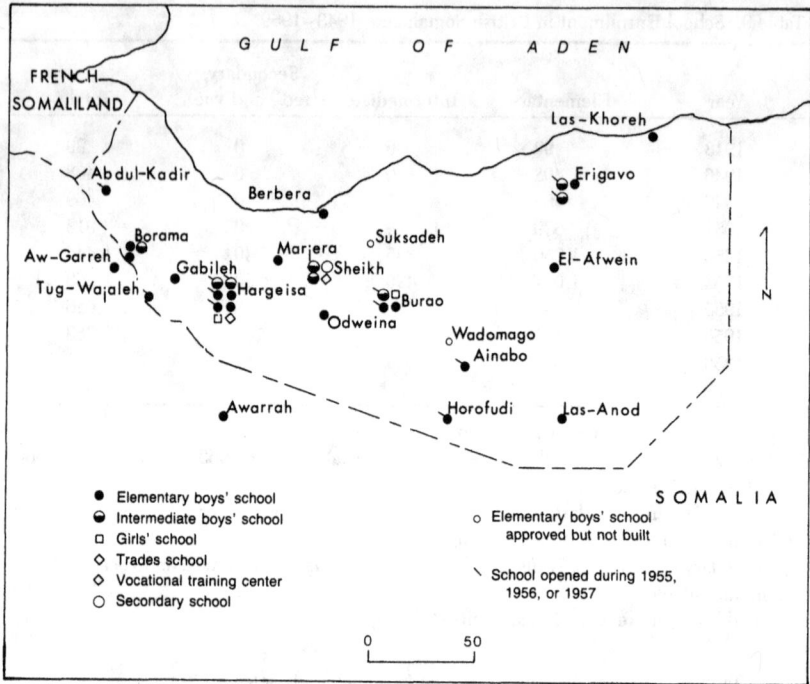

Map 3. Schools in Somaliland Protectorate, 1955–1957
Source: British Somaliland, Education Report, 1957

by the education that was supposed to "make them more successful"
herders and cultivators.

The Second World War not only gave impetus to the expansion of trade
and the acceleration of other internal socieconomic processes, but also
had other repercussions for the protectorate. The most critical of these
was the unification of all Somali territories except Vichy Djibouti under
British military rule and the subsequent rise of contemporary Somali nationalism. In spite of the fact that the Somalilands were under unified
British rule, each territory still had its own British administration. The
protectorate had its own military governor in Hargeisa. The Haud and the
Reserved Areas (see Map 4) were administered from Jigjiga by the British, who shared that city with the Ethiopians until 1954. The Ogaden remained attached to Somalia (as Italian Somaliland was known) under its
British headquarters in Mogadishu.[38]

Of all the colonized Somali lands, Somalia had known the most interventionist colonial policy. Italy, weak and a latecomer to colonialism, and
craving for its own empire, had intended to transform Somalia into its
settler colony. Between the early days of this century and the beginning

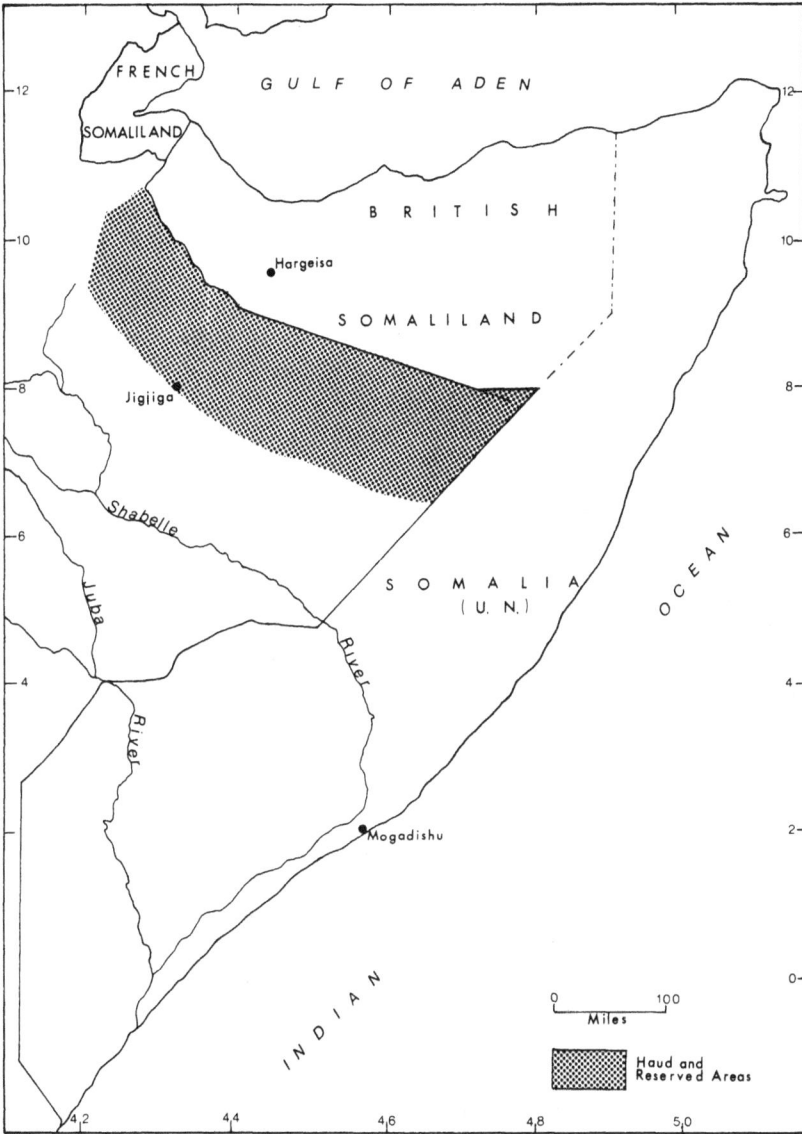

Map 4. The Haud and Reserved Areas

of World War II, it had envisaged various "development" schemes. At long last, a plantation economy emerged in parts of the riverine areas.[39] In sharp contrast to the British administrators of its northern colonial neighbor, the Italian administration appropriated land and employed forced labor early on; the use of forced labor was intensified during the Fascist regime. The humiliating defeat of the Italian Fascists lent new spirit to the many laboring people in the colony. In direct contradiction to Italian colonial policies, the British military administration began recruiting and training Somalis for junior positions in government. They also removed the ban on local politics. Through this liberalizing process a new cadre of Somalis emerged, hardened by the oppressive and discriminatory policies of the Fascists, enlightened by the propaganda of the Allies and the British "liberation," and aware of the struggles of other colonial peoples.

The indignation of the past, the upheavals of the East Africa campaigns, the defeat of their oppressors, and the growing awareness of the world at large created a classically fertile ground for the emergence of nationalist movements.[40] In 1943 the first modern nationalist movement, the Somali Youth Club, was founded. Not surprisingly, all of the founding members came from that stratum known by some as the "middle class." With the blessing of and under the watchful eye of the military administration, the club's membership grew to an estimated 25,000 by 1946.[41] In the following year the club changed its name to Somali Youth League and became a full-fledged political machine with offices and officers in all the Somali lands except Djibouti (French Somaliland). The league had a four-point program: (*a*) uniting all Somalilands and eradicating tribalism; (*b*) educational development; (*c*) keeping a clear eye on Somali affairs; and (*d*) developing a script for the Somali language.[42] Two events injected more spirit into the league. First, the United Nations deliberations on the future of the colony aroused patriotic fervor, particularly during the visit of the U.N.'s Four-Power Commission delegation in 1948. Despite the Somalis' demonstrated anti-Italian sentiments, Britain, France, and the United States voted for a U.N. trusteeship under Italian tutelage. This was done in the context of the cold war, to welcome Italy back into the Western camp.[43] In spite of the disheartening vote of the Four-Power Commission, the United Nations for the first time specified an independence date for a trusteeship, which was to be 1960 for Somalia. Second, while these deliberations were going on, and again over the objections of the western Somalis (who appealed to the British government), in 1948 Britain handed over the Ogaden to Ethiopia.

The days when the Somalilands could be carved up without the people's notice and protest were gone forever. The 1948 transfer of the Ogaden stirred strong emotions in southern Somalia and even in the quieter British Protectorate in the north. The protectorate, in contrast to southern Somalia, saw little state intervention, political oppression, and economic restructuring in the rural sector, conditions which were central to the rise of nationalist movements in the south. The emerging and aspiring petite bourgeoisie in the protectorate had few state-erected obstacles to overcome in their desire for greater self-aggrandisement. As was suggested earlier, they eagerly awaited the return of the British during the brief Italian occupation. Two factors converged during this time which rendered whatever nationalistic tendency these groups may have had inconsequential.

First, the British military administration established the Protectorate Advisory Council in 1946, the forerunner of local government councils, immediately after reoccupation. This administrative initiative preempted and went far beyond the dreams of most members of the trading and bureaucratic strata. Equally important was the eagerness of the administration to expand and develop education. These steps were, as the governor noted in 1947, clearly aimed at creating and promoting a collaborationist class for purposes of indirect rule, but it also had a disarming effect. Members of the council were selected by the governor. Potential council members had to be amenable to the general policy orientation of the administration. They also had to be "acceptable" to and "representative" of the clans of the protectorate if the council was to have any legitimacy. Elements of the protectorate petite bourgeoisie were the only group who could reasonably satisfy this seemingly contradictory rule. Among the notable members were Jirdeh Hussein M.B.E. (Master of the British Empire), Haji Ibrahim Egal M.B.E. (whose son Mohamed Ibrahim Egal later led the Somali delegation to the constitutional conference in London and then became prime minister of the Somali Republic in 1967), Michael Mariano, Haji Dahir Elmi, Haji Ibrahim Nur, and Sultan Abdirahman Sultan Deria. With the exception of Michael Mariano (a Christian Somali) and Sultan Abdirahman, these members were among the wealthiest merchants in the protectorate. Jirdeh Hussein and Haji Dahir Elmi became members of the board of directors of the Somali National Bank after the country became independent.[44]

Second, the nascent trading and bureaucratic groups could not have been better situated and better served during this period, given the new commercial opportunities and the lessened administrative restrictions. These groups were of no help to the administration in its attempts to intervene into pastoral production, yet the administration was pleased with their progress and the absence of major conflict.

Despite the apparently conflict-free environment that prevailed in the protectorate, there existed a handful of dissident Somalis who had gained awareness of the nationalist movements occurring in southern Somalia and elsewhere in the colonial world. These people, including some overseas Somalis, began to organize. Their first organization was called the Somaliland National Society, which was renamed the Somali National League in 1947. The Somali Youth League also had offices in the protectorate. The attitude of the administration towards these organizations was condescending at best; a government report of 1946 stated: "During the year some so-called nationalist activity has been apparent which lacks able guidance. . . . Many of the members of the Somaliland National Society are uneducated youth in towns who lack employment and hold this as a grievance for which the government is responsible."[45] This treatment was in sharp contrast to the kind of support the nationalist movement received from the British military administration in southern Somalia. Nevertheless, the propaganda of these organizations had little appeal, and the nationalist fervor waned for some years in the absence of any pressing political or economic problem around which Somalis could rally.

The 1948 Ogaden transfer proved to be too mild a source of grievance. It took the transfer of the Haud and the Reserved Area to Ethiopia in 1954, in combination with the progress made towards independence in southern Somalia, to deliver the message home and propel the petite bourgeoisie into the center of the nationalist movement. At long last a cause was found around which people could mobilize. As soon as the terms of transfer between Britain and Ethiopia became public knowledge, huge demonstrations took place in all parts of the protectorate. Public donations were collected to enable a Somali delegation to go to London and New York to petition to Whitehall and appeal to the conscience of the world community.[46] These efforts bore no fruit in terms of retrieving the lost territories. One of the tenets of the Anglo-Ethiopian agreement which brought the western Somalilands (Haud and the Reserved Area) under the rule of Imperial Ethiopia guaranteed Somali grazing rights in the region. But the British administration soon found it had little leverage with Ethiopia and was helpless in the face of Ethiopian violations of the agreement.[47] The failure to regain the lost territories coupled with Ethiopian violations of the agreement and the increasing awareness of the people about their national predicament left only one choice for those who were aspiring for political leadership, to seek self-government. After some negotiation with the administration, elections for self-government were held in February 1960, and subsequently the protectorate's first legislative assembly was formed. Immediately after these elections, with the approaching independence of Somalia, the Protectorate Assembly unanimously called for independence and unification with Somalia.[48] The assembly asked the governor to arrange for selected delegates to travel to London in order to make a formal request for independence to the colonial secretary. The request was granted, and a constitutional conference was held in the Colonial Office.[49] The colonial secretary granted the request for independence, and June 26, 1960, was set as the date of independence, just a little over a month after the conclusion of the conference.

The sudden collapse of British colonialism in Somaliland was attribut-able to the convergence of a number of strategic, economic, and political conditions. First, Somaliland lost its strategic value to Britain, particu-larly after the Indian subcontinent became independent. Although a large contingent of British troops were still in Aden, the danger of being cut off from their meat supply, which had haunted authorities in the past, had long since become irrelevant. Second, the Somali delegation was fully aware of the underdevelopment of Somaliland and of the country's built-in dependency on Britain. For example, of the total protectorate expen-ditures of £2,390,767 in 1958–59, £1,385,583 came from United Kingdom grants.[50] With a colonial government eager to relinquish colonial hegem-ony over the protectorate, a petite bourgeoisie anxious to take over the colonial state, and with neither Imperial nor colonial economic interest groups present to complicate the negotiations, the process of decoloniza-tion went smoothly and swiftly.[51] After seventy-six years of colonialism, Somaliland gained independence on June 26, 1960. Five days later the Somali Republic was formed as a union of the former Italian and British territories.

Conclusion

Nationalists, African socialists, and some Marxist social commentators have depicted colonialism as an attempt to forestall African development. In an attempt to correct this misconception, Freund suggests that despite the transfer of resources from the continent and its subsequent impover-ishment, colonial capitalism also had a progressive edge, that of develop-ing the forces of production.[52] The general nature of this discussion tends to conceal the variability of the effects of colonial capitalism. The final determinants of the effects of colonial capitalism on colonial societies de-pended on three interrelated factors: the economic prospects of the colony and the potential profit for the Imperial country; the noneconomic—that is, strategic—value of the colony; and the strength or weakness of pre-capitalist resistance to colonial intervention. The development or lack of development of the forces of production was a product of the interplay among these conditions. If a colony had a high economic potential—as did Zimbabwe, the Shaba region in Zaire, and the copper belt of Zambia and the Kenya highlands—colonial capitalist intervention was intense, lead-ing to the development of the forces of production. In such colonies the cost of suppressing precapitalist resistance was a worthwhile exercise, given the potential economic returns. If, on the other hand, the colony was economically unattractive but strategically valuable, little develop-ment of the productive forces occurred, particularly when the state had to

face a strong precapitalist resistance. These are only two of many possible
scenarios. The latter case seems to reflect conditions in Somaliland. As
was seen earlier, the prospect for colonial economic development in
Somaliland was grim, but the territory was deemed vital to British colonial strategy. Poor economic potential combined with strong and persistent precapitalist resistance circumscribed the level of development of
the productive forces in British Somaliland.

Some analysts suggest that in the absence of the development of capitalism in such societies as Somalia, precapitalism has survived and consequently buttresses stagnation and underdevelopment.[53] The preceding
discussion of the Somali condition indicates a different explanation for
underdevelopment. It will be recalled that the precolonial pastoral economy and society had a number of salient features. First, it was an economy oriented to the production of use-values. Second, there existed neither a landlord class nor a state establishment; and surplus extraction was
extremely limited to the "price" differences between bartered commodities. Third, this society had developed specific forms of herd organization
and management which ensured survival and reproduction. These techniques were a response to the demands of a precarious ecosystem. In
spite of the unsuccessful attempts by the state to reform pastoral production and the *seemingly* unaltered precapitalist facade which persisted, the
colonial period saw critical changes in the protectorate's political economy
which substantially altered Somali precapitalism. The first and foremost
of these changes was the expansion of the single-sector economy into a
three-sector one: pastoral, peasant, and town. Second, the era of statelessness vanished as the colonial state was established. Third, through the
provision of veterinary and water services and the commoditization of
livestock, the traditional pastoral-ecosystem relationship was ruptured.

Of what consequences were these changes for the territory's future economic development? First, out of the expansion of trade and the establishment of the colonial state gradually emerged a class of merchants and
state bureaucrats who had a claim on pastoral production. Second, the
provision of veterinary services and minor water developments in the pastoral sector partially mitigated nature's influences over pastoral life. This
blended well with the time-tested pastoral tendency (practice) to accumulate livestock. Part of the increase in the livestock population was
marketed, but most remained on the range. This horizontal expansion of
livestock production led to the exploitation of marginal areas and the overcrowding of traditional grazing lands. Third, most of the meager surplus
(rent) captured by the merchant and the state class was not invested in
productivity-enhancing enterprises in the urban sector. In other words,
the state and merchant capital were not progressive forces in terms of lay-

ing the foundation for a new and regenerative regime of accumulation. Such productive investments could have relieved the strain on the rural economy. Fourth, the increase in the price of imported necessities forced the expansion and intensification of rural production without concomitant enhancement of the productive forces.[54] This in no way means that changes did not occur in rural production. Rather, interventions in rural production such as disease control through veterinary services merely intensified precapitalist methods of resource exploitation, while the soil and water conservation schemes had a marginal impact on peasant production. With rural producers inextricably linked to the mercantile system and with no hope of the "exit" option, these pressures continually pushed production to marginal areas. This interpretation of northern Somali rural transformation under colonial capitalism does not belittle the initiatives of rural producers; instead, it stresses the contextual nature of human action.

In the end, the articulation of the Somali society to the world capitalist system was sealed. The days when pastoralists could withdraw from the market, even briefly, and live alone on pastoral products had passed. Furthermore, Somali rural producers became an integral part of a national economy dominated by merchant capital, both at the level of the state and in the private sector. Consequently, the future development of the agrarian sector was inextricably intertwined with the accumulation strategy of the state-mercantile class.

4

The Civilian Postcolonial State and the Agrarian Sector, 1960–1969

> Men make their history, but they do not make it just as they please; they do not make it under circumstances chosen by themselves, but under circumstances directly encountered, given and transmitted from the past. The tradition of all the dead generations weighs like a nightmare on the brain of the living.
>
> Karl Marx
> *The Eighteenth Brumaire*

> A development strategy indicates the general orientation of a regime with respect to the accumulation function. First, a development strategy indicates . . . which class . . . will take the main responsibility for expanding the economy, and hence benefit from the accumulation of capital. It also suggests . . . which classes . . . will have to bear the major part of the burden of socio-economic change.
>
> Richard Sandbrook
> *The Politics of Basic Needs*

During the struggle for national liberation, the nationalist ideology had the vast majority of the African body politic believe that colonial domination was the cause of their poverty and suffering and that "independence" was the panacea for these maladies. Very often, in those early days of independence, the discussion of development policy revolved around what ought to have been done. Instead of engaging in such a normative exercise, it is more fruitful to map the conditions, both objective and subjective, that the fledgling postcolonial society inherited. As Ake notes, a closer examination of these conditions will yield better insights into the rationale behind the particular orientation of any development policy.[1]

One of the inherited products of the colonial era was not only the postcolonial state but also the social classes that formally controlled it.[2] Materialist analysts note the centrality of the state in the development process, particularly in underdeveloped societies, where it is the controller of surplus. Following the lead of Hamza Alavi, analysts indicate various degrees of subservience of the postcolonial state to metropolitan capital.[3] Michaela von Freyhold, in particular, suggests that the governing class in the postcolonial society (as distinct from the ruling class) is a junior partner of the ruling metropolitan classes.[4] Moreover, some of the "domestic" policies of the governing class which may seem to contradict the interest of the ruling class, such as nationalization, do not necessarily do so. Nationalization, according to von Freyhold, is merely an attempt by the governing class to tighten its control over the producers. Revising his earlier analysis of the Kenyan state, Colin Leys notes that the postcolonial state is not necessarily and inherently an obedient servant of metropolitan capital.[5] In fact, in certain cases it can act and has acted on behalf of the local bourgeoisie, in contradiction to the design of metropolitan overlords. These presumably contradictory functions of the postcolonial state are not necessarily antagonistic. It is likely that the conclusions of von Freyhold and Leys reflect two particular historical junctures. The postcolonial state is neither inherently dependent nor inherently independent from metropolitan capital. The incorporation of colonial societies into the world capitalist system circumscribes the economic and political latitude available to the postcolonial state and society. The nature and the function of the postcolonial state are contingent upon the *balance* of internal class forces, which are themselves a product of colonial history, and the level of *development* of the productive forces.

Chapters 2 and 3 illustrated the underdevelopment of productive forces in colonial Somaliland. In the absence of a productive and dynamic domestic economy which could generate "sufficient" surplus for accumulation, the postcolonial state relied on external sources (foreign aid) to generate almost all its resources for economic growth. Such reliance on foreign aid had a number of lasting effects on the nature of the postcolonial political economy. First, it made the postcolonial state more responsive to the dictates of aid donors. Second, the postcolonial development strategies (reflecting the views of the donors and the governing class) bypassed rural producers, the bedrock of domestic production, and failed to generate alternative productive domestic sources of accumulation. Third, the failure to develop domestic sources of accumulation and the "neglect" of pastoral and peasant production intensified the state's dependence on foreign aid. The centrality of foreign aid as a source of domestic accumulation, to use Bates' analysis, created a peculiar form of rent-seeking society.[6] The competition between members of the governing petite bourgeoisie for strategic state offices, in order to get access to aid funds, became the central locus of politics. Consequently, the postcolonial state, rather than being embedded in the productive fabric of the Somali economy, was suspended over it.

The analysis in this chapter and the next one (to be read together) give primacy to state agrarian policies for the simple reason that the postcolonial state dominated the direction of agrarian (under)development. This is not to neglect or disregard the significance of peasant-pastoralist initia-

tives, but to underline the context within which such enterprises operated. After all, human action is contextual, as some of the detailed discussion in Chapter 5 confirms. These chapters unravel the astonishing
similarities between the development strategies of the parliamentary government of the 1960s and those of the present regime, in spite of their
opposing ideological stances. The rural development policies of both regimes have been biased against the peasant and the pastoralist. Furthermore, I will argue that the suspension of the postcolonial state over the
Somali economy is not so because of the precapitalist proclivities of the
peasant and the pastoralist, but rather, because of the creation (during
the colonial era) and perpetuation (during the postcolonial era) of a disarticulated Somali economy.[7] Hyden is quite correct when he talks about
the weakness and the suspension of the postcolonial state but is wrong in
his contention that its weakness and reliance on metropolitan capital is
due to the *ability* of African rural producers to evade state agrarian policy
and the market economy. The un(der)development of the productive
forces and the pursuit of a particular form of petit bourgeois accumulation
in a disarticulated economy underlie the weakness of the postcolonial
state in relation to "metropolitan" capital, as this analysis illustrates.

This chapter consists of six parts. The first briefly narrates the political
and the administrative organization of the postcolonial state. Second, I
sketch the fiscal basis of the postcolonial state and its relations to rural
producers and the world economy in the late 1950s and early 1960s. The
third section outlines the conditions of the rural economy. The fourth part
examines the economic development (agrarian) strategy the state adopted
in order to expand its resource base; it also assesses the impact of this
strategy on rural producers. Fifth, I argue that the collapse of petit bourgeois parliamentary democracy in 1969 was an inherent but not an inevitable outcome of the struggle between various factions within the petite
bourgeoisie for state control and hence state resources. Finally, I conclude the chapter by looking into the nature of the military coup.

The Organization of the Postcolonial State

On the first day of July 1960, the former British and Italian colonies
joined to form the independent Somali Republic. The two state appa-
ratuses were integrated into a unitary administration. The new republic
had three branches of government: the legislative, the executive, and the
judiciary (Fig. 12). The parliament, or National Assembly, consisted of
thirty-three deputies from the north and ninety deputies from the south.
The Somali National League controlled the majority of northern seats,
while the Somali Youth League dominated the south. Other, smaller po-

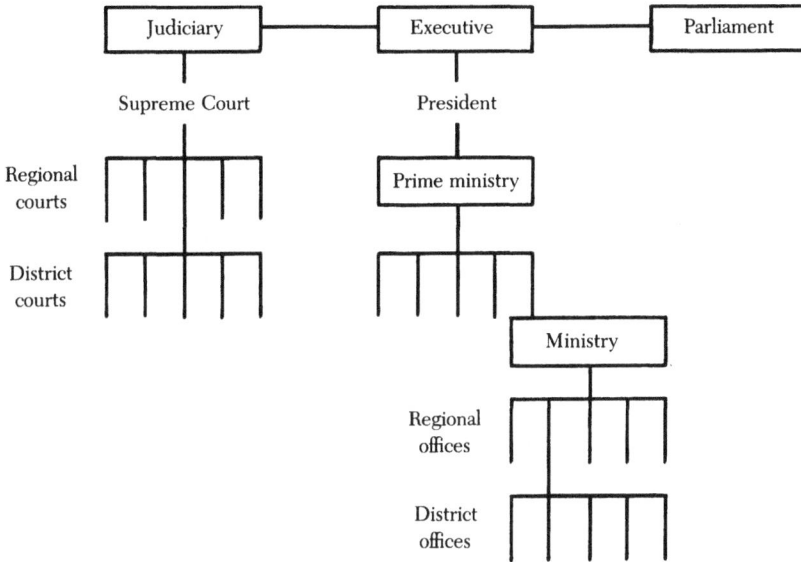

Figure 12. Postcolonial State Apparatus

litical parties, such as the United Somali Party and the Hizbia Digile Mi-
rifle (HDMS), had few members in the parliament. Members of parliament were elected every four years by a universal sufferage. Despite the
regional differences between the two main political parties, there was no
fundamental philosophical or ideological difference between them.[8] The
executive branch was headed by a president (elected from among the
members of parliament), who appointed the chief minister. The chief
minister, or prime minister, in turn, nominated his cabinet, which was
subject to the approval of the National Assembly. The executive branch
had twelve ministers and their regional and district representatives. The
regional branches were accountable to their respective ministers. Similarly, each region and district had its own locally elected legislative councils. Despite the existence of these locally elected bodies, the regional governors and the district commissioners—representative of the Ministry of
Interior of the central government—had monopoly on regional and district administration. Although the local legislative councils had both economic and financial responsibilities, the representatives of the central
government had a virtual veto power over their decisions, as most localities were dependent on the central government. Members of the judi-
cial branch, though appointed by the government, were "independent"
from it.

In the former British Protectorate (the northern region or the north henceforth), we have seen that merchants, teachers, and others who owed their very existence as a social category to the colonial economy led the independence movement. The Somali political leaders participating in the independence negotiations had no substantive disagreements with the Colonial Office. Their only grievances against the British were the transfer of Somali territory to Ethiopia and the lack of economic development.

In the trusteeship territory of Somalia (the southern region or the south hereafter), the Italian colonial administration, under the watchful eye of the U.N. Trusteeship Council, tutored Somalis in state affairs. The U.N. General Assembly prescribed that "the Western framework . . . had to be adapted to the traditions of a people to whom modern concepts of the state and democracy were alien."[9] The administering authority—Amministrazione Fiduciaria Italiana della Somalia (AFIS), as it was known—took note of the instructions and carefully prepared Somalis to replace Italians in the administration of their country without any structural changes in the economy of the territory. In the sphere of politics, however, an electoral process was introduced which satisfied the demands of such "aspiring natives" as traders and civil servants. Paying heed to the guidelines of the General Assembly, the colonial administration held the first general election in the territory, in which a territorial legislative body was elected. The Somali Youth League won most of the seats and dominated the new territorial government. Somali ministers took command of the administration except in foreign affairs and security, which were beyond the purview of the first modern Somali government.

The Fiscal Basis of the Postcolonial State

The Somali petite bourgeoise which took control of the state in 1960 had inherited a state that was weak in relation to the rural producers and also to its fomer colonial overlords. In neither region of the country had the colonial administration succeeded in transforming peasant and pastoral production into full-fledged commodity production. The vast majority of the Somali people were rural producers who had full access to the means of production (land). The failure of these administrations is indicated by the absence of any form of direct taxation on production. For example, in the case of the Italian colony indirect taxes constituted about 73 percent of the state's locally generated revenues between 1950 and 1958.[10] In the British Protectorate indirect taxes, mainly in the form of customs duties, accounted for more than 80 percent of the local revenues from 1955 to 1959.[11] Thus, the inherited postcolonial state was deeply rooted in the sphere of circulation, to use Kitching's notion.[12] In essence, state capacity to extract resources from local producers was tightly circumscribed by colonial history.

Table 11. Italian Budgetary Assistance to Somaliland, 1950–1958 (in thousands of Somali
shillings)

Year	Territorial revenues	Revenues from Italian grants	Total revenues	% of total from Italy
1950	21.8	118.6	140.4	84.5
1953	31.4	65.7	97.1	67.7
1956	44.2	57.1	101.3	56.4
1958	520.0	49.7	101.7	48.9

Source: A. A. Castagno, Jr., *Somalia*, Carnegie Endowment for International Peace Series, no. 522 (New York: Carnegie Endowment for International Peace, 1959), p. 380.

Another weakness of the postcolonial state, intricately related to the first, was its dependency on foreign assistance for its fiscal health. Locally generated revenues continuously fell short of meeting the recurrent expenditures of the state. This financial insolvency was part of the colonial legacy. As we saw in Chapter 3, the protectorate administration critically depended upon the Imperial Treasury. The Italian administration in the south was equally dependent on its home treasury for budgetary subsidies; as Table 11 indicates, grants from the Italian treasury made up between 84.5 and 48.9 percent of the colony's revenues in 1950 and 1958, respectively. Furthermore, as expenditures outstripped locally generated revenue in spite of some fiscal discipline exercised by the government,[13] subsidies from the imperial countries were necessary long after independence. To balance the government's budget, Britain and Italy made contributions of more than 138.7 million Somali shillings,[14] which amounted to more than 31 percent of the national budget of the first three years of independence. Thus, from the very beginning the postcolonial state was not able to meet its recurrent fiscal and long-term development needs from local sources. Accumulation based on domestic production was of much less significance than foreign aid. Consequently, the state became all the more central not as an instrument for the legitimization and reproduction of domestic exploitation but rather as a source of accumulation itself. Politics and therefore the state were "suspended" above society.

The Conditions in the Rural Economy

The fiscal problems of the postcolonial state were symbolic of the general underdevelopment of the productive structures of the economy which it had inherited. How underdeveloped was the economy? The agrarian productive structure, such as it was, consisted of (1) the plantation sector (bananas and sugar cane), (2) the pastoral sector, and (3) a small but important peasant sector.

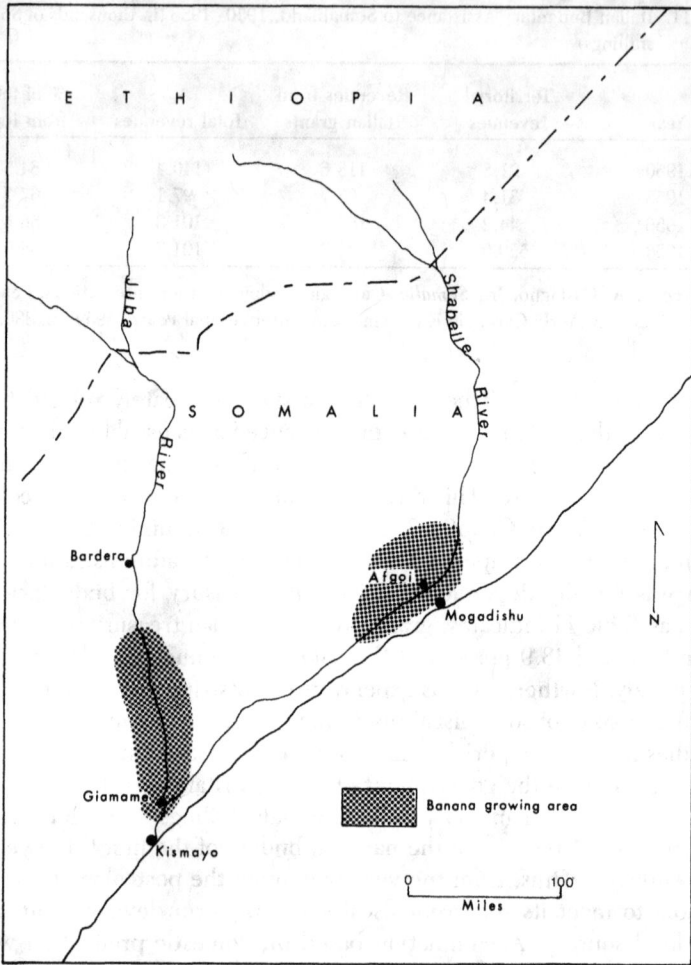

Map 5. Banana-Growing Areas in Southern Somalia

The plantation sector, mainly bananas for export, had been introduced into the south in 1928. There were two banana-growing areas in the country, Afgoi and Giamame, both on the banks of the only two permanent rivers (see Map 5). In 1930 Somali banana exports were exempted from Italian import duty.[15] This new economic enterprise was derailed by the Second World War, when most of the plantations reverted back to bush. Once the war was over, the plantations were resuscitated, although recovery was slow. Enjoying a competitive advantage in Italy because of the Italian tax exemption for Somali imports, bananas became the colony's single most important export crop. In 1950, plantations took up only 2,800 hectares, which produced 28,000 tons of the fruit; thirteen years later, banana plantations covered 11,000 hectares, and fruit production had increased to 110,000 tons (Table 12). In 1963 bananas accounted for about 45 percent of all the country's exports. In spite of the expansion of both the plantations and the volume of fruit produced, the proportion of exports accounted for by bananas by value remained relatively stationary from 1958 to 1963. This was in large part due to the declining price of Somali bananas. The average price at the Somali ports for a kilogram of bananas in 1949 was 155 lire. Fourteen years later the price was only 91 lire (Table 13).

Before 1960 banana plantations were entirely owned by Italian colonialists. It was only after independence that ownership changed partially, and by 1964–65, 350 of the 450 banana plantations were Somali-owned. Despite this overwhelming numerical superiority, the Somali farms had a much smaller area than the 250–350-hectare average size of the Italian plantations. More critically, however, the Italian planters had a monopoly over exports through their associations, the Societa Azionaria Concessionaria Agricoli di Genale, or SACA, and the Societa Agricoltori Giuba, or SAG).[16]

The other plantation crop was sugarcane. The first sugar plantation opened on a commercial basis in 1927 when an Italian firm, SAIS, established a small sugar refinery on the banks of the Shabelle River. In the early years, the firm produced relatively small quantities of sugar and sugar products despite the existence of a large internal market. It was only in the late 1950s, as indicated in column 7 of Table 14, that the firm began to produce significant amounts of the product to meet more than 50 percent of local demand. The large increase in productivity (in tons/hectare) in the late 1950s was brought about by heavy use of fertilizer and better farming methods. In spite of these improvements in productivity and the existence of a local market, only a small part of the plantation area was still in use during this period. Of the 24,000 hectares of prime agricultural land on the banks of the Shabelle River, the firm had irrigated only about 7,000 hectares, and as shown in Table 14, only a fraction of that was planted in cane. Some of the remaining land was used for grapefruit, cotton, peanuts, and food grains.[17]

Livestock was the second most important Somali export commodity at the time of independence. More significantly, some estimates have suggested that more than 65 percent of the Somali population depended on stock-raising for their subsistence.[18] The national livestock population was estimated in 1963 at 11 million head.[19] This figure may be a low estimate of the Somali herd, since earlier authorities such as Glover had suggested

Table 12. Production and Export of Bananas in Somalia, 1950–1963

	Production			Exports			
Year	Area (ha)	Tons	Tons/ha	Tons	% of total banana production	Value (thousands of So. sh.)	% of all exports accounted for by bananas
1950	2,800	28,000	10.0	22,065	78.8	—	—
1951	3,600	34,000	9.4	25,200	74.4	—	—
1952	3,800	40,000	10.5	32,030	80.1	—	—
1953	6,200	60,000	9.7	30,178	50.3	—	—
1954	6,700	55,000	8.2	43,389	78.9	—	—
1955	8,000	73,400	9.2	48,278	65.8	—	—
1956	8,800	65,000	7.4	36,515	56.2	—	—
1957	8,600	60,000	7.0	42,565	70.9	45,859	44.2
1958	8,498	83,000	9.9	55,848	67.3	58,906	45.3
1959	8,500	85,000	10.0	58,763	65.7	65,000	44.6
1960	9,100	91,000	10.0	73,735	81.0	74,430	45.3
1961	11,000	98,000	8.9	84,316	86.6	90,267	48.0
1962	12,000	107,000	8.8	75,555	70.6	80,149	44.1
1963	11,000	110,000	10.0	94,512	85.9	101,000	45.0

Sources: T. G. Shirname, Report to the Government of Somalia on Food and Agricultural Economy, FAO Report no. 2088 (Rome, 1965), p. 16. Data for last two columns (except 1963) from Somali National Bank, Report and Balance Sheet, 1962 (Mogadishu, 1963), pp. 114–15; data for 1963 from Somali Republic, Planning Commission, Short-Term Development Programme, 1968–1970 (Mogadishu, 1968), p. 24; no data is available for 1950–56.

Table 13. Average Price of Bananas at Somali Ports, 1949–
1963, Fixed by Azienda Monopolio Banane (AMB)

Year	Lire/kg	% annual decline of price/kg
1949	155	
1950	140	9.7
1951	137	2.1
1952	127	7.3
1953	123	3.1
1954	115	6.5
1955	112	2.6
1956	106	3.4
1957	101	4.7
1958	98	3.0
1959	94	4.1
1960	94	4.3
1961	92	2.1
1962	92	2.2
1963	91	1.1

Source: IBRD, "The Economy of the Trust Territory of Somaliland," January 1957, and Ministry of Agriculture and Animal Husbandry, cited in Shirname, *Report to the Government of Somalia on Food and Agricultural Economy*, p. 16.

Table 14. Sugarcane Production and National Imports of Sugar, 1950–1963

Year	Production Area (ha)	Production Tons	Production Tons/ha	Sugar imports (tons)	Total sugar consumed (tons)	Local production as % of total consumed
1950	1,264	3,580	2.8	—	—	
1951	2,000	5,016	2.5	—	—	
1952	2,500	5,160	2.1	—	—	
1953	3,000	4,015	1.3	—	—	
1954	3,500	8,361	2.4	—	—	
1955	3,200	10,400	3.3	—	—	
1956	3,500	8,891	2.5	—	—	
1957	1,146	10,003	7.0	—	—	
1958	1,230	11,049	9.0	8,315	19,364	57.1
1959	1,300	11,549	8.9	13,525	25,074	46.1
1960	1,300	11,500	9.6	10,471	21,971	52.3
1961	1,200	11,785	9.8	11,001	22,786	51.7
1962	1,300	11,885	9.1	19,572	31,457	37.8
1963	—	—	—	17,622	—	

Source: Shirname, *Report to the Government of Somalia on Food and Agricultural Economy*, pp. 12, 13.

91

Table 15. Main Export Commodities of Somalia, 1957–1962 (thousands of Somali shillings)

Product	1957	1958	1959	1960	1961	1962
Live animals						
Amount	20,372	22,117	32,920	40,927	51,476	66,648
% of total	19.6	21.6	22.6	24.9	27.4	37.0
Meat & meat products						
Amount	1,394	2,915	3,053	2,948	3,267	2,060
% of total	1.3	2.2	2.1	1.8	1.7	1.2
Hides, leather, skins, & untanned products						
Amount	13,422	13,218	20,250	15,323	11,861	11,584
% of total	12.9	10.2	13.9	9.3	6.3	6.4
Cereals						
Amount	3,177	2,436	129	57	116	95
% of total	3.1	1.9	0.1	<0.1	0.1	0.1
Sugar & sugar products						
Amount	1,554	336	148	26	2	11
% of total	1.5	0.2	0.1	<0.1	<0.1	<0.1
Bananas						
Amount	45,859	58,906	65,001	74,430	90,286	80,149
% of total	44.2	45.3	44.6	45.3	48.0	44.5

Source: Somali National Bank, *Report and Balance Sheet, 1962* (Mogadish, 1963), pp. 106–7.

a much higher figure (16 million) for the British Protectorate alone. In spite of the empirical indeterminacy, livestock was the most precious material asset in view of the size of the human population that depended directly upon it.

Livestock exports accounted for more than 80 percent of the export trade of the north; in the south, livestock export was second only to bananas. In 1957 exported livestock and livestock products represented 33.8 percent of the country's total export value, as shown in Table 15. In that year livestock and livestock products were clearly second to bananas in export earnings. Five years later, however, live animals and livestock products had come to account for more than 44.6 percent of the total value of all exports, thus eclipsing bananas as the leading export commodity. While banana farm gate (f.o.b.) prices had shown tremendous decline, livestock increased significantly (both in volume and value) in the late 1950s and early 1960,[20] owing mainly to a buoyant market in oil-rich Saudi Arabia. Most significantly, livestock required no preferential treatment (unlike the banana exports, which relied on import subsidies from Italy for their competitiveness).

Finally, a small but growing proportion of the rural population was engaged in the cultivation of food crops. In the early 1960s it was estimated that 15–20 percent of the country's population made a living as peasants, the great majority of whom were found in the southern part of the country. Except in the northwest, where primitive ox-drawn ploughs were employed, the hoe and other more rudimentary instruments were used to cultivate the peasant farm. The negligible amount of cereal and cereal exports (as indicated in Table 15) between 1957 and 1962 notwithstanding, Somali was primarily a net food importer. In 1957, 14 percent of the south's imports consisted of foodstuffs and beverages.[21] In 1961, 25 percent of the country's imports was food, 70 percent being cereals.[22] Table 16 indicates that cereal imports to the southern region almost tripled in the years between 1958 and 1962, partly because of the tremendous increase of the population of Mogadishu during the first years of independence. The population increase was partly a result of the concentration of state administrative apparatus in the new capital. (No population figures are available for Mogadishu during this period.)

The increase in food imports also reflected the inability of peasant agriculture to respond to increased local demand in spite of the fact that there existed no marketing boards or parastatals to depress food prices artificially. This increase in food imports also represented changes in the food tastes of city-dwellers.

Most food imports were destined for urban consumers, as the high proportion of rice—72 percent of the imported cereals[23]—suggests; rice is

Table 16. Somali Imports of Cereal and Cereal Products, 1958–1963

Year	Northern region		Southern region		Total country	
	Tons	So. sh.[a]	Tons	So. sh.[a]	Tons	So. sh.[a]
1958	11,005	8,956	7,984	8,025	18,986	16,980
1959	14,782	13,345	13,754	12,022	28,536	25,367
1960	15,557	12,785	14,378	11,699	29,935	24,484
1961	11,974	10,167	16,248	13,440	28,222	23,607
1962	13,840	13,432	21,845	19,636	35,687	33,068
1963	—	—	—	—	47,664	38,024

Source: Shirname, *Report to the Government of Somalia on Food and Agricultural Economy*, p. 7.

[a] In thousands.

principally an urban food commodity. Although food imports, shown in Table 16, do not indicate the proportion of the country's food needs that such imports constitute, when the estimates of maize and sorghum production of the southern region are combined with these imports, the overall food situation of the region become much clearer. Between 1958 and 1962 the southern region became increasingly dependent on food imports, as the last column of Table 17 shows. The sharp decline in domestic cereal production in 1961 and 1962 was primarily responsible for the precipitous increase in imports, although the quantities imported did not compensate for the shortfalls of domestic production. The large amount of food aid donated to the country in 1961 is not included in the import figures shown in Table 16. Such aid must have bridged the gap between domestic food requirements and the total food available through local production and non-aid imports. The dramatic decline of local production during 1961–62 was in part due to the floods that devastated the south, since domestic production of maize and sorghum went up to an estimated 226,000 tons in 1963.[24]

Neither the Ministry of Agriculture, which made the estimates shown in Table 17, nor the Food and Agriculture Organization had any explanation for the sharp vacillations in production and acreage in this entire period. It is probable that the climatological cycles endemic to the region accounted for some of the fluctuations, particularly in production. Moreover, in spite of the lack of detailed figures on retail price changes of imported commodities before, during, and after World War II, it is reasonable to assume that the pastoralists and peasants in the south faced the same sort of conditions that had forced their northern counterparts either to begin to cultivate or to expand their farm sizes.

In spite of its potential for expansion, the Somali agrarian economy was not producing a large surplus which could be tapped for future accumula-

Table 17. Production of Maize and Sorghum in the Southern Region, 1950–1962

Year	Maize Ha	Maize Tons	Sorghum Ha	Sorghum Tons	Total production	% of total food needs of the south met by imports[a]
1950	23,000	17,200	49,500	32,000	49,200	
1951	12,000	9,800	30,000	12,700	22,300	
1952	25,000	28,000	60,000	45,000	73,000	
1953	13,000	8,000	30,000	9,000	17,000	
1954	25,000	20,000	300,000	100,000	120,000	
1955	79,000	54,000	437,000	56,000	110,000	
1956	71,600	50,000	313,400	50,460	100,460	
1957	76,600	48,610	652,400	117,900	166,510	
1958	66,600	46,570	324,900	65,030	111,600	6.70
1959	80,000	45,000	305,000	63,800	108,000	11.22
1960	90,000	55,000	326,500	62,000	117,000	10.94
1961	70,000	20,000	350,000	15,000	35,000	27.75
1962	80,000	48,000	340,000	16,000	64,000	25.45

Source: Ministry of Agriculture and Animal Husbandry, cited in Shirmane, *Report to the Government of Somalia on Food and Agricultural Economy*, p. 9.
[a]Calculated from column 4 of Table 16 and column 6 of this table.

tion and expansion. For example, in 1962, the country's earnings from livestock and livestock products were able to cover only the essential cereal imports, thus leaving little for accumulation.[25]

Agriculture and Development Policy

The fiscal weakness of the postcolonial state meant that the scope of its future activity was inevitably constrained. Independence as a nation, with some expensive additional trappings such as the three branches of government and the enlargement in the number of lower-level government employees, implied increased state expenditures. These expenditures had to be matched by increased revenues, either through more extraction from rural producers or through soliciting increased amounts of foreign assistance. The state's capacity to utilize the first option was complicated by a variety of historical factors. First, in the early years of independence, the state had neither the administrative capacity nor the coercive capability to enforce any new form of direct taxation on pastoralists and peasants. Second, any new direct taxes imposed on rural producers during this period would have contradicted the political spirit and the propaganda that lent legitimacy to the petite bourgeoisie during the struggle for independence.

Without a lucrative local source of revenue and in view of the promises of services made to the public during the final days of colonial rule, the aspiring petit bourgeois politicians seem to have set a deadly trap for themselves.[26] During the first year of independence, there was some discussion by the new administration of becoming "fiscally responsible," thus reflecting the material realities of the incipient state. Consequently, from 1960 to 1963, the budget deficit was proportionally and progressively trimmed down.[27] The popular pressures and expectations generated during the nationalist period, however, militated against such austerity. As a result, state expansion was inevitable in spite of a state treasury that was essentially unable to meet its standing obligations. The attempts made by the postcolonial state to grapple with these contradictions found expression in its economic and social policies.

One of the first projects of the postcolonial state was to solicit funds from "friendly" countries and agencies to buttress its precarious position. Indeed, it was remarkably successful in persuading the international community to contribute to its cause. Yet, in seeking aid, it did not rely solely on the altruism of the donor community; rather, the prevailing cold war political climate enabled the government to play East against West.[28] This exercise paid off handsomely, as indicated in Table 18, in the contributions granted during the first three years of independence.

In addition to these substantial grants, the Somali Republic was also able to secure enormous financial and commercial loans to the tune of 520.35 million and 198.6 million shillings, respectively. Italy and the Soviet Union made the largest contribution of aid; the U.S.S.R. contributed 61 percent of the financial loans and 21 percent of the commercial loans,

Table 18. "Free" Foreign Aid to Somalia, 1960–1963 (millions of Somali shillings)

Donor	1960	1961	1962	1963	Total	% of total foreign aid
Italy	29.6	58.9	56.8	56.8	202.1	36.3%
U.S.A.	8.6	21.8	71.4	71.4	173.2	31.5
U.K.	16.0	30.5	30.3	0	76.8	14.0
U.N.O.	2.0	12.1	16.0	16.0	46.1	8.0
E.C.A.	0.4	13.5	0.6	8.5	23.0	4.0
U.A.R.	1.5	4.6	5.0	5.0	16.1	3.0
U.S.S.R.	0	0	0	5.4	5.4	1.0
G.F.R.	0	0	0	3.5	3.5	0.6
Other	0.2	3.8	4.8	0	8.8	1.6
All donors	58.3	145.2	184.9	166.6	555.0	100%

Source: Somali Republic, *Government Activities from Independence until Today* (Mogadishu, 1964), p. 90.

Note: These figures include ordinary budget subsidies.

Table 19. Sectoral Allocation of the Resources of the First Five-Year Plan, 1963

Sector	Millions of So. sh.	% of total expenditure
Transport	410	29.3
Agriculture	250	17.8
Industry	220	15.7
Housing, settlement, and water supplies	115	8.2
Education	92	6.5
Irrigation, drainage, and flood control	90	6.4
Banking and credit	75	5.4
Health and veterinary services	43	3.0
Cadastral survey, investigation, and research	40	2.9
Post and telecon	16	1.4
Information	10	0.7
Social welfare and community development	6	0.4
Statistics	6	0.4
Tourism	2	0.1
All sectors	1,400[a]	100.0[a]

Source: Somali Republic, *First Five-Year Plan, 1963–1967* (Mogadishu, 1963), p. 10.
[a]Totals given are those of source; exact totals are 1,375 and 98.2, respectively.

while Italy contributed 6.5 percent and 72 percent of the loans, respectively. The total sum of all foreign assistance amounted to more than $100 million in loans ($1 U.S. = 6.7 Somali shillings).[29]

As soon as the initial fiscal constraints eased, the postcolonial state expanded its plans for economic development. With technical assistance from the United Nations, the first five-year plan was made public in July 1963. In spite of the government's earlier claim of the sufficient availability of foreign assistance, the amount of aid at its disposal at the time of the plan's publication was later scaled down to 676.8 million Somali shillings, or little over $100 million in grants and loans (almost half of it being a loan from the Soviet Union). This amounted to less than 50 percent of the expected expenditure of the plan.[30] Despite this setback, the authorities were still confident that additional assistance would be forthcoming to cover the plan's expenditures.

According to the plan, as indicated in Table 19, three areas were given priority: transport, agriculture (including irrigation and flood control), and industry. These priority areas accounted for more than 69 percent of the total plan expenditures. The main stated objective of the government was to modernize, expand, and upgrade the productive capacity of the economy in order to improve the standard of living of the people.[31] However, the 250 million Somali shillings allocated for agriculture does not adequately reflect the primacy of agriculture in the plan. This agricultural priority is more adequately indicated by the fact that related sectors such as irrigation and transportation, which were intended to facilitate agricultural development, absorbed more than a third of the entire allocation of the plan.

Congruent with the prevailing development theories of the time, the authorities believed that the agricultural economy consisted of two sectors, the modern and the traditional. The plantation economy constituted the modern sector, while the traditional economy was represented by the peasantry and the pastoralists. In broad terms the main agrarian problem, according to the plan, was underutilization of resources, which was more acute in the traditional sector.[32] For the banana plantations, there were three chief difficulties that needed to be overcome. First, Somali bananas were not competitive in the international market.[33] Second, banana exports were tied to a single market (Italy), which hampered further expansion of the industry. Finally, the country was dependent on bananas as its single export crop. Thus, in order to make Somali bananas more competitive in the international market, the five-year plan set out to reduce the cost of transportation and production. Resources were allocated to improve feeder roads that linked the plantations to the ports,[34] while other cost-reducing approaches included harbor improvements and the provision of irrigation and credit to the industry (note the size of the budgets for transportation; irrigation, drainage, and flood control; and banking and credit in Table 19). None of the plan's agricultural budget was specifically earmarked for the development of bananas or sugar. The rationale for this omission was that banana plantations were privately owned, while the plan was a blueprint for public investment. This disclaimer notwithstanding, the plantation industry actually benefitted enormously from the development program in the form of irrigation, credit services, and improvements in transportation, all of which were publicly funded.[35]

In spite of these attempts to make Somali bananas more competitive in the European markets, very little progress was made in practice on this score, as the study commissioned by the Food and Agriculture Organization in the final year of the plan indicates.[36] Morevoer, the same study also demonstrated that Italy remained as important a market as it had been prior to the plan. This, in effect, means that during the five-year-plan period no new major markets opened up.[37] This is all the more telling in light of the fact that the Suez Canal was closed after the Six-Day War, which forced banana shipments around the Cape of Good Hope. In addition to these plan failures, the country remained solely dependent on this single export crop. The agricultural diversification that was so clearly needed never materialized.

The entire budget for agricultural development was designed to be

Table 20. Allocation of the Agricultural Budget of the First Five-Year Plan, 1963

	Millions of So. sh.	% of total expenditure
Crop production		
State farms	110	44.0
Settlement of nomads	25	10.0
Agricultural research	20	8.0
Central machinery pool	20	8.0
Grain storage & marketing	15	6.0
Plant protection	10	4.0
Agricultural extension	10	4.0
Date cultivation	7	2.8
Manures	2	0.8
Total for crop production	219	87.6
Other		
Animal husbandry	14	5.6
Forestry	14	5.6
Fisheries	3	1.2
Total for other uses	31	12.4
Total agriculture budget	250	100.0

Source: Somali Republic, *First Five-Year Plan*, p. 47.

used to establish modern agricultural enterprises and to develop "modern islands" amidst the vast traditional sector. The allocation of the plan's agricultural budget as shown in Table 20 partly indicates how the modernization of the traditional sector was to be carried out. More than half of the funds earmarked for crop production went into the establishment of state farms. Initially three in number (Tugwajaleh food-grain farm, cotton and oil seeds farms in Lower Juba), they were intended to bring more arable land under cultivation and were to be a prelude to the settlement of nomads. The rationale behind the adoption of a state farm strategy was the fact that in Somalia "peasant farming is yet in early stages of development."[38] Therefore, the main function of these farms was import-substitution, to increase the production of food and nonfood commodities in order to reduce imports. For instance, the Tugwajaleh farm was intended to experiment with wheat production under rain-fed conditions. These farms were also intended to be the modern islands of agricultural development. Because of the lack of data on state farm production, it is not possible to gauge how many of the planned production goals were attained at the end of the plan period. What is clear, however, at least in the case of Tugwajaleh farm, is that no modernity diffused to the surrounding countryside.[39]

Peasants at Work

Soviet-Made Agricultural Machinery in Disuse in the Tugwajaleh State Farm

The modernization of the traditional peasant sector was analogous to the intensification of commodity production.[40] A critical prerequisite of the commoditization was the need for a modern land-tenure law. Although the plan did not elucidate what "modern forms of land tenure" meant, it is apparent that private ownership of farmland is what the authorities had in mind.[41]

With that framework in mind, a number of new research and extension centers were initiated and some old ones were rehabilitated, notably the Bonka Farmers' Training Center, near Boidoa, the center of Afgoi, the one at Abu Rin, and the seed-production station at Tugwajaleh state farm. One of the main objectives of the Bonka program was to train and produce leaders in peasant agriculture (a watered-down version of the famous "progressive farmer").

The modernization of the peasant did not fare better than the state farm program. The number of "modern islands" were too few, and the resources at their disposal too scarce. These conditions did not enable them even to begin the modernization program, which, if successful, would have given the state de facto control over peasant production without physically expropriating the means of production. Despite the assistance of the Food and Agriculture Organization in grain marketing and storage, no marketing parastatal emerged. Apart from some initial success, as in the training of 750 farmers annually for a two-week period,[42] there is little evidence to suggest that the program made much headway in intensifying commoditization of peasant production. The land-tenure law that was such a central part of the strategy never materialized during the plan period, as Prime Minister Egal lamented in 1967.[43]

Pastoral production constituted the other half of the traditional sector. In contrast to the peasant economy, the pastoral economy was highly involved in the market. In fact, livestock exports began to rival bananas as the country's main export commodity by 1964–65. In spite of the high degree of pastoral commercialization, the state was convinced that although the marketable livestock surplus was small, still only about 50 percent of it was sold.[44] The pastoralists' retention of this unmarketed surplus was due to their traditional practice of holding large herds as a hedge against disaster and also due to the prestige associated with large herds. Furthermore, the lack of efficient market organization acted as an important disincentive to selling more animals.[45] Modernization of this sector was therefore coterminous with increased market penetration of pastoralism. It was assumed that such deepened market penetration could be brought about by reducing the risk of losing livestock to disease and drought through the provision of water and veterinary services, and also

The Camel—Central to Pastoralist Mobility

by the development of marketing facilities, such as holding grounds, and improved transportation. (Again note the centrality of the large budget allocations to transportation, which was not only for improving the competitive position of Somali bananas, but was also designed to play an important role in modernizing the traditional sector.)[46] The formation of the Livestock Development Agency in 1965–66 was to be a catalyst in this process.[47] Furthermore, the authorities considered pastoralism to be symbolic of tradition at its height and consequently planned to make a beginning at transforming pastoralism into settled communities. The modernization of pastoralism was expected to have three important consequences. First, it would result in increased marketing of surplus stock. Second, an increased off-take rate would reduce overstocking and hence relieve pressure on the ranges. Finally, increased surplus livestock sales would benefit both the pastoralists and the state.

Whatever the pastoralist's purportedly traditional proclivities may have been, it is quite apparent that they continued to sell larger numbers of the stock primarily in response to favorable prices. Between 1961 and 1964, the value and the number of marketed livestock increased by 111.8 percent and 85.5 percent, respectively.[48] This trend continued until the end of that decade, except in the 1965 drought year. It is not certain, however, whether the tremendous increase in the number of marketed livestock

Table 21. Comparative Prices of Livestock in Hargeisa and
Mogadishu, 1967

	Price/head (So. sh.)	
	Mogadishu	Hargeisa
Camels	300	500
Cattle	125	250
Sheep	35	80
Goats	30	75

Source: B. J. Hartley et al., *Agriculture and Water Survey:
Livestock Development Survey*, UNDP and FAO report no. MR/
54396 (Rome, 1967), p. 52.

implied a higher off-take rate or was merely a reflection of the natural growth of the herd population.[49] What is certain is that the meager public investment (not quite 2% of the total government expenditure)[50] and limited private investment did make available large tracts of previously waterless grazing areas to pastoralists.[51] Such horizontal expansion of production could have been responsible for a portion of the increase in marketed animals due to the increase in herd size.

The high livestock prices which prevailed in the 1960s and which induced pastoralists to part with more of their livestock (according to Konczacki) favored the northern region of the republic. As Table 21 indicates, in 1967 the price of a head of cattle in Hargeisa, in the north, was twice as much as that of a head of cattle in Mogadishu, in the south. The enormous difference in prices was due mainly to the proximity of the port of Berbera in the north to the lucrative Arabian market. This price difference had the effect of attracting to the northern region's ports, particularly Berbera, livestock from deep in the southern region (Map 6).

As is clear from the above discussion, pastoralists responded remarkably well to the buoyant market of the first decade of independence.[52] The success in further commercialization of pastoralism, an objective of the development plan, was in part a result of the provision of water and veterinary services. Nevertheless, commercialization of pastoralism did not have the intended effect—that further market penetration would remove more livestock from the range and therefore help ameliorate the deterioration of the range. In fact, greater pastoral involvement in the market had quite the opposite effect. For example, given the location of the principal livestock herd in the northern region (see Map 6), and coupled with the lack of an improved transportation system, livestock from many regions were continuously driven through the northern range and marketed there. This had a devastating effect on the northern ranges. In 1967 the

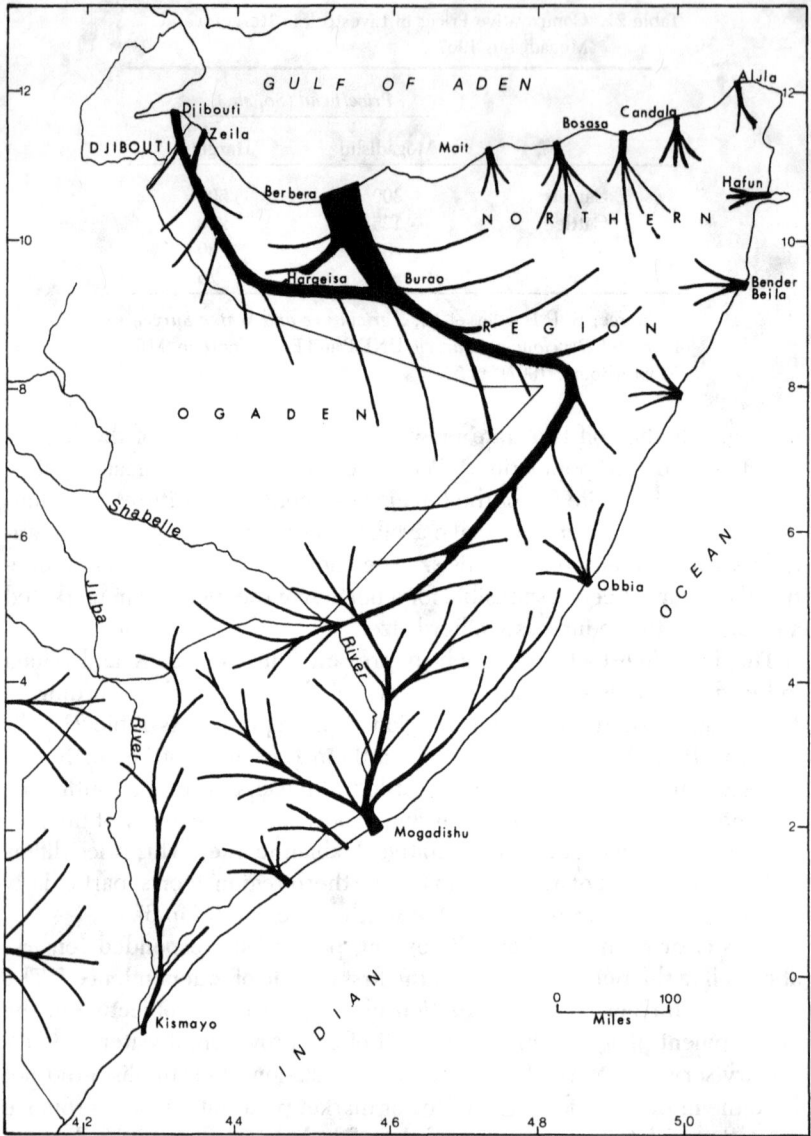

Map 6. Livestock Export Routes in Somalia
    Source: B. J. Hartley et al., *Agriculture and Water Survey: Livestock Development
    Survey*, UNDP and FAO Report no. MR/54396 (Rome, 1967), p. 49. Note: Thick-
    ness of the route lines does not show the exact proportions of animals at any given
    port; however, thicker lines indicate main outlets.

Sheep in the Hargeisa Livestock Market, 1986

Livestock Market in Hargeisa on a Busy Day

Food and Agriculture Organization report warned that, given the degree of range deterioration, a major drought would have catastrophic consequences.[53] The cost of ignoring this warning was enormous during *Dabadeer* ("endless"), the drought of 1974.

In summary, a disappointing overall performance of the first five-year plan was sprinkled with few successes. In the modern agricultural sector both sugar and banana production increased. In the case of sugar, output increased from 117,300 metric tons in 1962–63 to 350,000 metric tons in 1966–67, making the country almost self-sufficient. In contrast, banana increases were more modest.[54] Owing to the lack of comparable data on domestic food production in the traditional sector, it is difficult to make as certain a judgement, but if cereal imports can be used as an indicator of local food production, then domestic production of food stagnated during the plan period.[55] Second, the peasant's ability to increase his or her production in response to the developing domestic food market may have been blocked by certain critical constraints on production such as primitive tools (hoe) and the unavailability of modern agricultural inputs (fertilizers and irrigation) to the peasant.

Finally, if the First Five-Year Development Plan was intended to improve local productive capacity so that reliance on foreign assistance would be reduced, then no detectable gains were made. When the second development plan (1968–70) was introduced, the government still depended on foreign assistance to balance its annual budget. Moreover, the second plan, which had as its main objective the completion of the projects initiated in the first plan, was to be almost entirely funded from foreign sources.[56] Reliance on foreign assistance had a number of far-reaching consequences for the state's development strategy. First, the total amount of aid promised by the donors was never delivered.[57] Second, the selection of what constituted agricultural development projects, in both the first and second plans, was determined by the donor countries. For instance, with the first plan most of the Italian aid (grants and loans) directly assisted the banana and sugar industries, which were Italian-owned.[58] Similarly, significant amounts of the Soviet loan went directly to the establishment of state farms,[59] which explains, in part, the apparent neglect of the traditional sector. Furthermore, the potential and real resistance of the pastoralists and merchants to direct state intervention and control in pastoral production foreclosed any attempts that may have been made. If the neglect of peasant and pastoral production was due to the conditionality of foreign assistance and the resistance of rural producers to state intervention, the same cannot be said of the failure to implement other projects. As the Short-Term Development Program indicated, this failure was due to bureaucratic ineptitude.[60]

In sum, by the closing years of the 1960s, it had become apparent that the two exercises in development planning neither produced fruit nor created alternative sources of accumulation. Indeed, development planning seems to have accentuated the state's reliance on foreign assistance.

The Crisis of Petit Bourgeois Democracy and Accumulation

The poor performance of Somalia's development plans (1960–1970) reflected the incapacity of the governing petite bourgeoisie to create domestic sources of accumulation. The "failure" of economic development policy underlay the emerging crisis of petit bourgeois politics. What was the origin and the nature of this crisis? We have already seen that there were two major political parties (SYL and SNL) who dominated the political scene at the time of the independence. These parties shared the same ideological and philosophical view of the state and economic development. In the election of 1964, the number of political parties increased to twenty-four, who fielded 793 candidates for the 123 parliamentary seats. During the 1969 parliamentary election, again, the number of parties multiplied to sixty-two with 1,002 candidates in the contest.

This increasing fragmentation of national politics was seen by a knowledgeable commentator as the resurgence of traditional particularism in the Somali Republic: "It is this 'clanship' in the technical sense, rather than tribalism, which commands allegiance and frustrates the achievements of much that is in the national interest."[61] Lewis contends that it is the amazing capacity of the traditional social structure to absorb the modern without massive dislocation that brought about the demise of democratic government. Although most people do not deny the resiliency and tenacity of precapitalist ideologies, this explanation seems to suggest that "clanship" or tribalism is independent of other social processes. Hence, it presumes two untenable propositions. First, it presumes that at low stages of capitalist development, social class and class interest are both subordinate to clan and tribal interest. Second, it removes the individual politician from the context of his or her social class, which he or she may or may not represent, and therefore reduces politics to a contest of clans and their champions. For this school of thought the "reemergence of tribalism" explains the atrophy of parliamentary politics, and vice versa.

Other writers, such as Shivji, Meillassoux, Mamdani, and Saul, have suggested ways of avoiding this tautology.[62] Instead of beginning their discussion with an analysis of political parties, they focus attention on the nature and composition of social classes and their relations to each other and the state. In this scheme, understanding the role of the colonial state in the process of colonial capitalist accumulation is critical. Such an appreciation of colonial social history is central because the contradictions which emerged out of colonial capitalism informed the politics of national liberation and beyond.

A more careful examination of African liberation movements reveals that there was indeed a significant difference in the degree of involvement among Africans with the colonial economy. Some Africans, such as merchants and civil servants (including the armed forces), were intensely involved in the colonial capitalist economy, and their aspirations for accumulation and promotion were thwarted by the colonial state and the metropolitan bourgeoisie. Others, such as peasants and workers, were subject to the exploitation of both the colonial state and metropolitan bourgeoisie as well as the African petite bourgeoisie. These two social groups—the petite bourgeoisie and the "popular classes"—constituted the principal anticolonial forces. Thus, the national liberation movement should be viewed as a struggle in which various social groups with contradictory interests formed a united front against the colonial state.

How is it, then, that these social groups with different and particular grievances against the colonial state came together and jointly confronted the colonial state? This problem was temporarily mitigated by the fact that despite the economic and political changes that had taken place under colonialism, African societies were *relatively* untransformed economically. As a result, the differentiation of the African population was not significantly advanced, and the contradictions between these groups were not yet as apparent. The principal contradiction was that between the colonial state and African society. Thus, the secondary nature of the contradictions between the petite bourgeoisie and the popular classes made possible the necessary solidarity of the African population and the use of community ideology.[63]

This amalgam of contradictory forces held firm during the Liberation movement, since little armed struggle was involved which could have brought these contradictions to the surface. In most countries independence was a product of negotiation rather than the barrel of a gun. In these societies it was the petite bourgeoisie which inherited and laid claim to the postcolonial state "on behalf of the people." The petite bourgeoisie was not, of course, a homogeneous mass.[64]

Once the principal contradiction between African society and the colonial state was "resolved," another wave of struggle over control of the postcolonial state was unleashed. This struggle was among the members of the petite bourgeoisie themselves. In some cases it was resolved before the gaining or granting of independence, while in others it had to wait somewhat longer. The question was frequently which fragment of the petite bourgeoisie would dominate the postcolonial state and society. In

countries such as Kenya, where the level of colonial capitalist development was high and the petite bourgeoisie quite advanced and diverse, the
bureaucratic fragment which came to man the state apparatus was not
able enough to appropriate state power for its particular needs.[65] In other
words, the postcolonial state was made to serve petit bourgeois accumulation as a diverse entity and not only the bureaucratic fragment. Elsewhere, colonial capitalist development was not as advanced and hence petite bourgeoisie diversity narrow, and the bureaucratic fragment often
dominated the state. Such was the case of Mali.[66]

These two examples indicate that popular democratic politics is alien to
petit bourgeois accumulation, since that kind of politics would offer other
social groups such as peasant and workers some leverage in the political
process or alternative channels (parties) to challenge the hegemony of the
petite bourgeoisie. In both Mali and Kenya, the name of the general interest (African Socialism) was invoked to silence dissent. Once the class
nature of accumulation was "emasculated" and class ideology condemned,
the value of ethnic ideology became apparent in demoralizing and fractur-
ing the solidarity of the working people. The colonial game of divide and
rule is thus reinvented.

In the Somali case the struggle for state domination among the Somali
petite bourgeoisie took a slightly different form. Here the level of colonial
capitalist development was extremely low and the bureaucratic segment
of the petite bourgeoisie too small and ill-equipped to take control of the
state on its own behalf. The Somali petite bourgeoisie consisted of livestock merchants and traders and civil servants. All of them were either
involved in trade or employed by the state, and neither group was strong
enough materially to capture the state alone. The merchant and trading
category was large and illiterate, and because of the underdevelopment of
Somali capitalism, this group had not yet broken all its ties with the pastoral community. Moreover, because of the nature and organization of
pastoral trade, the merchants occupied a strategic point between the pastoral economy and the outside world. This proved vital and to the advantage of the trading class during National Assembly elections (in both British and Italian Somaliland). This victory for the trading group in no way
implied defeat for the fledgling bureaucratic stratum. In some cases individual bureaucrats who were supported and nominated by the merchants
were elected to the parliament. In short, this "undifferentiated stratum,"
trader-bureaucrat, dominated the postcolonial civilian state.

The triumph of the trader-bureaucrat class at independence may have
seemed like a flawless class coup, but this was not the case for a variety of
reasons. First, given the underdevelopment of the Somali economy, there
were no "White Highlands" or "Copper Belt" which could have been na-

tionalized to provide a haven for this class. The small banana plantation in the southern region was essentially off-limits, since its nationalization would have meant forsaking the large Italian budgetary subsidy. Second, locally there existed no other important productive economic enterprises that could have been appropriated; the only possibility was import-export trade, which was based on bananas and livestock. Nationalizing this trade would have amounted to an act of sabotage against the trading group. Third, any takeover by the state would have alarmed aid donors and jeopardized potential aid from Western countries and private Western investment, which was badly needed.

In the absence of nonpublic sources of accummulation, state revenues, including foreign assistance, became the bone of contention. This meant that those who had access to the appropriate offices could reward themselves and their clients. The competition for profitable state offices unleashed a deadly race among the petite bourgeoisie. The race was not between the bureaucratic and the trading factions but (in most cases) among individuals within the petit bourgeois class. In a classic sense, this class, fragmented into the smallest units possible (individuals), was "entangled in an *insolvable contradiction.*" The state, which mediates conflict between classes in advanced capitalist societies, was here the object and the price of the struggle (appropriation of the state). Without the mediating services of the state, petit bourgeois parliamentary democracy was inimical to this brand of petit bourgeois accumulation (that is, private accumulation within the public sector), and as will be seen shortly, the system's reproducibility was problematic.

One way to have access to state funds was to be a representative in a parliament or, even better, to hold a cabinet post. This race for parliamentary seats explains the increase in both the number of political parties and the number of candidates in the 1964 election. Of the twenty-four parties, only four were able to win seats in the second parliament. The new prime minister, Abdirazaq Hussein, made attempts to curtail the bleeding of the public purse, but this was doomed to failure. After the presidential elections of 1967, the new president called upon Mohamed I. Egal, the new prime minister, to form the new government. For the new leadership, the war on corruption and abuse of public resources was not a priority, since they had their attention turned to a more profitable affair, the parliamentary elections of 1969. In preparation for these elections, the prime minister summoned what he called the "First National Advisory Council" in 1968. The main purpose of the council, according to the president, was "not [a concern] with parties or faction" but the "need to assist the constitutional bodies in their task for formulating and applying the country's laws by the direct expression of public opinion."[67] The proclaimed purpose notwithstanding, the meeting was an earnest effort by the prime minister to position his ruling clique in a strong position for the upcoming elections. Members of the advisory council were handpicked by the supporters of the government and were local opinion-makers. In other words, this was a clear attempt by the ruling clique to gain control over the state electoral process and to prevent it from further disintegration.

In spite of this invention of the Advisory Council and other changes in the electoral by-laws, the prime minister's hopes did not materialize, at least not immediately. The failure to prevent further erosion of the electoral process was in part due to the fact that it had become common knowledge that the 1969 election was not a contest between competing ideologies, but a race for the greatest personal access and use of state resources. As a result, many senior civil servants resigned from their jobs and threw their lots into the electoral game. The proliferation of political parties to sixty-two was a product of this exercise. In the absence of any philosophical or ideological differences among the petite bourgeoisie, clan background was the only factor that distinguished between parties and candidates. The appeal and utility of clan ideology to the individual petit bourgeois under such circumstances is best summed up by Saul:

It is precisely this intraclass competition for control of the state and for related economic advantage which activates the diversity of fractions [of petite-bourgeoisie] produced "in the sphere of practice alone." . . . As regards the modernizing constituencies—this referring to the attempt to create some popular base for sustained political activity—a utilization of "tribal" ploys can also seem particularly attractive to the petite-bourgeoisie politicians.[68]

The effectiveness of the "tribal ploy" to mobilize voters had its limits, given the fact the competition was intense even within clans. For example, since most people realized that this exercise in petit bourgeois "democracy" had nothing to offer the country, it became part of the norm that any personal costs incurred, including time spent in going to the polling station, had to be paid for by the contending individuals. In all cases the tribal appeal had to be supplemented with distribution of cash to influential individuals. The greatest financial cost was incurred during the last days of the campaign, when nomads and peasants had to be collected and maintained in kraals located near the polling stations. In many cases these voters were trucked in from Western Somalia (Ogaden). The elections of 1969 were very expensive as a result of this. It was estimated that some candidates had spent as much as $30,000 during the campaign in a country whose annual national budget was $30 million. Furthermore, it has been reported that the prime minister expended more than $1,250,000 of public funds in payment to members of the assembly between January and October 1969.[69]

The Somali Youth League emerged victorious from the elections, with

73 out of the 123 seats. Immediately after the result of the elections were made public, a feverish competition ensued among those who secured seats in the third parliament to recoup their electoral expenses and a lot more. The way to do so was to have access to the central chambers of state power, and to be a member of an opposition party was not a profitable venture. This explains the rapidity with which all those in the opposition parties (except former prime minister Hussein) crossed the aisle to join the ruling party.[70] The damage to the petit bourgeois democratic ideology by this incessant competition for resources was profound and fatal. The myth about the national interest being served by elected members was finally exposed for what it essentially was, as Lewis so lucidly articualted:

> The democratic parliamentary system which had seemed to combine so well with traditional Somali institutions, and had begun with such verve and promise, had turned distinctly sour. The National Assembly was no longer the symbol of free speech and fair play for all citizens. On the contrary, it had been turned into a sordid marketplace where deputies traded their votes for personal rewards with scant regard for the interests of their constituents.[71]

Moreover, whatever semblance of democracy remained was shattered when the newly appointed Supreme Court chief justice reversed an earlier decision by the court and refused to take up cases accusing the government of electoral fraud. The chief justice claimed that his court had no jurisdiction over such matters.[72]

In a nutshell, this endless search and competition for state resources swiftly transformed what seemed to many political commentators of the time to be a promising multiparty democratic society into one of Africa's single-party states. Given how expensive it had become to run for a parliamentary seat, the ruling clique was quite conscious of their increasing leverage over any future candidate for high public office. Having such leverage, however, was not a sufficient condition for the reproduction of the system. State revenues that could have been used to induce candidates to support the government were very limited. Furthermore the possibility existed under this political system that enough disgruntled members could bring the government down, as happened in 1964 and 1967. Therefore, it was imperative that important changes in the political process be brought about to save the system from consuming itself. The interest of the individual petit bourgeois had run counter to the interest of the class. In essence this meant shedding the "democratic," if not the electoral, paraphernalia and imposing a petit bourgeois dictatorship on the Somali society.[73]

The maintenance and the reproduction of this dictatorship by the ruling clique required the use of the coercive machine of the state, the army.

Shortly after the elections, the prime minister made well-publicized inspection trips to the military headquarters in Mogadishu. It has also been reported that he had made plans to instruct some of the senior military officers to leave for a training period to the Soviet Union,[74] which had been training the Somali army since the early 1960s. This was an attempt by the prime minister to replace the army leadership with officers sympathetic to his views. Before this scheme bore any fruit, on a fateful afternoon, in the town of Las Anood, President Sharmakee was gunned down by one of his security guards. The prime minister, who was on an unofficial visit in the United States, hurried back home to take charge of the election of a new president to ensure his own political future. This he was able to do in the caucus of the SYL, where his choice, Haji Musa Bogor, a wealthy merchant, was accpeted as the party candidate for the presidency. The Haji's election by the National Assembly was certain. The bargaining in the SYL caucus symptomized the decay of petit bourgeois parliamentary democracy. If all the previous internecine struggles within the petite bourgeoisie had not made the need for discipline apparent, this last act did. The night before the parliament was to vote on the next president, and long before the ruling clique had achieved its wish for discipline, the military intervened and took over state power on October 21, 1969.

The Coup: Some Concluding Remarks

Why did the military intervene? There is, of course, a large literature on military coups. What follows is a brief overview of the various "themes" put forth to elucidate the causes and the rationale behind military coups. The more conventional interpretations of military coups suggest two scenarios.[75] First, it is thought that military coups result from the breakdown of the immature political processes and institutions of newly independent nations. In other words, political paralysis in these societies pushes the military to center stage. Second, others contend that in "backward" societies the military alone has the qualities, the organizational discipline, and the "modernizing impulse" to propel it into the center of state power.

The insertion of the military into politics is of course the result of the "malfunctioning" of the political institutions of these "backward" societies. As Decalo pointed out, these two "different" explanations are, in fact, the two sides of the same phenomenon.[76] He brushes aside the "uniqueness" of the military as a "modern island" in an ocean of "tradition" and "backwardness." The main weakness of these expositions, Decalo contends, is that they overlook what is frequently the most important cause of military coups, namely the "personality factor": "Hence, detailed examination of motivations for coups reveals that the main weakness of attempts to explain them by pinpointing major areas of systemic stress is that insufficient weight is placed on the personal motives of ambitious or discontented officers, who have a great deal of freedom and scope for action in fragmented, unstructured, and unstable political systems."[77]

Put differently, the competition for state domination is between ambitious individuals. It is usually the case that the man with the sword wins the trophy. In spite of the importance of the "personal ambition" factor, however, Decalo's elaboration is not in conflict with the main theoretical thrust of the works he set out to criticize.

Another analyst of military coups suggests that the armed forces take over state power in order to protect their class interest—that is, military-class interest.[78] Lofchie's proposal is indeed a real advance in making class interest the central issue. However, the military class argument glosses over the differentiation within the military in terms of pay. More critically, it fails to relate the class nature of the military to the relations of production and cannot explain the split that usually develops between the troops during the coup, and countercoups. Mamdani in a trenchent rebuttal to these theories dismissed both the class-based explanation of military coups as well as the personal-ambition factor. He argues that the inability of the petite bourgeoisie to consolidate and become hegemonic as a class underpins the political crises of neocolonies like Uganda.[79] The fragmented character of the petite bourgeoisie which leads to political crisis is the product of its colonial heritage:

This fragmentation is not just a result of its specific historical function, but also its dependent character: it cannot establish effective control over the nationally generated surplus, which is primarily appropriated by imperial capital. Such fragmentation gives inordinate strength to the section of the class that directly controls the state apparatus. The political struggles between opposition factions typically center on the method of accumulation: whether it should be creation of state property or private property.[80]

In the Ugandan case, it was the nonbureaucratic fragment that lost the day. Some of these losers made contacts with army officers. The leaders in the army had become conscious of their strategic position as a result of the increasing use made of the military by the ruling bureaucracy to suppress other social groups.[81] It was this amalgam of forces that produced the 1971 military coup in Uganda. Clearly, then, it is not the military as a class which takes over state power, but a segment of it in collaboration with factions from the other classes.

In spite of the materialist nature of his analysis, Mamdani foreclosed the likelihood of some progressive segment of the military stepping in alone or with the collaboration of other segments, to preempt the forging of that reactionary block. As another commentator points out, how else can one explain those very rare instances when a group within the military allies itself with other progressive social groups?[82] Ahmed Samatar appears to be suggesting that this had happened in Somalia, although he is very much aware of the contradictory nature of such an alliance.[83] In sharp contrast to the Ugandan case, the Somali petite bourgeoisie had not "sufficiently evolved" to constitute the antagonistic camps that Mamdani so succinctly portrayed. The degree of fragmentation of this class was so pervasive that Mamdani's hypothesis needs to be modified.

In Somalia, it seems to have been the case that a small group within the military leadership made the decision to take over state power without the initial support of any portion of the civilian petite bourgeoisie. Little, if anything, is known about the initial motives of the twenty-four members of the Supreme Revolutionary Council, and the few commentaries written on the subject are speculative at best. Apparently, however, the junta which led the coup initially appeared to be philosophically and ideologically monolithic; once the immediate crisis was over, however, conflicting and contradictory views concerning the purpose of the coup emerged. I suggest that some of the younger members of the junta, who were instrumental in the plan and the execution of the coup, constituted the "progressive" wing. It was because of their influence that the regime veered to the left and tapped both the populist and the progressive elements of the intelligentsia. The senior officers in the Supreme Revolutionary Council, who were more traditional and reactionary in their views, were able to prevail over their junior lieutenants after a brief period of time (1969–73) and took control of the state.

In sum, it is my contention that in spite of the influence of the progressive elements in the Supreme Revolutionary Council earlier on, the imposition of military rule merely marked a *restatement* of that peculiar, foreign-assistance-based form of *disarticulated accumulation* under the repressive tutelage of the military bureaucracy. The productive base of the Somali economy, pastoral and peasant production, which was neglected by the development strategy of the parliamentary regime, remained almost as peripheral under the postcoup "revolutionary" strategy.

5

The Military and the Agrarian Sector, 1969–1984

In fact, the structure of our society and the present framework of our economy contain the only possible alternative for a rapid economic and social rise. In Somalia there are no classes in the Marxist sense; rather, we are nomads, farmers, small employees, and soldiers.

Siyaad Barre
October 21, 1970

In the colonial days we were able to argue with the colonial authorities and question the merits of their ideas. Occasionally we won the arguments; and the officers used to heed what we had to say. Nowadays, neither can we utter a word to the authorities nor resist if all our properties are taken. Despite humiliation, abuse, and injustice, we must always exude our admiration for these rapacious and venal authorities.

Hassan
eighty-year-old poor peasant
February 12, 1984

The discussion in Chapter 4 underlined the dependency of the postcolonial civilian state on foreign assistance and its impact on Somali development strategy. Given the predominantly agrarian nature of the national economy with the concommitant absence of any significant working class and with a politically immobilized peasant and pastoral population, the military clique that captured state power did not depend on the political support of these classes for its survival. Consequently, the regime's development strategy was not responsive to the needs of these classes. In contrast to its predecessors, the military regime increasingly drew a larger proportion of its development funds from domestic sources.[1] Paradoxically, the increased reliance on local sources did not alter the relationship between the state and rural producers. This contradiction was made possible by the initial general public enthusiasm for the change of government. Increasingly though, the regime's strategy came to be based on the excessive use of coercion.

In discussions of Somali policy between 1969 and 1975, the claim has been made that in its early years, the military regime was "revolutionary" and responsive to the needs of the popular classes. Basil Davidson, a long-time supporter of and sympathizer with progressive movements, declared that Siyaad's regime was a people's government worthy of the support of progressive people.[2] Apologists of the ruling military and of Siyaad in particular, such as Luigi Pestalozza, were quick to claim that the "Somalian revolution" was an authentic and popular socialist revolution.[3] A recent commentator, Ahmed Samatar, indicated that the early period, 1969–73, was characterized by an intense internal power struggle within the Supreme Revolutionary Council (SRC) which was concluded with the triumph of Siyaad (chairman of the Supreme Revolutionary Council) and his camp.[4] The emergence of Siyaad's clique consequently led to the gradual evaporation of whatever popular base the regime had. The defeat of the Somali troops in the 1977–78 Somalo-Ethiopian War, with the resultant internal strife in the army, merely intensified state repression.

These three authors—Davidson, Pestalozza, and Samatar—underline the accomplishments of the regime, such as the admirable way the regime managed the 1974–75 drought, the national literacy campaign of the same year, and the expansion of social services. Despite these accomplishments, it is one of the contentions of this chapter that even in those early "days of legitimization" and popular support, popular input into the decision-making process was cosmetic at best. More critically, the regime's development program, in spite of its socialistic claims, either bypassed the overwhelming majority of the population, the peasants and pastoralists who are the bedrock of the Somali economy, or intensified its exploitation of them, or hampered indigenous responses to the crisis of the rural economy. The simultaneous marginalization and exploitation of the rural producers by the militarized state was made possible by three factors: (*a*) foreign aid remained the main source of development funding, (*b*) the military regime showed little interest in improving the productive capacity of small producers, and (*c*) rural producers were unable either to withdraw from the commodity economy or to find alternative channels to the market and the state.

This chapter consists of three parts. The first is a brief discussion of the "new" forms of state organizations, with particular emphasis on regional and local level structures and their responsiveness to local people. The second part examines the regime's agrarian development strategy. Finally, the last part is a detailed look at the conditions of rural producers (peasants) in the northwest region under the tutelage of the "revolutionary" regime. Particular attention is paid to their responses to the deteriorating capacity of the rural economy to provide them with sustenance.

The Structure of the Postcoup State

One of the first acts of the new regime was to dissolve the parliament and the executive and judiciary organs of the old state. The Supreme

Revolutionary Council (SRC), made up of twenty-four officers, became the sole and ultimate law- and policy-formulating body. It was assisted by the Council of Secretaries (civilian ministers), who were hand-picked by the supreme council. Members of the Council of Secretaries were primarily civilian administrators and technocrats who were entrusted with the routine operations of the state bureaucracy. At the regional and district level the previous governors and commissioners were deposed and replaced with military men. For the first one and a half years these officers administered their respective localities without much input from the resident population. It was only in 1971 that Regional and District Revolutionary Councils were formed to assist the new leadership. The governors and commissioners selected the members of these councils, and they automatically became the chairmen of these bodies. Governors and commissioners were accountable to the SRC and could not be removed either by the local council or by the public. In other words, the public had no immediate protection against the possible abuse of state power by regional and local authorities. Furthermore, the rhetoric of decentralization and popular participation notwithstanding, local policy formulation and implementation, despite initial inputs by the council members, became the sole prerogative of the council chairman. The redundancy of the council members was brought to light and clearly illustrated during a debate in the Gabileh District Revolutionary Council.

In an interview I conducted in northwest Somalia in 1984, a member of the first council in the Gabileh District informed me that it became apparent to council members by the second meeting of the council that the chairman was the sole authority and that they were expected not to challenge his policies.[5] During that meeting, some council members inquired about the implementation of the council's policy decisions made during the first meeting. The chairman was not enthusiastic about their queries and dismissed their questions. During that same meeting, moreover, the chairman brought to the council's attention a new agricultural tax circular promulgated by the SRC. Members of the council argued that this tax must have been intended to apply to irrigated agriculture only, as the levy was too high for rain-fed farming, Gabileh being a rain-fed farming district. The council suggested that the chairman should request further clarification from the SRC. The chairman reacted by telling council members that SRC policy pronouncements were not subject to the scrutiny of local councils. He added that if they did not join with him in the implementation of the tax law, he would proceed and no longer require their participation. According to two other councilmen who wished to remain anonymous, this meeting terminated any illusions they had about the conditions of their participation in the local decision-making process.

This format prevailed until 1976, when the SRC created the Somali Socialist Revolutionary Party.[6] The process of party formation lacked genuine popular input, just as in the case of the revolutionary councils. The emasculated unions of state employees (made powerless by the Law of Twenty-Six Articles, which instituted the death penalty against strikes) were ordered to send their representatives to the central party conference. In this conference the Socialist Revolutionary Party was "institutionalized," and delegates elected various party officers. Siyaad Barre was elected party secretary, the chairman of Politburo, the president of the Democratic Republic, and the commander-in-chief of the armed forces.[7] With the creation of the party, the SRC was disbanded, only to reappear in party attire.

At the regional and local levels the same process was repeated, and governors and district commission-cum-party secretaries were appointed by the central government. During my fieldwork informants emphasized to me that although local "elections" were held to choose members of the Local People's Assembly, known as the *Dagaan*, the process was nothing more than a farce. Voting was conducted by depositing ballots into separate boxes for each candidate, and ballot-box guards were on hand to watch how individuals voted.[8] One person who joined the party in the early period reported that although he had lost faith in the organization, he was not able to resign for fear of severe repercussions.

The "decentralized" administrative and authority structure which was instituted in the late 1970s is shown in Figure 13. The district party committees were inducted into the party authorities; they were not accountable to the working people. The district party secretary, who was formerly known as the district commissioner or the chairman of the District Revolutionary Council and was usually a uniformed officer, was appointed by the Politburo and was therefore accountable to it. As indicated in Somalia's Rural Development Strategy of 1981–90, the secretary supervises and coordinates political and administrative activities and is also responsible for law, order, and security.[9] Law, order and security had become a dominant preoccupation of the government since the war of 1977 with Ethiopia and increasingly in the last four years override all other local and national concerns.

The concern over national security has further strengthened the hand of local authorities. In contrast to the party, the Local People's Assembly is an "elected" body; to run for election, however, one must be a party member and have its approval. The chairman of the Assembly and the party secretary are both responsible to the regional governor/party secretary. The Local Assembly has the legal authority to establish village councils.[10] The two standing subcommittees are responsible for the economy

```
                          ┌─────────────────────┐
                          │   Local government  │
                          └─────────────────────┘
                                    ↕
                          ┌─────────────────────┐
                          │   Regional governor │
                          └─────────────────────┘
        ┌──────────────────────┐        ┌──────────────────────┐
        │ District party       │        │ Local people's       │
        │ secretary            │        │ assembly chairman    │
        └──────────────────────┘        └──────────────────────┘
                   ↕
        ┌──────────────────────┐        ┌──────────────────────┐
        │ District party       │        │ Local people's       │
        │ committee            │        │ assembly             │
        └──────────────────────┘        └──────────────────────┘
        ┌──────────────────────┐        ┌──────────────────────┐
        │ Subcommittee on      │        │ Subcommittee on      │
        │ economy and          │        │ social affairs       │
        │ cooperatives         │        └──────────────────────┘
        └──────────────────────┘
                          ┌─────────────────────┐
                          │   Village council   │
                          └─────────────────────┘
```

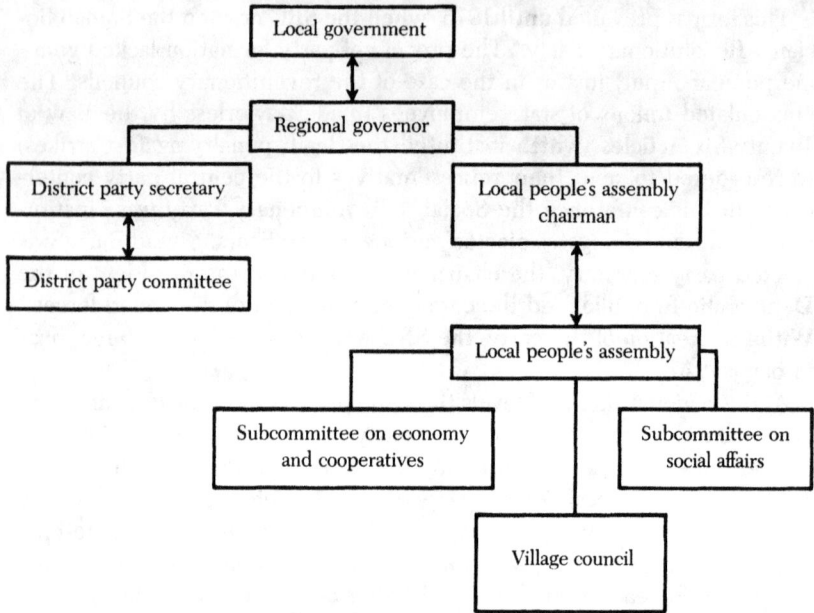

Figure 13. Structure of Local Government Administration since 1976–1977

and cooperatives and social affairs such as public health, justice, and education. Finally, the village council is responsible for planning and executing development schemes at the village level.

In spite of this appearance of decentralized state structure and the potential for popular input in determining development strategy, all of the local council participants I interviewed unanimously agreed that the new village councils have only two functions: collecting tribute from the villagers and notifying them of new government dictates.

The Postcoup Agrarian Development Policy

The new five-year development plan announced for 1974–78 described itself as "much more ambitious not only in its scope but also in the emphasis given to the mobilization of local resources. To illustrate, the total envisaged investment in the present programme is So. sh. 3,863,357,000, while that of the previous programme for 1971–73 was around So. sh. 999,943,000 only—in other words the amount expected from internal resources alone, which is So. sh. 1,260,393 (32.6% of the total), is greater than the global investment of the previous program."[11] Unlike previous civilian governments, the military regime drew an increasingly larger proportion of its development revenues from local sources in its first two de-

Table 22. Proportion of Development Funds from Local versus Foreign Sources, 1963–1982

Development plan period[a]	Local revenues		Foreign revenues	
	So. sh. (millions)	% of total	So. sh. (millions)	% of total
1963–67	0	0	1,400.0	100.0
1971–73	118.9	16.2	615.8	83.8
1974–78	1,260.3	32.6	2,602.9	67.4
1982–86	3,199.0	20.0	13,050.0	80.0

Sources: Development Plans, 1963–86.
[a] No information was available for 1968–70.

Table 23. Proportion of Development Funds for Agriculture and Livestock, 1963–1982

Development plan period	Agriculture		Livestock	
	So. sh.[a]	% of total	So. sh.[a]	% of total
Pre-coup				
1963–67	250.0	17.8	43.0	3.0
1968–70	53.9	7.7	45.9	6.5
Post-coup				
1971–73	146.6	14.7	59.4	5.9
1974–78	1,124.5	29.1	162.1	4.2
1982–86	4,782.8	29.1	2,433.3	14.9

Sources: Development Plans, 1963–82.
[a] Millions of Somali shillings.

velopment programs (Table 22). Central to the regime's "revolutionary" and increasingly locally financed economic development program was the development of the rural sector (agriculture and livestock).[12] The importance of the rural sector was reiterated in the plans of 1974 and subsequent programs and strategy. An indication of the state's commitment to the rural sector was the increasing proportion of the total development resources that were earmarked for that sector, as shown in Table 23.

The Livestock Subsector

The livestock pastoralism subsector is the most important sector in the Somali economy; it is the dominant earner of foreign exchange, and it also provides the livelihood of 60 percent of the Somali population. In spite of its centrality, the pastoral sector has been of low priority to the state, as is demonstrated by the decline in the proportion of development funds allocated to it in the third and fourth plans (5.9% and 4.2%, respectively). These appropriations are in direct contradiction to the claims of the plans.

Regardless of the cyclical decline in development funds for pastoralism,

Table 24. Distribution of Development Funds to Livestock Development Projects,
1971–1973 and 1974–1978 (thousands of Somali shillings)

Project	1971–73	1974–78
Animal health program	5,402.8	2,435.0
Joint rinderpest campaign	3,396.0	—
Parasite treatment center	265.0	1,777.2
Training school for animal health assistants	3,919.0	4,834.8
Central veterinary research station	2,638.0	7,847.1
Feasibility study on pilot ranches[a]	113.0	—
Hides and skins development[a]	4,139.0	6,261.8
Kismayo holding ground[a]	2,640.0	8,762.7
Purchase, sale, and export of livestock[a]	2,795.0	—
Staging points on Burao-Berbera road[a]	215.0	4,488.8
Marshalling yard at Kismayo[a]	172.0	—
Fodder production[a]	800.0	—
Development of small ports[a]	308.0	—
Pilot project: livestock[a]	32,583.0	—
Check-treatment-quarantine stations	—	6,119.4
Tsetse fly control	—	317.5
Veterinary pharmaceutical project	—	1,224.0
Trans-Juba Livestock Development Project[a]	—	80,350.0
Multipurpose ranches[a]	—	7,338.4
Feedlots project[a]	—	14,797.8
Dairy farms (Mogadishu and Hargeisa)	—	7,953.0
Artificial insemination centers[a]	—	3,476.0
Model poultry farm[a]	—	4,103.0
All projects	59,385.8	162,086.5

Source: Somali D. Republic, Development Plans, 1971–73 and 1974–78.
[a]Project designed to improve marketing of livestock.

the absolute amount of money earmarked for this sector more than doubled between 1971–73 and 1974–78, and increased over forty times between the third and the current (fifth) development plans. Given the "socialist" proclamation of the regime, how were these vast amounts of money to be expended? In other words, what was the objective of the state's pastoral/livestock development strategy and how different was it from past strategies? A glance at the livestock development projects of 1971–78, shown in Table 24, is illuminating. In spite of the significant increase in the number of projects since the 1968–70 plan, the orientation and purpose of development did not change. In the "prerevolutionary" era, the dominant purpose of livestock development was the intensification of marketed output from the pastoral sector. Despite the rhetoric, there was no change in the objectives of the pastoral development under the third and fourth plans. Of all the development projects specified in Table 24, in the 1971–73 plan, 73.7 percent of the resources set aside for pastoral development was specifically aimed at facilitating or improving livestock market operations. In the 1974–78 plan, 79.9 percent of the resources were again devoted to the same purpose. Moreover, livestock trade was the only major economic sector that remained in private hands after the wave of nationalizations in the early 1970s. Unlike other parastatal agencies set up during this period, the Livestock Development Agency was purposely designed not to compete with or replace the established patterns of private livestock traders and trade.[13] The state's lack of revolutionary resolve in this critical area is said to have been due to its unwillingness to tamper with the country's single most important foreign-exchange earner.[14] It was suggested that this policy was in part a product of the real and potential strength of livestock traders, as demonstrated in 1981, when traders went on strike and refused to assemble animals for export because of the imposition of a 25 percent *ad valorem* tax. The Livestock Traders Association forced the government to back down on this issue.[15]

Although early development programs had referred to the deteriorating conditions of the range,[16] it was not until the devastating drought and famine of 1974–75 that any attention was paid to the plight of pastoral production. The first major form of state intervention into pastoral production was the Northern Range Project. Despite its ambitious goals, at the end of the first phase of implementation, the project was deemed a near total failure from the vantage point of the traditional pastoralists.[17] In effect, the project intensified range expropriation by individuals who were more involved in livestock trade.[18] The Northern Range Project (1975–1980) and the Central Range Project (1981–88) notwithstanding, methods of pastoral production and development retained their dualistic character; that is, there was increasing production for the market without a concomitant advancement of the methods of production.[19]

In spite of the development program's emphasis on livestock marketing, livestock exports between 1972 and 1981 showed no increase for the two main export animals—sheep and goats (Table 25). Sheep and goat exports reached their peak in 1972 and never recovered from the effects of the Dabadheer, as the 1973–75 drought is known. Only in cattle exports to Arabia were sustained increases recorded. This was largely a product of the shift of livestock from the riverine regions which had previously been marketed across the border in Kenya and had not been considered exports by the government. The general stagnation of livestock exports, some hint, demonstrates that at long last a critical point may have been reached in terms of the capacity of the range to accommodate increasing numbers of livestock.[20]

The price of livestock exports increased enormously while the quantity of livestock exported stagnated. Due to the fantastic increase in demand for meat in Saudi Arabia, by the late 1970s, fewer Somali animal exports

Table 25. Live Animal Exports from Somalia, 1971–1981 (thousands of head)

Year	Sheep	Goats	Total small ruminants	Cattle	Camels
1971	622	564	1186	59	26
1972	816	819	1635	81	22
1973	709	675	1386	68	29
1974	663	575	1238	31	24
1975	793	743	1536	40	34
1976	385	381	766	58	33
1977	465	461	926	55	33
1978	739	715	1454	77	22
1979	717	705	1422	68	13
1980	747	734	1481	93	17
1981	685	680	1365	117	14
1982	730	719	1449	157	15
1983	559	557	1116	44	8
1984	339	337	676	8	4

Source: J. Holtzman, "The Economics of Improving Animal Health and Livestock Marketing in Somalia" (USAID, Mogadishu, 1982), p. 3, and Central Bank of Somalia, *Monthly Bulletin*, September 1985.

were generating more than three and half times the revenues of 1972.[21] For example, during 1972, when live animal exports peaked, they brought in 88.2 million Somali shillings in export earnings. Six years later fewer sheep and goats were exported, but their value stood at 447.3 million Somali shillings.[22] It is apparent from the increases in the price of livestock exports that pastoral production, despite the quantitative decline in live animal exports, had done very well against inflation.[23] What is not so clear, however, is the proportion of increase in the price of these exports that livestock merchants retained and how much of that profit they transmitted to the producers. Vali Jamal seems to suggest, inferring from aggregate national statistics, that the producers have benefitted from the export boom.[24] Others note that merchants were passing substantial parts of the gains to the producers, as evidenced by the increasing number of bank deposits in such towns as Burao.[25] Holtzman is less certain, although he suggests that it is unlikely that the barter terms of trade in the pastoral sector had deteriorated.[26] Aronson, although less emphatic that Swift, contradicts the hypothesis that pastoralists have not lost ground.[27]

It is my opinion, after one year of field research in 1983–84 and another in 1986 and 1987, that Swift's suggestion of the deteriorating pastoral terms of trade is credible. For instance, although producer prices for livestock kept pace with inflation in the boom years of the 1970s, pastoral terms of trade deteriorated in the 1980s as livestock prices stagnated at $42 per head of sheep. In the meantime, the Mogadishu consumer price

Cattle Became an Important Export Commodity in the 1970s

Livestock Carrier Anchored at Berbera Harbor

index (1970 = 100) rose to 1007.40 in 1984 and further to 1379 by 1985. Food prices soared by 115 percent in 1984 alone and peaked at 1002 percent during that year. This is particularly the case at the retail level when one considers not only the price of livestock sold but also the skyrocketing prices of consumer commodities upon which pastoralists depend (e.g., 1 kilogram of sugar in 1972 was 3 Somali shillings, while in 1986 its cost was close to 80 Somali shillings). The price of these commodities is tied to the black-market rate of exchange, while livestock exports are linked to the official rate of exchange. At any given time the black-market exchange rate was at least three times the official rate,[28] although that gap has been narrowed due to a recent IMF-induced devaluation of the Somali shilling.

The scenario works as follows. A pastoralist sells sheep to a trader and usually gets no more than 50 percent of the price paid at the livestock market in Jedda (Saudi Arabia).[29] The trader must remit a portion of the foreign exchange (usually 70%) back to Somalia through the national bank at the official rate of exchange. Through taxes, the government gets about 10–15 percent of the total value. The trader then invests the unremitted foreign exchange, 20–25 percent, in merchandise such as rice and sugar, which are imported at undervalued prices to Somalia[30] and then sold at exorbitant prices in the "open" market. The pastoralist, who is a consumer of these commodities, must pay these prices. In fact he or she may pay an extra penalty, as it is usually the case that pastoralists are not paid for their animals until the final sale is made in Jedda, despite the fact that the trader takes full possession of the animals in Somalia.[31] During 1983–84, it was not uncommon for the prices of consumer commodities to rise significantly (up to 10%) within a month. In sum, I fully concur with Aronson's conclusion that "the Somali nomad is thus neglected; with no changes in technology and no ability to break the government alliance with the traders, he is immobilized in a production system that threatens maladaptation and breakdown."[32]

The "revolutionary" development programs of the socialist regime were revolutonary only in speeding up and intensifying the process of pastoral commoditization that began long before the country became independent.

The Agriculture Subsector

Although only 20 percent of the Somali people are engaged in peasant agriculture, the regime's allocation of development funds for agriculture has almost doubled, from 14.7 percent in the 1971–73 plan to 29.1 percent of the 1982–86 plan (Table 23). A fundamental component of the government's agricultural development strategy from the very beginning was the promotion of food-crop production. More specifically, the regime's aim was to attain self-sufficiency in sorghum, maize, vegetables, and edible oils, and to increase the production of rice, wheat, cotton, and grapefruits.[33] It should be noted that sorghum, maize, and oil seeds were produced by peasants. Thus, the primacy of food self-sufficiency implicitly meant improvement of peasant production. The government's intention

Harvest Time—Sorghum (Pile at Farmer's Left) is the Chief Crop in the Northwest Region

to help rejuvenate peasant production was explicitly spelled out by the former vice-president of the country (who is currently in detention):

Prior to the October Revolution, agriculture suffered a severe setback, and thousands of farmers lost interest in farming, owing to the lack of any incentive-generating measures from the past regimes. Somalia today is one of the very few nations in the world which opted for a judicious return to the workers tilling the land. It is anticipated that the efforts made towards the development of agriculture will soon reverberate with positive results, and not only in Somalia.[34]

The "new" strategy suggested that low producer prices were not the only obstacles to increased production in the peasant sector; so were poor "cultural" methods of farming.[35] The task of agricultural development was therefore to find new methods of improving peasant production.

Despite its bold and revolutionary tone, the rhetoric of the strategy did not translate into a real commitment to the development of peasant production. A cursory look at the agricultural development projects in Table

Table 26. Distribution of Development Funds to Agricultural Projects, 1971–1973 and
           1974–1978 (thousands of Somali shillings)

Project	1971–73	1974–78
Agricultural extension service[a]	3,092	2,528.4
Agricultural cooperatives[a]	0	47,961.0
Strengthening research[a]	3,000	20,078.5
Plant-protection service	4,707	20,159.8
Agro-meteorology[a]	0	982.0
Grain storage and marketing	3,315	6,310.0
Farm machinery[a]	0	35,551.6
Rice-production program	0	8,153.0
Agricultural crash program	15,000	112,500.0
Pilot farm for irrigated agriculture	0	1,924.2
Afgoi-Mordinle Project	0	16,358.9
Fanole Irrigation Project	0	241,961.2
Balad Irrigation Development	0	160,000.0
Banana development	60,000	20,000.0
Integrated agricultural development[a]	0	44,319.5
Grapefruit seed multiplication	0	545.0
Grapefruit cultivation	6,000	89,518.1
Date plantation	0	7,073.0
Sugarcane plantation	0	101,096.0
Study of swamp reclamation	0	5,400.0
Jowhar Off-Stream Storage	0	35,000.0
Dredging and canal desilting	0	7,085.0
Bardere Reservoir	0	140,000.0
Seed multiplication[a]	2,555	0
Cotton	10,051.0	0
All projects	107,720.0	1,124,505.2

Source: Somali D. Republic, Development Plans, 1971–73 and 1974–78.
[a] Peasant-oriented development project.

26 illustrates that peasant farming was not a development priority. In
spite of the doubling of the agricultural share of development funds, peasant production scarcely benefitted from these increases. For example,
in the 1971–73 plan, only 8.3 percent of the total funds for agricultural
development were spent on projects that were peasant-oriented. In the
1974–78 program, the proportion was 13.5 percent. A closer examination
of these peasant-oriented projects indicates that such projects as agricultural extension services, seed multiplication, and agricultural research
had very little impact on the small rural producer.[36] In interviews with
over seventy-five peasant households in the Galooley, Sanlawaha, Saarey,
and Ijawaaji areas of Gabileh District, I did not find a single household
that indicated having been contacted by an agricultural extension agent.[37]

Agricultural extension service was nonexistent when the regime came to power in 1969, and sixteen years of military rule had not changed the situation.

Agricultural extension service was not the only means which the state devised to "reach" the peasant. Two other projects—agricultural cooperatives and the integrated agricultural development projects—were central elements of modernizing traditional agricultural production. A closer look at examples of these two, a cooperative and an integrated project, will demonstrate the marginality of peasant production. Both of these projects are in the northwest in Gabileh District (Map 7).

Given the scarcity of modern agricultural inputs, the lack of a developed extension system, and the dispersed and individualistic nature of peasant production, the government decided that traditional agriculture could be transformed only by vigorously encouraging the formation and development of agricultural cooperatives.[38] The National Cooperative Law of 1973 laid the legal basis for the establishment of these institutions under the Ministry of Agriculture.[39] (At present, cooperatives come under the party Structure.) Three forms of cooperatives were envisaged: multipurpose cooperatives, group farming cooperatives, and production cooperatives. The multipurpose cooperative was conceived of as an umbrella organization for a variety of lower-level organizations. Its initial purpose was to initiate an educational program in order to convince individual peasant producers of the value of cooperative farming. Once the social terrain was prepared, the next stage of cooperative development was to be undertaken, that of group farming. At this stage peasants would still privately own their land and livestock but would be expected to share things like agricultural machinery, draft animals, and sprayers. The common use of these inputs was intended to prepare the groundwork for the final and most advanced stage of cooperative development, the production cooperative. In this final stage, land and other production resources were to be commonly owned and used.

How much progress has the Somali Cooperative Movement made since its foundation in 1973–74? The following assessment is based on interviews and discussions with cooperative members in rural Gabileh between December 1983 and March 1984. Gabileh is the most important agricultural district in the northern region. These interviews were supplemented by fieldwork in Kurtinwarei and Mogadishu in the southern region.

In Galooley, the cooperative movement, at the multipurpose level, started in 1973, when members of the government traveled there and called meetings for the peasants. A state official delivered lectures about the superiority of cooperative farming to individual efforts and described

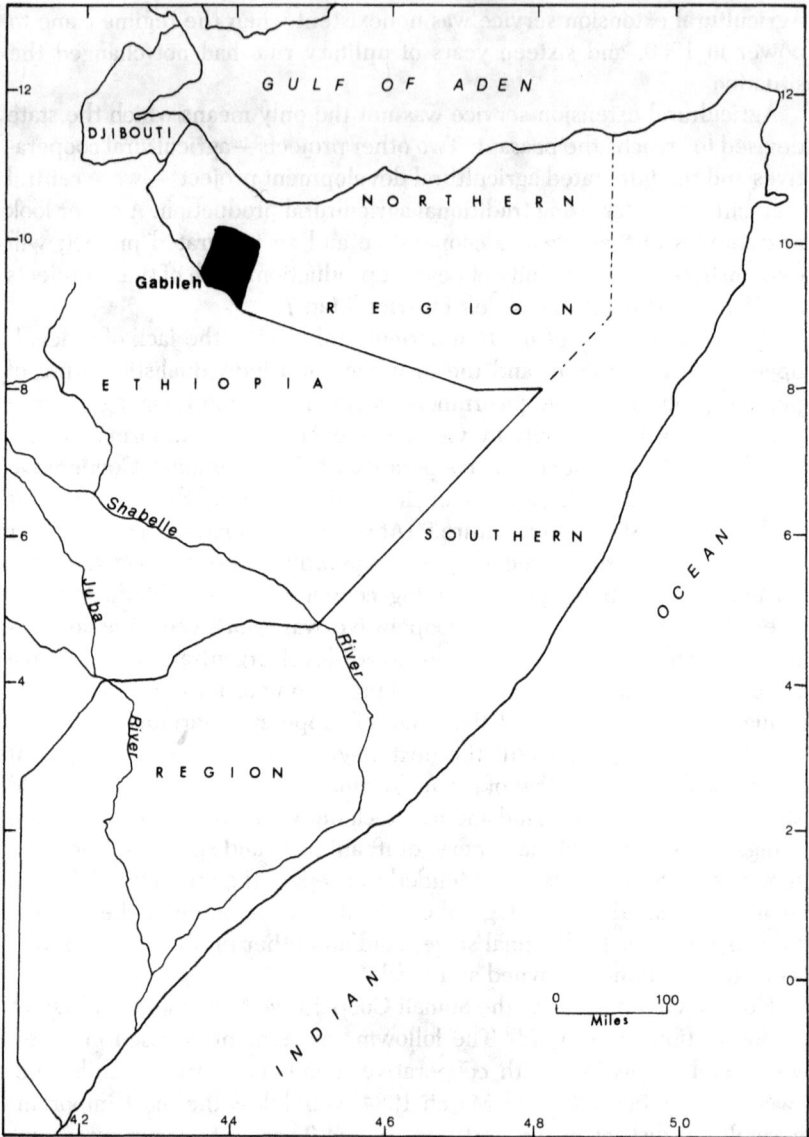

Map 7. Gabileh District

the government's willingness to help cooperative development provided
peasants organized themselves. With some suspicion, the Galooley peasants formed their first multipurpose cooperative. State contributions were
forthcoming in the form of a tractor (the tractors distributed came as aid
from North Korea) and 30,000 Somali shillings. This money was used in

the construction of the cooperative center. With the peasants providing labor, the center was completed in 1974. It consisted of four rooms; one was used as cooperative office, the second as a meeting room, the third as a garage for the tractor, and the fourth for grain storage. With the encouragement of state officials, Galooley members of this multipurpose cooperative were asked to advance to the next higher stage of cooperative, that of *Tacabwadaag* (semiproduction co-op). Ideally, the formation of Tacabwadaag was based on the premise that the state would provide vacant agricultural land to the members, who would cultivate it collectively, with remunerations based on labor contribution. Since there was no such land to be had in Galooley, peasant members contributed a small portion of their land to the Tacabwadaag. This land was cultivated, using free tractor time which the state donated and peasant labor. At harvest, after those who worked in the common farm were compensated, a small surplus remained which was stashed away as a common reserve. Again in 1976, there was another surplus. One must bear in mind that these surpluses were possible because those who labored on the farm had their own fields and did not have to rely on the cooperative for their entire reproductive needs. Rainfall was poor in 1977, and so was the harvest. Consequently in the winter of 1977–78, there was a scarcity of grain, and even those who had money to pay the high prices were not always able to obtain it. Fortunately for those members of the Tacabwadaag, the common reserve met their needs.

In spite of this moderate and tangible success, state involvement and participation, which was critical in encouraging and mobilizing the peasants, vanished from the rural scene. This departure, in part due to the preoccupation of the state with the Somalo-Ethiopian War of 1977, marked the end of the cooperative era. Today, despite the establishment of impressive offices in the capital and regional centers, cooperatives of any form are absent from the scene except when state authorities revive the structures temporarily to extract "development contributions" from the peasantry.

If the cooperative movement has wilted on the vine, the Northwest Region Agricultural Development Project, or NWAP (part of the program for integrated agricultural development noted in Table 26) has survived to the present. The project covers the agricultural parts of the northwest region shown in Map 8. NWAP was a very important element of the government's program towards self-sufficiency in grain. It is mainly an elaborate follow-up of the bunding work done by the British Somaliland administration in the 1950s and the U.S. Agency for International Development in the early 1960s.[40] Most of the funding for the first phase of the project (72%) came from a $10 million loan from the World Bank; it is currently in the second phase, also funded by the World Bank. The purpose of the

Map 8. NWAP Area
　　Source: SOGREAH, *Northern Region Agricultural Development Project*, Main Re-
　　　port (Grenoble, France, June, 1983)

project was to construct bunds to reduce the rate of soil erosion and con-
serve water for farm use. Its initial target, in Phase 1, was to construct
bunds on 25,000 hectares and rehabilitate old ones on another 2,000 hectares (about 120,000 hectares are under cultivation in the area). It also
included a small-scale experimental gulley-erosion-control program and

Misuse of Land Induced by the Forces of the Emerging Economic Order Led to Deforestation and Gully Erosion

other services such as the restoration of the Abu Rin demonstration farm.[41] The first phase of NWAP started in 1978 and lasted for six years. In the Second National Farmer's Conference in October 1983, the project management reported that it had protected 28,957 gross hectares on 4,714 farms from soil erosion.[42] The protected area, as shown in Figure 14, is much larger than the farm area. As the report notes, the performance of the project was superb and had exceeded its planned targets for the first phase by 107 percent. Moreover, yields in bunded farms increased between 2.40 to 13.74 quintals per hectare over unbunded farms.[43] According to the report, the project also performed very well in its nonbunding works, such as the construction of human and animal water points (concrete reservoirs and earth-dam reservoirs, respectively).

Are these claims of accomplishment matched by actual performance of the project in the field? This is not an easy question to answer, particularly since the management of the project does not evaluate and examine the facts behind the data reported by the field team. My field data on this subject are supplemented by information gathered during my brief association with NWAP.[44] In assessing its performance I must describe the nature of the project itself. NWAP has its headquarters in Hargeisa, where

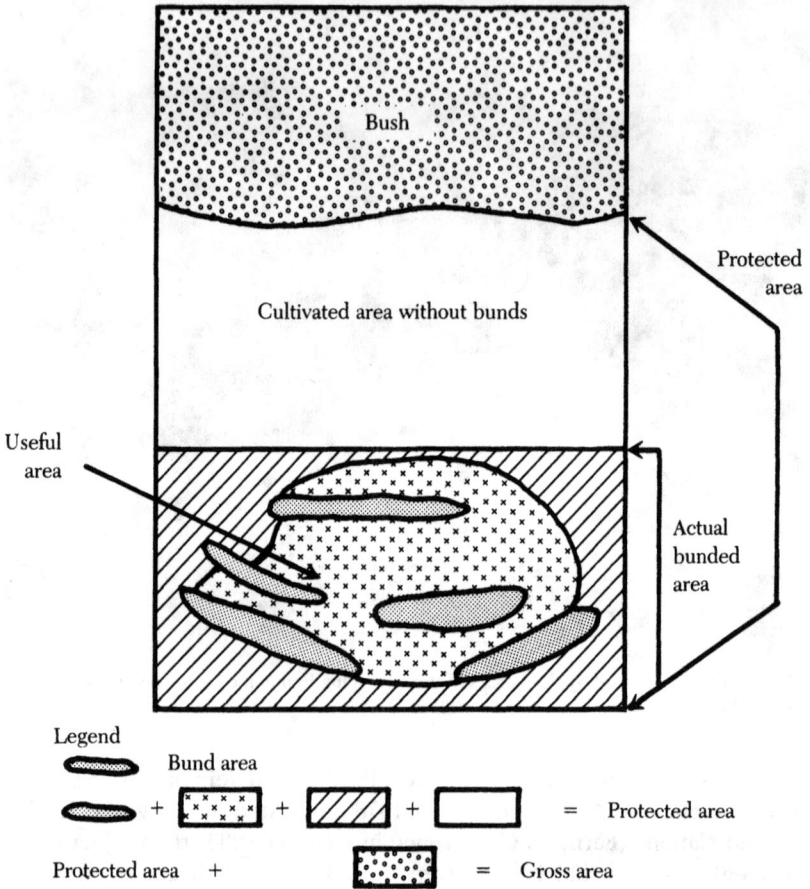

Figure 14. Bunded Farm
         Source: SOGREAH, *Northwest Region Agriculture Development Project*, Technical Report no. 10 (Grenoble, France, March 1982)

its general manager and other auxiliary administrative and technical experts are based. The field crew consists of a mobile team, equipped with heavy earth-moving machinery such as bulldozers. The mobile team's function is to construct and repair bunds and earth dams used as animal watering points. The team is led by a director stationed in Gabileh. The team started its fieldwork in Ijaara in 1978, and according to project reports, it was to be part of the normal working procedure that the team would move from one farming community to another only after it had completed all the necessary work in the first community.

The local office in Gabileh had the power to decide where the team went after it finished its work in Ijaara. My data indicates that the decision was contingent upon which community provided rent, the "sweetener." Usually, the sweetener consisted of a "gift" to the team in the form of cash. In fact, in the course of time the team (apparently, with the blessing of the administration) began to "suggest" to prospective communities that they deliver a certain amount of money in advance if they wanted the services of the team. For instance, in the case of Gogeisa the magic figure was 50,000 So. shillings. After some negotiations between the team and Gogeisa elders, the sum was scaled down to 24,000 shillings.[45] In many cases, once bunding work started in a community, each peasant had to bargain further with the team. One grievance of the peasants in the areas I visited was that if the team was not content with the bribes, it usually moved to another community where the offers were more generous. Such premature moves left many farms unbunded although the service had been paid for. In order to attract the team back to their community, the peasants would have to be more generous. A second grievance, verified by my observations, was that the number of bunds constructed on a farm was not a product of technical calculations but subject to the discretion of the team. Third, in farms where gulley erosion occurred, the team did nothing to retard its progress. This was clearly the case in Saarey. Fourth, in many cases the cultivation area was not leveled after bund construction, as called for by the project. This left many farms in a state of poor drainage. After rain, parts of these farms became ponds while adjacent areas stood dry. Fifth, the community animal watering points were too poorly constructed to be of any use during the winter months. Sixth, in the case of human water points, the project management contracted with merchants to do the construction. The merchants, in turn, hired peasants within the community to do the job. Three out of four human water points this author visited were in disrepair. When I asked the peasants whether they could have done a better job had the contract been awarded to them, the answer was a unanimous yes.[46] They also suggested that the cost of construction of the water point would have been lower. Although these water points were expected to provide drinking water for people during three months of the winter, the ones I visited were dry at the height of the winter season, December and January. As for the quantitative increases of production in bunded farms, I have no evidence to either substantiate or refute the claims of the project management.

The apparent willingness of the peasants to offer payoffs demonstrates the importance they attach to soil and water conservation—that is, to the improvement of farmland. One wonders then why the peasants did not bring these abuses by the field team to the attention of the general manager, who was ultimately responsible for project performance? Peasants and community leaders made attempts to meet with the general manager, but their requests were turned down numerous times. They later turned to district authorities such as the party and District Assembly for help, again to no avail. [47]

The defunct cooperative movement and NWAP were the only two developmental interventions in the northwest peasant sector by the military regime. The agricultural marketing parastatal, Agricultural Development Corporation, established in 1971, never became an important factor in agricultural production in this region. Likewise, the highly venerated self-help schemes (building hospitals, waterworks, etc.), which were so widespread in towns in the early days of the regime, did not affect the agrarian sector. [48] In the northwest, and in Gabileh District in particular, not a single self-help scheme was carried out in the countryside. The marginalization of the northwest peasantry by the "revolutionary" agrarian development strategy of the 1970s symbolizes the state's real disinterest in peasant production all over the country. This relationship between the state and the peasantry in the northwest and the peasants' reaction to it demonstrate that these producers were not delighted with their "free" mode of production, contrary to the contention of one recent theorist. [49] In spite of their neglect, the peasantry contributed to state revenues, both through taxes and through "development contributions." [50] From the very beginning, the regime chose a bimodel agrarian development strategy. [51] Huge state projects were the nucleus of its program. Even in the case where such projects involved the production of food grains, the peasantry was bypassed. Such was the case with the state rice farms and the crash programs.

The Crisis of the Rural Sector and the Response of the Peasants

The peasantry in northwestern Somalia is not content with the regime's agrarian policy, which attaches peripheral importance to peasant production. In spite of their neglect by the development program, peasants are an integral part of the economy. In other words, the linkages between the peasant sector and the rest of the economy are such as to preclude peasants' exercising their purported "exit" option. Given their relationship to the commodity economy, the development strategy, and the increasing prices of consumer commodities (a product of the inflation of 1970s), how did the peasants respond to their marginalization? In other words, how did they manage their linkages with the larger political economy, and what impact did this response have on the farming methods and the socioeconomic structure of the peasant community? What follows is an attempt to gauge the course of this process in the northwest region and in Gabileh

District in particular. One must not infer from the following discussion that the response of the peasantry or of some of the peasantry in the northwest necessarily typifies peasants in the country as a whole.[52]

A brief historical capsule of the forces operating in rural areas of the northwest is essential in order to appreciate the nature of peasant response to the deepening crisis of rural production and reproduction. Gabileh District is located at an elevation ranging between 2,000 and 5,000 feet above sea level—that is, from the Guban ranges to the Ogo plateau. By Somali standards, it is ecologically one of the richer parts of the country. Significant areas of the district receive enough rainfall to allow the cultivation of sorghum and maize on an annual basis. Although the district experiences climatic variability, its economy is the most agriculturally based in the northern region; about 30 percent of the regional population are peasants. The people of this district, like others in the northern region, were historically pastoralists, and a large number (no estimates available) are still engaged in that activity. The transition from pure pastoralism to cultivation started in earnest around the turn of the century, as noted in Chapter 2. This movement towards cultivation was a response to the increased risks of pastoral production, brought about in part by the changing political configuration of the Horn. In the first forty years, the transition from pastoral to peasant production was a slow and uneven one. Mixing pastoral and peasant production temporarily alleviated the riskiness of the pastoral economy. Farming enhanced the food self-reliance of the pastoral household. Instead of the customary barter of animals for grain, several members of the household were left to grow grain, while others remained with the herd. Cultivation also provided a disease safety valve for the pastoralist in periods when most of their herds were decimated. The reliability of that safety valve, however, depended very much on good rains in the spring and summer to guarantee a sufficient harvest.

The regional economy underwent another major crisis during and immediately after the Second World War (see Chapter 3). The response of the pastoralists and the emerging peasantry to this crisis was to intensify cultivation. Although the expansion of cultivation temporarily mitigated some of the immediate impact of the crisis on rural production, it also generated new difficulties. With increasing rural population and the concomitant expansion of cultivated areas in the last four decades, pastoralists lost much of what had formerly been communal pastureland to permanent cultivation.

Residents of the small settlements on the Ogo plateau of Gabileh are part of a peasantry numbering from 12,000 to 15,000 households who are products of this historical process.[53] The plateau peasant settlement areas

of Galooley, Sanlawaha, and Ijawaaji were selected for closer study. A
peasant settlement in the northwest consists of a number of farming families who reside together, not on their individual plots but in a nucleus area
adjacent to their farmland. There is no official statistical definition of a
settlement. Historically, a peasant settlement consisted of a group, usually more than four households, residing in the same nucleated farm area.
The settlement I examined ranged in size from the minimum of four families to a maximum of twenty-five. Seventy-five households were selected
from seven settlements in the area to evaluate the response of the peasantry to the crisis.[54]

The critical problems which plague the rural areas in Somalia include un-
reliability of rainfall, plant diseases, soil erosion, lack of agricultural extension services, and high consumer prices. The toll of these problems is
such that the peasant household is almost always on the verge of destitution. There have been crop failures on the average of once every four
years since 1960, and there is no guarantee that production in a good year
will cover the lean ones. The situation is further compounded when one
takes into account the extent of the droughts in the mid-1960s, in 1973–75,
and in 1978–79, in which both livestock and crops were devastated.
These conditions were coupled with significant population growth (2.5%)
and the increasing prices of such commodities as sugar, tea, clothing,
dates, rice, kerosene, and tractor time. For instance, in 1971–72 one hour
of tractor time rented for 15–20 Somali shillings; in 1984 the rate was almost 200 shillings. There were similar increases in the price of rice and
other commodities. Peasants were progressively caught in a squeeze not
much different from the one experienced by their parents during the Second World War. One important factor that marked the conditions of the
late 1960s and the 1970s was the inability of these peasants to expand cultivation, owing to their primitive farming technologies (such as the use of
ox-drawn wooden ploughs) and the increasing scarcity of arable land.[55] It
became increasingly apparent that old methods and strategies of mitigating the risks of the rural economy had lost their effectiveness and that new
departures were necessary.
   Under these difficult conditions a handful of peasants began to experiment with the cultivation of kat, or chat (*Caltha edulis*), in the late 1960s.
The leaves of this shrub are a mild stimulant, popular in urban areas. Kat
in its natural state flourishes in elevations of 5,000–8,000 feet above sea
level. However, it grows well in a wide range of ecological regions, accepting a variety of soil and rainfall conditions, although wet and poorly
drained soils are not suitable. It is propagated from cuttings from branches,
in spite of the fact that it is a fruit-bearing plant. Normally it takes four to

five years for the plant to mature, but harvest can be made as early as the end of the second year. The life span of the plant is about twenty years.[56]

During the early experimental phase (1966–76), only a few peasants had more than a couple of hundred plants. The adoption of kat farming by the plateau peasantry was very slow in this period. However, as the drought of the 1970s devastated the rural economy, as the prices of consumer commodities skyrocketed (in 1972 the price of a kilogram of sugar was 3 shillings; in 1983–84 it was about 30–36 shillings), and as the kat market expanded, those who grew kat on their farms found themselves in a strategic position. As the brief biographies at the end of this section of the chapter will show, these individuals improved their income substantially.[57] As a result, kat farming gradually became a viable cash crop in the northwest, particularly in Gabileh, from the late 1970s to 1983.

As the income earning power of kat became known (1978–79), many members of the urban petite bourgeoisie, such as merchants and state officials, also invested some of their resources in kat production. In fact, some of the largest kat farms in the region were owned by members of this class. Indeed, as shown in Table 27, the involvement of the average peasant in kat production was not substantial. Of the seventy-five families in my sample, 16 percent did not grow kat, and 75 percent had less than six *qoodis* each under this crop.[58] Only 7 families, or 9.3 percent, had what can be considered substantial kat fields. The high rate of adaptation of kat cultivation (84% of all families) by the peasants is due to the fact that

Table 27. Kat Production in Rural Gabileh, 1983–1984

Area planted in kat (in qoodis)[a]	No. of peasant families	% of families
0	12	16.0
1	9	12.0
2	25	33.4
3	10	13.3
4	10	13.3
5	2	2.7
6	2	2.7
7	1	1.3
8	3	4.0
9	0	0
10	1	1.3
	75	100.0

Source: Field data, 1984.

[a] A qoodi is a local unit of farm area: it is the area a pair of oxen can plough in a day's time, usually a little less than an acre.

Table 28. Farmland Ownership and Distribution in Rural Gabileh,
1983–1984

Qoodis of farmland	No. of families owning	No. of families cultivating
1–2	0	0
3–4	2	3
5–6	5	6
7–8	4	5
9–10	6	6
11–12	2	3
13–14	3	5
15–16	6	5
17–18	1	3
19–20	5	6
21–30	16	18
31–50	15	8
51+	10	7
Total	75	75

Source: Field data, 1984.

Galooley is the area where the first experiments in kat cultivation occurred. The larger growers are all members of a group who started kat
cultivation in the early or mid-1970s. Moreover, these large growers usually came from that segment of the rural population who owned more than
20 qoodis of land. As shown in Table 28, forty-one out of the seventy-five
households in my sample owned more than 20 qoodis of farmland.

The age of kat plants in the sample ranged from one to sixteen years.
This range of adoption occurred within as well as across households. For
example, the age of kat plants in one plot ranged from one to seven years
old. This graduated adoption strategy reflects, mainly, a combination of
two factors; (a) peasants' wariness about getting too involved in an un-
tested enterprise, and (b) the growing knowledge of the fantastic benefits
accruing to those households who were at an advanced stage in the process of kat cultivation.

The production of this commodity helped to mitigate the pressures on
peasant production and reproduction in several ways and had an important impact on the peasant economy and the district beyond. The production of kat for sale in towns and cities of the region had begun to reverse
the deteriorating barter terms of trade against peasants. The tenacity of
kat prices in staying at parity with inflation (in 1971–72 the price of one
pound of kat was 3–6 shillings; in 1984 it was 100–200 shillings) enabled
growers to buy such commodities as sugar, kerosene, and cloth and also
retain some of the grains they had had to sell in the past. The kat plant is

less sensitive to rainfall variation than sorghum or maize, and for the growers it had become a temporary solution to the crisis of rural production; some even called it a famine preventer. In the pre-kat days milk and sorghum had to be sold to obtain cash in order to buy other commodities, but income from kat eliminated the need for such sales, and milk and grain consumption by kat growers increased. In addition, kat-growing peasants contend that income generated from kat sales enabled them to bring more of their land under cultivation. This, they argue, is because with income from kat they can afford to hire tractors, which can cultivate more land than an ox-drawn plough. My field data support this contention. Table 29 shows the number of peasant households that hire tractors to cultivate their farms. Except for seven families who were still using traditional ox-drawn ploughs and two others who were still using hoes, the remaining sixty-six families used hired tractors for cultivation. Of these sixty-six families some had begun hiring tractors only in the last few years. It must be remembered that tractors were used for sorghum and maize cultivation and not kat.

Because of the income it generated, kat production began to give land-ownership in the district a new meaning. Not only did it create an incipient land market, but also engendered a new land rush, as demonstrated by the privatization of arable dry-river banks (mostly by nonpeasants), making rain-fed farmland a very attractive commodity.

The cultivation of kat, then, initiated a very slow process of incipient peasant differentiation. This is not to imply that prior to the introduction of kat there was no inequality, but the origin and the nature of traditional inequality was principally a product of such factors as the differential im-

Table 29. Families Hiring Tractors for Cultivation, Rural Gabileh

No. of years tractor hired	No. of families hiring
1	2
2	1
3	4
4	6
5	7
6	7
7	4
8	8
9	7
10	12
11	8

Source: Field data, 1984.

pact of epidemics and drought, the livestock-management skills of the household, traditional ties, household population sizes, and luck. In fact, landownership distribution (Table 28) and livestock distribution (Table 30) are, in the main, a result of these traditional contingencies. In the case of livestock distribution no particular relationship between kat cultivation

Table 30. Distribution of Livestock among Sample Households, 1983–1984

No. of animals	No. of families owning	No. of families selling in last 3 yrs.
Camels		
1	20	3
2	4	0
3	1	0
4	3	0
5	0	0
6+	4	0
Cattle		
1	3	13
2	8	5
3	5	4
4	7	1
5	1	1
6	9	0
7	6	0
8	5	0
9–15	19	0
16+	10	0
Sheep & goats		
1	1	0
2	0	2
3	1	1
4	0	0
5	1	1
6	1	0
7	2	1
8	2	0
9	1	0
10	1	1
10–15	2	1
16–20	2	0
21–30	2	0
31–50	2	0
51–70	2	0
73+	1	0

Source: Field data, 1984.

Table 31. Hire of Rural Labor and Kat Ownership, Rural
Gabileh, 1983–1984

No. of mos. labor hired	No. of families hiring	No. of those families growing kat
0–2	21	21
3–6	3	3
Year-round	2	2

Source: Field data, 1984.

and livestock ownership emerges. For instance, a peasant who had been growing kat for fifteen years (8 qoodis) had 55 sheep and goats and 12 cattle, while another peasant who had grown kat for five to eight years (4 qoodis) had 73 sheep and goats, 14 cattle, and 6 camels. A third peasant who had no kat plants on his field had 65 sheep and goats.

The first sign of any new differentiation in the rural sector makes its appearance in the form of purchasing labor power. As shown in Table 31, there is a definite relation between hiring labor and owning a kat field. This must not be taken to mean that there was no such practice in the countryside before the introduction of kat. Traditionally, owners of larger farms or livestock employed some labor, although this was rare in the countryside. Some features of the traditional relationship between employer and employee still prevail, such as providing food and shelter for the employee during the term of employment.

In the sample, all those households hiring labor were also engaged in kat production. There seem to be no direct relationship between the amount of labor time purchased and the amount of land involved in kat cultivation. For instance, the area planted in kat of the first category of employers listed in Table 31 ranged from 2 to 8 qoodis, with seven of them cultivating 3 qoodis of kat. Employers in line 2 of Table 31 owned between 4 and 5 qoodis. The two households who had one year-round employee cultivated 8 qoodis and 6 qoodis, respectively. Both of these families had been growing kat for ten years or more. One of these two employers owned 45 qoodis of farmland, while the other had a 100-qoodi farm. Despite the lack of any fixed relationship between the size of the kat farm and the amount of labor time hired, all of the twenty-six employing families had done so only since they began to make sufficient income from kat.[59] The absence of a clear relationship between amount of land planted in kat and labor time purchased notwithstanding, there is little doubt that those with larger kat fields earned a great deal more cash income than those with small kat plots. For the latter group of growers, kat-generated income merely supplemented their dwindling purchasing power. However, for the larger growers (above 5 qoodis), who had been engaged in

the production of this commodity for a longer period, earnings from kat
exceeded necessary consumption. In spite of the unwillingness of kat
growers to disclose their specific annual cash income from the crop, it
seems clear that the older and larger growers were accumulating money.[60]
The following short biographies of three growers will indicate not only the
uses made of the income from kat, but also the conditions under which kat
cultivation was first adopted and the changes it brought.[61]

I. X was born in rural Gabileh in the mid-1930s to a first-generation
    peasant family. At present only five of the eight children born to his
    parents are alive. He grew up in the countryside, and in spite of his
    frequent visits to the villages, such as Gabileh and Arabsiyo, he be-
    came a peasant herder, managing his livelihood along the same lines
    as his father. While still a young man, he briefly attended a Koranic
    school. He married his first wife just before British Somaliland be-
    came independent. Like other peasants in the region, he had to
    travel on foot to Jigjiga Plateau (Ethiopia) to purchase sorghum and
    stover in the all-too-frequent years when rains either came late or
    were not sufficient. With the increasing prices of commodities in the
    towns, which outstripped the price of whatever commodities peas-
    ants were selling, life in the country became exceedingly difficult.
    Under these conditions X decided to experiment with kat cultivation.
    In 1966 while in Arabsiyo village he saw some kat seedlings being
    sold and bought about a hundred seedlings. He planted them on his
    farm. After three difficult years when the small plants were often mu-
    tilated by children and animals, in 1969 he had his first harvest and
    sale of kat. At the time the price of a pound of kat was 1.50 shillings.
    The income generated by the first harvest was sufficient to cover the
    cost of basic consumer commodities his family purchased, and he was
    also able to lend some money to relatives. Furthermore, it enabled
    him to hire enough tractor time to cultivate more of his farm than he
    had before. During the following two years, he also gave seedlings to
    a number of relatives who gained interest in kat after they saw his
    success. Over the following few years he expanded the size of his kat
    holding. By 1977 he had 8 qoodis under kat. In 1982 the farm-gate
    price of a pound of kat was 25–30 shillings, and X, being one of the
    largest kat producers in the district, accumulated a sizable amount of
    money wealth. He made a pilgrimage to Mecca and built an eight-
    room townhouse in Gabileh. In that same year, he also married his
    second wife and spent a significant amount of money on the wedding.
    He has also hired a farm worker for about eight years.

At the time of my interviews (1983–84) X was using hired tractors on his
two farms. The second farm is about 25 miles away and was given to him

by his uncle. X also owns fifty-five sheep, fifteen goats, seven cattle, and five donkeys. He has two wives and fourteen children, one of whom is in Veterinary College in Mogadishu; a second boy is in intermediate school. Most of the remaining children are too young to help him in the field, but some look after his livestock around the settlement and collect drinking water from the tug (dry river) two and half miles away. X became a rich peasant because of the income generated by kat.

II. Y was born in rural Gabileh in the late 1930s to peasant parents. Four of the eight children born to his parents are alive. While still young and a helping hand to his parents, he also studied the Koran and Islamic teachings for six years. In his early twenties he moved to Gabileh town and was hired by a retail storeowner as a storekeeper. He remained in that job until the mid-1960s, when he and another storekeeper pooled their savings and started a small store of their own. The venture went bankrupt in 1970, and Y returned to his boyhood settlement, decided to make a living as a peasant, and bought a farm. The return to the countryside was not a joyous occasion. Rainfall during 1971 and 1972 was sufficient, and Y had a good enough harvest of sorghum and maize to meet his family's basic needs and to store a small surplus in his earthpit. Although the harvest provided basic grain rations for the family, they had to do with little or none of the commodities that were available in towns. In the following year Y bought about 150 kat seedlings, having seen a couple of other growers getting good returns from kat sales. By spring of 1975, he had his first harvest and earned enough to enable his family to purchase such commodities as sugar, tea, dates, and rice. He immediately increased his kat holdings. In 1983–84 he had 6 qoodis under kat, and the youngest of his plants were four years old. As his monetary returns increased Y assisted his two brothers in starting their own kat holdings. In the late 1970s he invested most of his savings and income in a tin-roofed brick house on his farm. Later on, he bought a plot of land in Gabileh town, planning to build another house on it. In 1982 he married his second wife. In the spring of 1984 he had two wives and eight children, four of whom were in Koranic school and two in fifth grade. His farm is 45 qoodis, and he has one employee throughout the year. He uses a tractor to plough his sorghum and maize fields. He also grows some onions and tomatoes, and owns one camel, eight cattle, seven sheep, and a donkey.

III. Z was one of fifteen children born to peasant parents in rural Gabileh. Only four of these are living today. He is forty years old and, like most peasants his age, inherited his farm from his parents. He also kept a large herd of livestock whose products, such as milk and sheep, supplemented the family's grain rations. Some of these products were sold to earn cash in order to purchase commodities like clothing, sugar, tea, and kerosene. The drought of 1974–75 devastated his herd, leaving him with one lactating cow. These were hard times, and since he only had enough grain for seed, his wife had to sell the milk from their one remaining cow in the nearest town in order to purchase grain to eat. Fortunately, the rains were good the following spring, and at the end of the growing season they had a good harvest of sorghum. It had become common knowledge after the drought that those peasants who had kat plots were able to recover from their loses quickly. Consequently, Z decided to join the "kat elite." Using money savings from sales of milk, he bought kat seedlings during the summer and a year and half later made his first kat sales. Once he realized his first income from kat, he set out to expand his kat holding and in the process helped some of his relatives with seedlings. Six years later he had built himself a tin-roofed, mud-walled single-room dwelling, though he still retains the family hut. He has a wife and four children between the age of six and two years. He farms 15 qoodis, 3 of which are planted with kat. The ages of his kat plants range from three to seven years. He also owns fourteen goats, three cattle, and a donkey.

These three households are not representative of the success of all kat-producing peasants in the district. They merely illustrate that those who went into kat production early on were able to significantly reverse their deteriorating material conditions. This does not imply that those late-comers with much smaller plots of kat, who represent the majority of kat growers, would, in time, have replicated the success of their fortunate companions, had the state not banned kat imports from Ethiopia and Kenya and ordered the destruction of kat farms in the spring of 1984.[62] The state's successful implementation of the kat-eradication campaign left peasants no choice but to comply with government dictates, without gaining a replacement cash crop.

For the majority of growers, kat-generated income had enabled them to purchase basic commodities and hire tractor time for cultivating their farms. This became especially important after 1981, when prices of most commodities skyrocketed; as we have seen, the cost of one hour of tractor time was 200 shillings in the spring of 1983, having more than doubled in four years. Although the majority of the peasants in the district were not kat growers, kat cultivation was spreading quickly.

The production of kat had a number of other effects on the countryside. First, in spite of the national land laws which ban land sales, it was common knowledge in the northwest region that kat production and sales had

Kat Eradication Campaign—Students, Women's Association Members, Civil Servants, and Others Brought to the Countryside to Cut Down and Burn the Kat Crop, March, 1983

made farmland a more precious resource and commodity. Farm sales increased, although they remained an insignificant amount of land transactions. Second, despite the claims of the government that kat was displacing food production,[63] there is no evidence to refute the contention of those who grew the commodity that their ability to produce grain was enhanced by kat. They argue that they were producing more grain than before the introduction of kat: income from kat enabled them to hire enough tractor time to cultivate more farmland than before. Moreover, they were able to resow if the initial seeds did not germinate. Finally, the increased number of shillings circulating in the kat-growing areas intensified the monetization of the rural economy and further strengthened urban-rural linkages.

Conclusion

In spite of its rural development rhetoric since its establishment in 1969, the "revolutionary" Somali military regime rarely intervened in peasant and pastoral production. How can this phenomenon be explained? A well-known social commentator, Hyden, noted: "In this respect, African countries are societies without a state. The latter sits suspended in 'mid-air' over society and is not an integrated mechanism of the day-today production activities of society."[64] According to this reasoning, the suspension of the African post-colonial state is a result of the existence of an independent peasant mode of production. It is therefore supposedly the autonomy of the peasant producer which underscores the suspension of the state. In other words, it is the ability of the tenacious peasant producer, defending a subsistence way of life against outside interference, that is the basis not only of the state's inability (weakness) to intervene and transform agricultural production but also of the demise of rural surpluses.

No one denies the importance of the precapitalist social relations in understanding contemporary rural development problems in Africa. This chapter has illustrated how the peasantry in the northwest region progressively involved itself in the production of a nonfood commodity, an activity which tied it more closely to the commodity economy and the state. If Hyden's logic held, these peasants would have resisted the adoption of kat and would have been content in their "liberating mode of production." Hyden asserts, moreover, that "the peasant experiences any public policy aimed at improving his agriculture as 'foreign' intervention."[65] The field observations of this study indicate that peasants are eager to accept productivity-enhancing policies, provided that they *benefit* from the gains and that they have a say in the decision-making process. The discussion of the regime's agrarian policies and strategies suggests that the state consciously decided to bypass peasant production. This chapter points to a reversal of Hyden's assertion of the rationale behind the suspension of the state. In a different context Raikes points out that Hyden's view "flies in the face of abundant evidence firstly that peasants are pushed out of the door by poor terms or sheer lack of goods to exchange for their produce and second that their flight . . . is less to subsistence than to the black market."[66]

It is my contention that the State's disinterest in the improvement of rural production (pastoral and peasant) is premised on two basic material conditions: (1) the availability of foreign aid to lubricate the state's development machinery and (2) the state's ability, because of its colonial origins, to extract resources from the rural sector without intervening in agricultural production.

The availability of foreign aid has had two effects. First, development aid is in most cases project-specific and has been usually anti–small producer. In such projects tremendous windfalls accrue to strategically situated bureaucrats.[67] Second, even in those rare cases where a project is small-producer oriented, as was the NWAP, those who control the state machinery (mostly low-paid bureaucrats and state employees) usually subvert project objectives and divest some of the funds to other uses. This private appropriation—that is, embezzlement and corruption of public resources—by state officials is one variant of what has been labeled "rent-seeking."[68] For most of Africa rents are derived from the undervaluation of peasant-produced commodities bought by state monopolies. In the Somali case foreign aid has been the main source of rent, although, in the pastoral sector, substantial windfalls accrue to livestock merchants who, with state collaboration, control access to export markets. In other words, elements of the bureaucratic and trading petite burgeoisie have been the main beneficiaries of these windfalls.

Critics of Bates's rent-seeking theory raise a central question not addressed by Bates, which is "whether the material and ideological conditions required for the *reproduction* of such rent-seeking society can be *continually* secured?"[69] In the Somali context, given the country's strategic location and the rivalry of the super and regional powers, foreign assistance is still forthcoming in substantial quantities, as shown in Table 32.[70] As for the domestic sources of rent, no one is certain how long pastoral production can sustain current forms and quantities of surplus extraction, given warnings that pastoral production has reached a plateau.[71] At the ideological level, current forms of rent and surplus extraction can be sustained only through continued repression.

Second, owing to its colonial origins, the state has been able to extract resources from rural producers, pastoralists in particular, without vig-

Table 32. Foreign Assistance to Somalia by Donors, 1984–1986 (estimates in millions of U.S. dollars)

Source	1984		1985–86	
	Amount	% of total	Amount	% of total
Arab Funds	47.0	19.0	88.0	12.6
U.S.A.	44.3	17.9	132.5	19.0
W. Germany	29.9	12.1	46.9	11.0
World Bank	27.3	11.1	95.6	13.7
EEC	23.2	9.4	51.2	7.3
Romania	14.9	6.0	51.6	7.4
Italy	11.4	4.6	85.0	12.2
France	8.0	3.2	13.0	1.9
World Food Program	6.0	2.4	12.2	1.7
UNDP	4.7	1.9	14.3	2.0
Finland	4.6	1.9	7.6	1.1
Denmark	4.3	.8	5.5	.8
Others	21.2	8.6	64.8	9.3
All sources	246.8	100.0	668.2	100.0

Source: U.S. Agency for International Development, *Country Development Strategy Statement for 1987* (Washington, D.C.: Government Printing Office, January 1985), p. III-10.

orously intervening at the point of agricultural production. Extraction in this case takes two forms; first, the state taxes commodities consumed by rural producers, and second, it taxes marketed rural produce such as livestock. Under this system of taxation the state can extract "surplus" without involving itself in rural production; in 1982, for instance, 82 percent of total state revenues came from such sources.[72] Foreign assistance in Somali reinforces this *historic* suspension of the state over the domestic productive processes.[73]

Since pastoralists and peasants are not self-sufficient, they have to stay in the commodity economy to gain access to essential commodities, although they realize its exploitative nature. Strangely enough, it is the ability of the state to extract resources from the rural sector without being instrumental in introducing productivity-enhancing methods and resources into peasant and pastoral economy that is the issue. This slow bleeding of the rural economy has its parallels in the industrial world, where the term "cash cow" has been coined.[74] The use of foreign assistance, whether donated by the Soviet bloc or by the West, to underwrite state-controlled "development" projects buttresses this system of extraction and has in fact ensured the reproduction of this peculiar form of petit bourgeois accumulation and underdevelopment. Freyhold's analysis of the subservient postcolonial state needs a slight reformulation to characterize the Somali case. Here, the global conflict between the superpowers gives the Somali postcolonial state a bargaining chip which it exploits to gain more resources from donors. In spite of this advantageous position, its dependence on external actors for the material conditions of its reproduction is unquestionable. Small producers who are immobilized in this system may adopt crops and/or methods of production that may not serve the "general public interest" but may temporarily alleviate the crisis of peasant and pastoral reproduction. The adoption of kat cultivation by the northwest peasantry is a case in point. Curiously, it is the incapacity of peasants and pastoralists either to withdraw from or to alter the prevailing power structure that underpins rural underdevelopment.

Finally, much as in the parliamentary era, the most central political issue has been the distribution of rent between different factions of the petite bourgeoisie. The governing clique was able, until recently, to maintain social peace by using a mixture of nationalist rhetoric and coercion in determining the dispensation of the largesse. But after the defeat of Somali troops in the Ogaden in the late 1970s, patriotic ideology lost its currency, and the conflict among the petite bourgeoisie over rent intensified. Consequently, various competing factions marshalled ethnicity as an organizing ideology. As the dividing line between the dominant groups and peripheral ones began to merge with clan boundaries, nationalist pretensions were discarded by the governing clique in favor of more repression. In the face of such tyranny, peripheral groups of the petite bourgeoisie organized regionally and tribally based armed resistance—the Somali Salvation Front and the Somali National Movement. These intraclass conflicts and the consequent repression reinforce the suspension of the postcolonial Somali state.

6

The Long Transition

If the ruling class has lost its consensus, i.e., is no longer "leading" but only dominant, exercising coercive force alone, this means precisely that the great masses
have become detached from their traditional ideologies and no longer believe
what they used to believe previously, etc. The crisis consists precisely in the fact
that the old is dying and the new cannot be born: in this interregnum a great variety of morbid symptoms appears.

A. Gramsci
Prison Notebooks

Defining the past is crucial to controlling the present and the future.

Guy Gran
Beyond African Famines

In a recent attempt to unmask the origins of "personal rule" in tropical
Africa, Sandbrook suggested that the "central conundrum facing postcolonial political leaders is how to govern and hold together unintegrated
peasant societies in the absence of legitimacy."[1] Such an explanation of
personal rule and Africa's economic stagnation is predicated on two conditions: (*a*) a weakly integrated peasant society and (*b*) rulers craving to rule
with or without legitimacy. This combination defines the social context of
the current crisis.

Sandbrook's contribution weaves together two disparate threads of the
neoclassical populist discussion of the African condition: Hyden's *uncaptured peasantry and economy of Affection* and Bates's *political basis of
agricultural policy*. This synthesis suffers from three fundamental flaws.
First, there is nothing in Sandbrook's text which explains the social history of the so-called unintegrated peasant society. Second, the continental
scope of his text forces the analysis to succumb to broad generalizations,
in spite of authoritative warnings of Sara Berry to the contrary.[2] Third,
although Sandbrook recognizes the destructive effects of personal rule on
capitalist development, he nevertheless says little about the important relationships between the genesis of peripheral capitalism and the emergence of personal rule.

The present regime in Somalia clearly practices "personal rule" par excellence. Somalia also suffers from the woes of economic stagnation and/or retrogression. Thus the Somali case *appears* to confirm Sandbrook's hypothesis. On the contrary, however, the social history of northern Somalia demonstrates two issues fundamental to this discourse: (1) that "personal rule" is a disguised and distorted form of (petit bourgeois) class domination under a particular kind of peripheral capitalism, and (2) that social disintegration is not a consequence of cultural and ethnic fragmentation, but is induced by the compulsive and corrosive intraclass struggle over private accumulation in the public realm. Such internal conflicts among the governing petite bourgeoisie undermine whatever hegemonic claims it had. This process ultimately ensures the supremacy of coercion and the (re)production of naked dictatorship as those who command state resources strive to cling to the reign of power, and it literally prepares the way for a multitude of "odd" regimes. In order to understand the root causes of this phenomenon, one needs to examine the structure of production and the politics of precolonial times, the manner in which such societies were incorporated into colonial capitalism, the degree of capitalist development (i.e., productive forces), the complexion of the postcolonial society's class structure, and its accumulation strategy. This chapter sketches the contours of these processes in Somalia.

On the eve of colonization, the social structure of northern Somali society precluded the existence of generalized exploitative relations between members of the pastoral community. The absence of such relations among the members of Somali pastoral society was historically determined by the egalitarian distribution of the means of production, livestock, and range resources, and the resulting production of use-values by all able-bodied members of the community. A salient characteristic of this society was the absence of state formation. In a nutshell, precolonial Somali society approximated Marx's Germanic mode of production.[3] Over the last century significant qualitative changes have taken place in the structure of this society. However, conventional social analysts of the Somali society continue to overlook changes such as those elaborated in the preceding chapters.[4] I have three principal objectives in this chapter. First, I will dispute the misleading theoretical premises of conventional Somalists—which emphasize the analytical value of tribalism and tradition—by contending that the concept of social class is more appropriate to the analysis of contemporary Somali political economy. Second, I will advance in broad theoretical terms the nature and the extent of the capitalist transformation of Somali society. Finally, I will argue that the imposition of colonial capitalism on Somali society and the subsequent development of peripheral capitalism had a formative influence on Somali politics and social reproduction.

Production, Exchange, and Class Relations in Northern Somalia

Livestock production, the central focus of pastoral life in precolonial Somaliland, is still the principal productive sector of the economy in northern Somalia. The persistence and centrality of this sector has often been pointed to as if it were evidence that Somali society in general and pastoralism in particular has remained "traditional" in spite of the influence of the modern market. This approach assumes historical continuity and confines social scientific analysis to the immediately visible forms of social phenomena—that is, the endurance of "tribalism" and nomadism. Accordingly, the changes which have taken place in the political economy of this society are represented as being quantitative changes that did not alter the essence of Somali tradition. The nature, the logic, and the impact of the global economic system of which Somalia is now a part is usually assumed away and considered unproblematic. The only exceptions to this kind of analysis are the works of Swift, Aronson, and Ahmed Samatar.[5] The approach developed in the previous pages contradicts this standard belief. I contend that the precolonial Somali tradition has been blown asunder by its incorporation into the world capitalist system. Livestock and pastoral production, which originally was principally geared for domestic use, has been commoditized, qualitatively transforming precolonial nonexploitative social relations into peripheral capitalist relations.

The argument in the scholarly literature has been that peripheral and peasant societies are not capitalist because of the absence of capitalist and working-class relations.[6] The supporters of this scenario also include some writers of materialist persuasion, such as the proponents of an independent peasant mode of production.[7] This contention is based on the presumption that the development of capitalism always manifests itself in such a way as to divorce working people from the means of production. This interpretation is too restrictive and somewhat ahistorical in that it fails to delineate the variety of forms which capitalist development can take in precapitalist societies. Also, this conceptual framework cannot explicate the contours of the long transition periods when primitive accumulation is in high gear. The flaws of the so-called peasant-mode-of-production schema should alert social analysts to be sensitive to the complexity of capitalist penetration into noncapitalist and peripheral societies.[8]

My contention, given the evidence presented in the last four chapters, is that the development of a peripheral capitalist economy in Somalia meant the emergence of clearly differentiated social classes. Of course, the demarcation of class boundaries is a very difficult task, since social classes are not frozen entities at the level of praxis, particularly in convulsive transitional periods. Class is not a fixed category[9] but a relationship between people in the processes of production and reproduction: as

Lenin noted, "Classes are large groups of people differing from each other by the place they occupy in the historically determined system of social production, by their *relations* to the means of production, by their *role* in the social organisation of labour, and, consequently, by the *share* of social wealth of which they dispose and the mode of acquiring it. Classes are groups of people one of which can appropriate the labour of another owing to the different places of which they occupy in a definite system of social economy."[10]

In postcolonial Somalia there exists a definite class relationship between Somali pastoralists and livestock merchants, conditioned by the way Somaliland was inserted into the global capitalist economy and the subsequent commoditization of livestock. The degree of commoditization of livestock in Somalia is advanced. Livestock exports from precolonial Somaliland were an insignificant trade item. Today the number of livestock sold in the market, either for nonpastoral domestic consumption or for export, exceeds three million head annually. This enormous growth of market relations occurred without the physical displacement of pastoralists by "commercial growers" and without an evident transformation of property relations. The absence of an emergent "classic" capitalist road has often led analysts to the uncritical conclusion that the merchant-pastoralist market relation is mutually beneficial, implying the existence of a kind of equality between the two groups. The presumed equality does not have a basis in reality.[11] The merchant class extracts surplus labor from pastoralists in the sphere of exchange. Exploitation through trade is nothing new, since it was through this method that significant amounts of capital were raised in the European capitalist transitions: "Merchant capital remained in the sphere of circulation instead of being invested in production, and the [pastoralists] were subordinated to merchant capital through exchange, not production relations."[12]

This "antiquated" method of surplus appropriation is not unique either to the initial primitive accumulation or to peripheral capitalist societies. Similar phenomena have been observed in certain sectors of advanced capitalist economies where capital "chooses" not to completely subsume the production process.[13] Scholars analyzing these situations use concepts such as "propertied labor" to distinguish between proletarianized labor and labor which has some access to the means of production but which is nonetheless exploited by capital. This construct, propertied labor, points to the plausibility that labor can be subjected to capitalist exploitation without separating it from the means of production. Does this therefore imply that Somali livestock merchants are capitalists and the pastoralists are propertied labor? The answer is in the affirmative because pastoralists yield surplus to the merchants and their reproduction is concretely tied to the international commodities market. In sharp contrast to conditions experienced by their precolonial or even early colonial pastoralist kinsfolk, contemporary rural producers do not have the luxury of withdrawing from the market, not even partially or occasionally.

The inequality in precolonial Somali pastoralism was Chayanovian and was not related to surplus extraction.[14] The growth of class relations in Somali society has undermined precapitalist egalitarian norms. Livestock-export merchants are among the chief beneficiaries of the development of class relations in Somalia. For example, the 923 merchants who exported livestock from the principal port of Berbera between 1981 and 1986 earned more than $30 million of profit.[15] These resources are not widely distributed even within the mercantile class. Only a minority of the exporters—29 men, to be exact—dominate the business. The surpluses which accrue to the merchants, via this trade, are the principal domestic source of accumulation. How these surpluses are deployed is privately determined by the individual merchants. It is common knowledge in northern Somalia that such surplus earnings have been invested mainly in real estate, trade, and other urban enterprises which do not enhance the productive capacity of the economy.[16] This is the classic circulation-based pattern characteristic of mercantilism.

In the last few years profits earned from livestock exports have stagnated as a result of the decline in livestock export prices and a drop in the number of animals exported.[17] The pressure of the current profit squeeze is an indication that the mercantile method of surplus extraction has run its course. Consequently, the claimant social classes—the state and the livestock merchants—are searching for new ways of expanding surplus extraction from rural producers by "advancing" rural productivity. Whatever form this rural development strategy takes, it is doubtful that pastoralists and peasants will have significant input in its design.

The peasants are the other group of rural producers in Somalia, although they are a smaller group than the pastoralists. In the years since the peasantry was created by broad regional and international forces, the northern Somali peasants located in the Gabileh, Borama, and Hargeisa districts have been securely tied to the market, although they do not not produce as large a surplus as their pastoral neighbors. In spite of this quantitative difference, they also constitute a propertied laboring class subject to the exploitation of the state and of merchant capital. Together, peasants and pastoralists form the most productive segment of Somali society.

Postcolonial Politics and the Crisis of Social Reproduction

The incorporation of the precapitalist pastoral society into the colonial capitalist economy has had lasting and far-reaching effects on Somali society; it led to the development of exploitative relations and the concomitant restructuring of precolonial politics and ideology. The broad distribution of the means of subsistence and the absence of exploitative and class-based state institutions gave precolonial Somaliland a unique decentralized political system rooted in the material needs of the basic unit of production, the pastoral household. This was the traditional social system which anthropologist Lewis termed a "pastoral democracy." The ethnic underpinnings of this political system had a qualitatively different social function in that society than does its contemporary caricature, tribalism.

The political structure of the stateless pastoral community mirrored its egalitarian material base. Community elders—that is, all mature adult men—"democratically" participated in the decision-making process. The council of elders was the focal point of community politics. The voluntary compliance of the populace was the chief means of accomplishing the council's decisions. These men did not control a centralized coercive machinery nor other resources which they could have used to reward or punish those who deviated from traditionally established norms and practices. Because established social institutions dominated by a particular ethnic group or social class were not present, they could not be used to focus or magnify whatever exploitative or repressive tendencies such communal organization had. Only during occasional conflicts between clans did the ethnically based political system develop into a temporary but organized coercive form. In summary, during the precapitalist era, no individual or group within the pastoral community was able to use the precapitalist political system regularly as an instrument to repress or exploit other members of the community. The broad communitarian social relations in precapitalist Somaliland were more akin to primitive communalism or even anarchy than pastoral democracy, as the following extract from a British colonial writer in East Africa suggests: "Somalis, Bawana, they no good: each man his own Sultan."[18]

The imposition of a British colonial state and the concomitant development of colonial capitalism fundamentally altered the logic of the precapitalist communal economy and its political superstructure. The British colonial state was a coercive and centralized force more powerful than any of the clan families. Its imposition had three contradictory and long-lasting effects on the social structure of the Somali society:

First, it was a force that superseded the political cleavages of the pastoral society. Consequently, it brought together dispersed Somali lineage groups together under a national umbrella.

Second, the colonial state, a capitalist state, was determined to insure the implantation of commodity relations within the pastoral society. The development of a Somali social group nurtured by the growth of capitalist relations and subordinate, at least initially, to the colonial project was inherent in this process. This new group was the incipient petite bourgeoisie.

Third, for the purposes of the colonial administration (its security and legitimacy with the Somali people), the colonial state had to reshape the precolonial political system and subordinate it to its dictates. Thus, there was the establishment of administrative boundaries which coincided with the presumed traditional tribal areas and the institution of chiefs (akils) who represented their respective clans in the governor's court. In this way, previously independent clans were gradually turned into vassals of the colonial state. Colonialism caricatured and ossified the precolonial political system and encouraged development of a powerful ideology which pitted one "tribe" against another in the competition for state favors. These developments gave the ethnic and community-based political system a permanency it had never possessed, and radically changed its foci and character.

Given the limited purposes of the British colonial project in northern Somaliland, the development of commodity relations meant the transformation of the logic of pastoral production from its use-value orientation to one that was increasingly geared to the market. In the absence of any other profitably exploitable resources, the slow but progressive commoditization of pastoralism (without the proletarianization of the nomads) severely circumscribed the development of capitalism and confined exploitative relations to the exchange circuit. When northern Somaliland gained its independence in 1960 and formed a union with the former Italian colony of Somalia, the governing classes were far from being hegemonic in the Gramscian sense.[19] This jumble of a class, the so-called petite bourgeoisie, whose members operated the state apparatus, had no direct roots in production. Reliance on circulation rendered the reproduction of this class, both in its simple and expanded forms, problematic. In the face of the growing numbers within the aspiring petite bourgeoisie, the rigid limits of the sphere of exchange as the main avenue of surplus created a very unstable social environment. At the same time, the capacity of the postcolonial state to devise a regenerative domestic source of accumulation was severely constrained by the legacy of its colonial heritage, the fragmented nature of the petite bourgeoisie (its dependence on circulation), and the resistance of rural producers to certain forms of state intervention they deemed disadvantageous. The hamstrung state with its Western view of development sought assistance from overseas in order to fund its development programs. It has been very successful in attracting the "generosity" of aid donors.

The success of the state in securing external resources to fuel its development projects inevitably reinforced the centrality of state power and state resources in the accumulation process. As a result of this centralization, the single most important national political question was who among the governing petite bourgeoisie would control the public purse and ultimately determine its use. The "modern" and inherited public mechanism for doing this was the parliamentary political process. In capitalist democracies, political parties are one of the vehicles through which opposing social forces influence societal accumulation strategies. The differing agendas of these classes echo their contrasting social locations or ideologies and account for the dissimilarity between political parties. Here the state is both the arena where social struggles occur and simultaneously the social force which ensures that class conflict does not go unchecked to consume the whole society. It therefore guarantees the continuance of the social system. In spite of the interclass and intraclass conflicts in developed capitalist societies, the hegemony of capitalist property relations has been established. Furthermore, the means of exploitation is economic, and the sources of accumulation are principally in the private sector. As a consequence of this social arrangement, the power vested in the state is the object of struggle between classes, but the state itself is neither the object of appropriation nor the source of accumulation for the hegemonic classes. In other words, it is inconceivable for any one class or fragment of a class to completely dominate state resources without precipitating grave social upheavals.

In sharp contrast to capitalist democracies, the peripheral capitalist and postcolonial Somali society completely lacked these crucial social "arrangements" between social classes and also the productive domestic sources of accumulation available to the capitalist hegemonic classes. In other words, the process of private accumulation and access to direct state control were fused into one, releasing centrifugal forces of immense destructive force.[20] The dearth of private and productive domestic sources of accumulation, the adoption of a peripheral capitalist development strategy, and the lack of substantive ideological differences between different segments of the governing class led various factions of the dominant but not hegemonic petite bourgeoisie to battle over the private appropriation of the public sector. Under these circumstances the parliamentary process which had seemed so well-suited to the Somali political environment atrophied as the incessant competition among the petite bourgeoisie for strategic and remunerative state offices intensified. The centrifugal nature of intraclass competition demolished whatever capitalist social cohesion the governing class had. Each individual petit bourgeois contestant was at war with the rest in order to completely appropriate state power. The only distinction between those competing for public offices was their ethnic heritage, since they shared similar social and class backgrounds and had the same ambitions. Ethnicity and other precapitalist relationships and belief systems had to be resurrected and deployed in order to distinguish the candidates in the competitive political marketplace of postcolonial Somalia. The proliferation of political parties in the 1960s was a manifestation of this process. Tribalism—or tribal politics, as the precapitalist social relationships are currently dubbed—is superficially precapitalist, since the social and material basis upon which such relationships were grounded had been completely *fanshened*.[21] It is no wonder that the articulated precapitalist Somali pastoral society with its egalitarian, republican social and political character degenerated under such compulsive competitive pressures. It gave way to a repressive and exploitative system, which has found its fullest expression in the current militarized and "tribalist" regime.

The transformation of a precapitalist ethnic and non-commodity-based political system into a coercive system of class domination in order to buttress the extra-economic appropriation of public resources by a specific fragment of the petite bourgeoisie reinforces the wedge between the state and civil society. It appears that these conditions will continue, at least in the short run. This seems guaranteed by several factors. First, the arbitrary, excessive, and violent use of the coercive machinery of the state— such as the planned destruction of kat farms in the northwest in the spring of 1984 and the more recent "collective" punishment of certain communities—contributes to the fragmentation of communities along ethnic lines. Second, overrepresentation of members of certain "ethnic" groups in strategic positions in the armed forces and other sectors of the public realm, and the consequent private appropriation of public resources by these groups, ensure the vitality of sectarian ethnic politics. Third, the abolition and distortion of precapitalist and bourgeois methods of legal and public management of social conflict, the breakdown of the public-security system guaranteeing personal safety and the basic civil rights of most citizens who are not related to the powers that be, and the lack of nonethnic forms of cultural and ideological frames of reference sustain and prolong the prevailing social crisis. Furthermore, this form of petit bourgeois dictatorship—which led to growing alienation between communities of differing "ethnic" backgrounds, between the state and civil society, and between warring factions of the petite bourgeoisie—is sustained by the massive injections of "development" assistance from overseas. Such assistance underwrites a large portion of the ordinary operations of the state and bolsters the relationship between the state and rural producers (characterized by neglect of peasant and pastoral production) discussed in Chapters 4 and 5. For example, currently more than 75 percent of the operating budgets of all of the social and economic ministries are funded by foreign assistance.[22] In addition, the Ministry of Defense, which allegedly consumes more than 50 percent of the state budget, is generously subsidized by foreign donors.

Peripheral-capitalist "tribal" politics came to prominence in the early 1960s as a means through which certain groups within the petite bourgeoisie gained access to the state apparatus and its resources under the pressures of the competitive political marketplace. The employment of ethnicity as a political ideology in peripheral-capitalist Somalia unleashed destructive forces which razed the parliamentary electoral process, fractured the governing class, led to the unprecedented emergence of a repressive and authoritarian regime, alienated communities from each other in ways previously unknown in Somali history, undermined the basis of state legitimacy, and, finally, threaten the very existence of contemporary Somalia as a country by swiftly and fatally maiming Somali nationalist ideology, the main supraclan cohesive fiber in this society.

Conclusion

The transformation of northern Somali rural life since the turn of the century entailed more than just agrarian change. It encompassed the entirety of the Somali political economy, material, cultural, and social. The development of peripheral-capitalist "tribal" politics and the mercantilist nature of accumulation spawned a politico-economic development strategy dependent on foreign sources, and led to the exploitation of rural producers in the sphere of circulation for its maintenance and to the demise of rural production. The evolution of the process carried with it the seeds of societal crisis in its fullest sense: endangerment of social reproduction.[23] This is the nature and the social history of the current Somali development crisis—a crisis of social reproduction which cannot be gleaned from the statistics of the Ministry of Planning nor from the tables of the World Development Report of the World Bank. It cannot be determined how long the dominant class will maintain the prevailing social chaos, the extra-economic and economic means of surplus extraction, and the foreign-assistance-based accumulation. Continuation of the current situation is contingent on the development of numerous social factors, such as the emergence of nontribal social movements guided by the recognition of the contradictions and the limits of peripheral-capitalist development, and the need for an accumulation strategy oriented to the fulfillment of the basic needs of rural producers. The prognosis for the immediate future is disheartening. The repression by the militarized "tribalist" regime deepens ethnic cleavages because communities and individuals seek refuge in the ruins of precapitalist social structures, which ironically re-inforces social fissures. This prolongs the dying of the deformed old and delays the birth of the new. The emergence of "regionalist" or "tribalist" resistance movements, the majority of whose members and leaders were associated with the military regime (such as the Somali National Move-ment and Somali Salvation Front), is symptomatic of this predicament.[24] This is not to imply that the present ruling faction of the petite bour-geoisie will retain state power indefinitely. On the contrary, it may and probably will be replaced by another faction, but that change is unlikely to produce a foreseeable change in the regime of accumulation. This is the social basis of the current legitimacy crisis and economic stagnation.

Notes
Bibliography
Index

Notes

Preface

1 On method, see Andrew Sayer, *Methods in Social Science: A Realist Approach* (London: Hutchinson, 1984).

2 John M. Johnson, *Doing Field Research* (New York: Free Press, 1975); William M. O'Barr, D. H. Spain, and M. A. Tessler, *Survey Research in Africa: Its Application and Limits* (Evanston, Ill.: Northwestern University Press, 1973); M. Watts, *Silent Violence* (Berkeley: University of California Press, 1983).

3 Jan Vansina, "Recording the Oral History of Bakuba, 1: Methods," *Journal of African History* 1, no. 1 (1960): 45–53.

4 V. Person, "Chronology and Oral Tradition," in M. A. Klein and G. W. Johnson, eds., *Perspectives on the African Past* (Boston: Little, Brown, 1972), pp. 3–16.

5 Vansina, "Recording the Oral History of Bakuba." Vansina indicates that such "a sample should never be random, for in history, two witnesses never have the same value and cannot therefore be considered as similar units one could choose at random."

6 J. Vansina, R. Mauny, and L. U. Thomas, eds., *The Historian in Tropical Africa* (London: Oxford University Press, 1964). See also Barbara Allen and W. L. Montell, *From Memory to History: Using Oral Sources in Local Historical Research* (Nashville: American Association for State and Local History, 1981), and J. Hoopes, *Oral History: An Introduction for Students* (Chapel Hill: University of North Carolina Press, 1979).

7 Abdi Samatar and Ahmed I. Samatar, "The Material Roots of the Suspended African State: Arguments from Somalia," *Journal of Modern African Studies*, 25, 4 (1987): 669–90.

8 Eric R. Wolf, *Europe and the People without History* (Berkeley and Los Angeles: University of California Press, 1982).

Chapter 1: Introduction

1 Ahmed I. Samatar, *Socialist Somalia: Rhetoric and Reality* (London: Zed Press, 1988).

2 D. D. Laitin and S. S. Samatar, *Somalia: Nation in Search of a State* (Boulder, Colo.: Westview Press, 1987).

3 John Lonsdale, "States and Social Processes in Africa: A Historiographical Survey," *African Studies Review* 24, nos. 2/3 (1981): 227–74.

4   Robert Bates, *Markets and States in Tropical Africa* (Berkeley and Los Angeles: University of California Press, 1981); Michael Lofchie and S. Commins, "Food Deficits and Agricultural Policies in Tropical Africa," *Journal of Modern African Studies* 20, no. 1 (1982): 1–26; Keith Hart, *The Political Economy of West African Agriculture* (Cambridge: Cambridge University Press, 1982).

5   For an excellent presentation and critique of the plurality hypothesis of the state see Ralph Miliband, *The State in Capitalist Society: An Analysis of the Western System of Power* (New York: Basic Books, 1969), ch. 1.

6   V. I. Lenin, *The Development of Capitalism in Russia* (Moscow: Progress Publishers, 1977); Henry Bernstein, "Concepts for the Analysis of Contemporary Peasantries," in R. Galli, ed. *The Political Economy of Rural Development: Peasants, International Capital, and the State* (Binghamton: State University of New York Press, 1981); Alain De Janvry, *The Agrarian Question and Reformism in Latin America* (Baltimore: Johns Hopkins University Press, 1981); J. G. Gurley, *China's Economy and the Maoist Strategy* (New York: Monthly Review Press, 1976); Michael Watts, *Silent Violence: Food, Famine, and Peasantry in Northern Nigeria* (Berkeley and Los Angeles: University of California Press, 1983).

7   E.g., I. M. Lewis, *A Pastoral Democracy: A Study of Pastoralism and Politics among the Northern Somali of the Horn of Africa* (London: Oxford University Press, 1961). An exception is Jeremy Swift, "The Development of Livestock Trading in a Pastoral Economy: The Somali Case," in *Pastoral Production and Society* (Cambridge: Cambridge University Press, 1978). For a useful and comparative piece, see John I. Iliffe, *A Modern History of Tanganyika* (Cambridge: Cambridge University Press, 1978), ch. 1.

8   Lewis, *A Pastoral Democracy.*

9   Lofchie and Commins, "Food Deficits." See also Food and Agricultural Organization, *The State of Food and Agriculture* (Rome, 1979), pp. 95–104. In the twenty years since Africa's independence a debate has been raging on the exact nature of the continent's "backwardness." The modernization, nation-building school argues that the African condition is due primarily to "traditionalism" and that the Western presence, in dismantling it, and was a modernizing force. For this view see David Apter, *The Politics of Modernization* (Chicago: University of Chicago Press, 1967); M. Yudelman, *Africans on the Land: Economic Problems of African Agricultural Development . . . with Special Reference to Southern Rhodesia* (Cambridge: Harvard University Press, 1969); Manning Nash, *Primitive and Peasant Economic Systems* (San Francisco: Chandler, 1966); George M. Foster, *Traditional Societies and Technological Change* (New York: Harper and Row, 1973). This does not mean that other themes do not abound in the debate. However, it seems that the ones recapitulated here are the front-line contenders. For this see Gavin Kitching, *Development and Underdevelopment in Historical Perspective: Populism, Nationalism, and Industrialization* (New York: Methuen, 1982).

10   Henry Bernstein, "Agrarian Crisis in Africa and Neo-Classical Populism" (Paper presented to the Postgraduate Seminar on Peasants, Institute of Commonwealth Studies, University of London, March 15, 1985); De Janvry, *The Agrarian Question*, ch. 10.
11   For a sample, see R. J. Berg and J. S. Whitaker, eds. *Strategies for African Development* (Berkeley and Los Angeles: University of California Press, 1986).
12   Goran Hyden, *Beyond Ujamaa in Tanzania: Underdevelopment and the Uncaptured Peasantry* (Berkeley and Los Angeles: University of California Press, 1980).
13   Keith Hart, *The Political Economy of West African Agriculture* (London: Cambridge University Press, 1981).
14   Bates, *Markets and States in Tropical Africa*, p. 120.
15   The World Bank, *Accelerated Development in Sub-Saharan Africa: An Agenda for Action* (Washington, D.C., 1981). See also the World Bank, *Land Reform* (Washington, D.C., 1974). Here the Bank contends that a major problem in African agricultural development is the traditional communal land tenure system because it is too rigid. Are rural people in countries where communal land tenure is a thing of the past vastly better off? This the Bank does not address. It is a theme I will examine later in this chapter. For a critical analysis of the Bank's report see the entire issue of *African Development* 6, nos. 1–2 (1982).
16   This assumption is implicit in the entire analysis except in the presentation of Hart. Although Hart does see the state in a different light than do the World Bank and Bates, nevertheless he fails to recognize the relationship between capitalist agriculture and rural poverty. This is a theme well articulated by DeJanvry regarding Latin America.
17   A. G. Hopkins, *An Economic History of West Africa* (New York: Columbia University Press, 1973), pp. 291–92. See also Gary Wasserman, *Politics of Decolonization: Kenya, Europeans, and the Land Issue, 1960–1965* (New York: Cambridge University Press, 1976); Colin Leys, *Underdevelopment in Kenya: The Political Economy of Neo-Colonialism, 1964–1971* (Berkeley and Los Angeles: University of California Press, 1975); Claude Meillassoux, "A Class Analysis of Bureaucratic Process in Mali," *Journal of Development Studies* 6, no. 2 (1970): 97–110; Michaela Von Freyhold, "The Post-Colonial State and Its Tanzanian Version," *Review of African Political Economy* 8 (1977): 75–89; Michael Crowder, "Whose Dream Was It Anyway? Twenty-Five Years of African Independence," *African Affairs* 86, no. 324 (1987): 7–24.
18   Gavin Kitching, *Classes and Economic Change in Kenya: The Making of African Petite-Bourgeoisie, 1905–1970* (New Haven: Yale University Press, 1980). This is one of the best materialist critiques of the neoclassical analysis of African underdevelopment.
19   Richard Sandbrook, *The Politics of Basic Needs: Urban Aspects of Assaulting Poverty in Africa* (Toronto: University of Toronto Press, 1982), chapter 2.

This is a good critique of the neoclassical populist, urban-biased literature which contends that workers in the urban areas are part of the privileged.

20 Watts, *Silent Violence*, pp. 148–86.

21 John Lonsdale and Bruce Berman, "Coping with the Contradictions: The Development of the Colonial State in Kenya, 1895–1914," *Journal of African History* 20 (1979): 487–505.

22 For an excellent but general illustration of different colonial methods of commodity penetration, see E. Sik, *The History of Black Africa*, 2 vols. (Budapest: Akademiai Kiado, 1966).

23 Bernstein, "Concepts for the Analysis of Contemporary Peasantries," p. 9.

24 M. Mamdani, "Extreme but not Exceptional: Towards an Analysis of the Agrarian Question in Uganda," *Journal of Peasant Studies* 14, no. 2 (1987): 191–225.

25 Michael Watts, "The Etiology of Hunger: The Evolution of Famine in a Sudano-Sahelian Region," *Mass Emergencies* 4 (1979): 99.

26 For various forms of direct or indirect state and capital intervention into the production process, see Bernstein, "Concepts for the Analysis of Contemporary Peasantries," p. 10, n. 23.

27 Walter Rodney, *How Europe Underdeveloped Africa* (Washington D.C.: Howard University Press, 1981).

28 Claude Meillassoux, *Maidens, Meal, and Money: Capitalism and the Domestic Community* (Cambridge: Cambridge University Press 1981), part 2.

29 Terrance Ranger, "Growing from the Roots: Reflections on Peasant Research in Central and Southern Africa," *Journal of Southern African History* 5, no. 1 (1978): 99–133.

30 Lenin, *The Development of Capitalism in Russia*, pp. 6–87 and 195–200.

31 Colin Leys, "The 'Overdeveloped' Post-Colonial State: A Re-evaluation," *Review of African Political Economy* 5 (1981): 39–48; Hamza Alavi, "The State in Post-Colonial Societies: Pakistan and Bangladesh," *New Left Review* 74 (July–August 1972): 59–81; Harry Galbourne, "The Problem of the State in Backward Capitalist Societies," *African Development* 6, no. 1 (1981): 45–70.

32 De Janvry, *The Agrarian Question*, ch. 3; Lenin, *The Development of Capitalism in Russia*, chs. 2–4.

33 Lenin, *The Development of Capitalism in Russia*, pp. 185–86.

34 P. Gibbon and M. Neocosmos, "Some Problems in the Political Economy of African Socialism," in H. Bernstein and B. K. Campbell, eds., *Contradictions of Accumulation in Africa: Studies in Economy and State* (Beverly Hills: Sage, 1985); emphasis added. See also the interesting and recent work edited by M. Chibnik, *Farm Work and Fieldwork: American Agriculture in Anthropological Perspective* (Ithaca: Cornell University Press, 1987).

35 James C. Scott, *Weapons of the Weak: Everyday Forms of Peasant Resistance* (New Haven: Yale University Press, 1985).

36 D. Goodman and M. Redclift, *From Peasants to Proletarians: Capitalist Development and Agrarian Transition* (New York: St. Martins, 1982), p. 112.

37 De Janvry, *The Agrarian Question*, p. 173.

38 Jonathan Barker, Introduction, in Jonathan Barker, ed., *The Politics of Agriculture in Tropical Africa* (Beverly Hills: Sage, 1984).

39 Lewis, *A Pastoral Democracy*, p. 33; also Colonial Office, *Somaliland: Report for 1958 and 1959* (London: H. M. Stationery Office, 1960), p. 49.

40 J. F. Griffiths, ed., *World Survey of Climatology*, vol. 10, *Climates of Africa* (New York: Sevier, 1972), p. 135.

41 I. M. Lewis, ed., *Abaar: The Somali Drought* (London: International African Institute, 1975).

42 Jeremy Swift, "Pastoral Development in Somalia: Herding Cooperatives as a Strategy against Desertification and Famine," in Michael H. Glantz, ed., *Desertification: Environmental Degradation in and around Arid Lands* (Boulder, Colo.: Westview Press, 1977), pp. 275–306.

43 S. Touval, *Somali Nationalism: International Politics and the Drive for Unity in the Horn of Africa* (Cambridge: Harvard University Press, 1963), p. 102.

44 Lord Curzon, *Frontiers* (Oxford: Clarendon Press, 1907), p. 41.

45 Swift, "The Development of Livestock Trading in a Pastoral Economy."

46 Swift, "Pastoral Development in Somali," p. 283.

47 M. Laurence, *New Wind in a Dry Country* (New York: Knopf, 1964).

48 Lewis, *A Pastoral Democracy*, p. 90.

49 I. M. Lewis, "The Dynamics of Nomadism: Prospects for Sedentarization and Social Change," in T. Monod, ed., *Pastoralism in Tropical Africa* (London: Oxford University Press, 1975), pp. 426–42.

50 Lee V. Cassanelli, *The Shaping of Somali Society: Reconstructing the History of a Pastoral People, 1600–1900* (Philadelphia: University of Pennsylvania Press, 1982), p. 179.

51 These peasants retained some animals, and some pastoralists retained herds primarily. This transformation was a gradual process and is still continuing.

52 An anthropologist working for one of the World Bank–sponsored National Range Agency projects told me in 1983 that most pastoralists he came in contact with were more than inclined to sell some of their herds but that they were too far removed from the reach of the traders.

53 Lewis, "The Dynamics of Nomadism," p. 432.

54 For the development of nationalism in Somaliland see Touval, *Somali Nationalism*.

55 Meillassoux, "A Class Analysis of the Bureaucratic Process in Mali."

56 These included the Agricultural Development Corporation, the Banana Board, and the Livestock Development Corporation, among others.

Chapter 2: Somali Pastoralism and the Development of the Colonial Economy, 1880–1937

1 Two of the most important are Eric Wolf, *Europe and the People without History* (Berkeley and Los Angeles: University of California Press, 1982), and Meillassoux, *Maidens, Meal, and Money*.

2 Lewis, *A Pastoral Democracy*, ch. 2.

3 A. H. Jacobs, "African Pastoralists: Some General Remarks," *Anthropological Quarterly* (1965): 144–54.

4 T. Asad, "Equality in Nomadic Social System? Notes toward the Dissolution of an Anthropological Category," *Critique of Anthropology* 11 (1978): 57–65; Bernstein, "Concepts for the Analysis of Contemporary Peasantries"; Eric Wolf, *Peasants* (Englewood Cliffs, N.J.: Prentice-Hall, 1966).

5 John S. Saul and Roger Woods, "African Peasantries," in G. Arrighi and J. S. Saul, *Essays on the Political Economy of Africa* (New York: Monthly Review Press, 1973), pp. 406–16. See also Philip C. Salzman, ed., *Contemporary Nomadic and Pastoral Peoples: Africa and Latin America* (Williamsburg, Va.: Department of Anthropology, College of William and Mary, 1982), p. ix.

6 B. Bradby, "The Destruction of Natural Economy," *Economy and Society* 4, no. 2 (1975): 127–61.

7 Lewis, *A Pastoral Democracy*, p. 32. For a lengthy explanation of the reasons for animal species mix, see Kenneth Ruddle, *The Crisis in Dryland Pastoral Economies: An Essay in Applied Human Ecology* (N.p., 1979), p. 836.

8 Colonial Office, *Somaliland: Report for 1928* (London: H. M. Stationery Office, 1928), p. 7.

9 Swift, "Pastoral Development in Somalia," pp. 278–79, and my field notes.

10 Interview with H. M. Madar, Gabileh, January 10, 1984. See also Richard Pankhurst, "The Trade of the Gulf of Aden Ports of Africa in the Nineteenth and Early Twentieth Centuries," *Journal of Ethiopian Studies* 3, no. 1 (1965): 55.

11 James C. Scott, *The Moral Economy of the Peasant: Rebellion and Subsistence in Southeast Asia* (New Haven: Yale University Press, 1976), p. 4.

12 Gundrun Dahl and Anders Hjort, *Pastoral Change and the Role of Drought* (Stockholm: Swedish Agency for Research Cooperation with Developing Countries, 1979), p. 18.

13 P. H. Gulliver, *The Family Herds: A Study of Two Pastoral Tribes in East Africa, the Jie and Turkana* (London: Routledge and Kegan Paul, 1955). See also Swift, "The Development of Livestock Trading"; Lewis, *A Pastoral Democracy;* and Dahl and Hjort, *Pastoral Change.*

Many analysts of African pastoralism labeled the "surplus" stock kept by pastoralists as the "cattle complex." See Melville J. Herskovits, "The Cattle Complex in East Africa," *American Anthropologist* 28 (1926): 230–72, 361–88, 494–528, 633–64. Only recently did researchers realize the value of the "surplus" stock to the survival of the pastoralists; see Hans Hedlund, "Contradictions in the Peripheralization of a Pastoral Society: The Maasai," *Review of African Political Economy* 15/16 (1979): 15–37; W. Deshler, "Native Cattle Keeping," in A. Leeds and A. P. Vayda, eds., *Man, Culture, and Animals,* AAAS Publication no. 78 (Washington, D.C.: American Association for the Advancement of Science, 1965).

14 Douglass L. Johnson, "The Response of the Pastoral Nomads to Drought in the Absence of Outside Intervention" (Special Sahelian Office, December

19, 1973). Also, Lee V. Cassanelli, *The Shaping of Somali Society: Reconstructing the History of a Pastoral People, 1600–1900* (Philadelphia: University of Pennsylvania Press, 1982), pp. 38–83.

15 This does not mean that these were frozen structures. Rather, as the group grew, new ones were formed.

16 Cassanelli, *The Shaping of Somali Society,* p. 21.

17 Richard Burton, *First Footsteps in East Africa* New York: Praeger, 1966), p. 31.

18 Lewis, *A Pastoral Democracy,* p. 1. For further explanation of stateless societies, see Robin Hortin, "Stateless Societies in the History of West Africa," in J. F. A. Ajayi and Michael Crowder, *History of West Africa* (New York: Columbia University Press, 1976), pp. 79–119.

19 Iliffe, *A Modern History of Tanganyika,* p. 21.

20 John Tosh, *Clan Leaders and Colonial Chiefs in Lango: The Political History of an East African Stateless Society* (Oxford: Clarendon Press, 1978), p. 17.

21 Lewis, *A Pastoral Democracy,* p. 197.

22 London, Public Record Office (hereafter PRO), CO 535 131/46/71, Swayne to Major Rayne, "Tribal Structure: Loyalty of Somali Chiefs," December 9, 1938.

23 Lewis, *A Pastoral Democracy,* p. 217.

24 For an elaboration of the nomads' lack of self-sufficiency, see Douglass L. Johnson, *The Nature of Nomadism: A Comparative Study of Pastoral Migration in Southwestern Asia and Northern Africa,* University of Chicago, Department of Geograhy Research Paper no. 118 (Chicago, 1969), pp. 11–12.

25 I am not aware of any research yet conducted on this westward trade.

26 Richard Pankhurst cited in Swift, "Pastoral Development in Somalia," p. 302.

27 G. S. P. Freeman-Grenville, *The East African Coast: Selected Documents from the First to the Earlier Nineteenth Century* (London: Rex Collins, 1975), pp. 21–22, 27–31.

28 There is little known about the commercial role of what has become known as the ruined Towns of Somaliland. See A. T. Curle, "The Ruined Towns of Somaliland," *Antiquity* 2 (1937): 315–27.

29 I. M. Lewis, "Lineage Continuity and Modern Commerce in Northern Somaliland," in Paul Bohannan and G. D. Dalton, eds., *Markets in Africa* (Evanston, Ill.: Northwestern University Press, 1962), pp. 365–85.

30 Burton, *First Footsteps,* p. 96. For an excellent discussion of trade in precolonial Somalia, see Ali A. Hersi, "The Arab Factor in Somalia History," (Ph.D. diss., UCLA, 1977).

31 Burton, *First Footsteps,* p. 96.

32 Swift, "The Development of Livestock Trading in a Pastoral Economy," pp. 461–63.

33 Karl Marx, *Pre-Capitalist Economic Formation,* 9th ed., trans. Jack Cohen, ed. Eric J. Habsbawn (New York: International Publishers, 1980).

34 A. M. Brocket, "The British Somaliland Protectorate to 1905" (Ph.D. thesis, Oxford, Lincoln College, 1969), p. 14. For other, similar incidents see Foreign Office, *European Captives among the Somali Tribes, 1866–69*, Foreign and Commonwealth Library (London, n.d.).

35 L. S. Stavrianos, *Global Rift: The Third World Comes of Age* (New York: Morrow, 1981), ch. 13. See also Bill Freund, *The Making of Contemporary Africa: The Development of African Society since 1800* (Bloomington: Indiana University Press, 1984), ch. 5.

36 For a detailed account of the British, French, and Italian maneuverings in the region, see I. M. Lewis, *A Modern History of Somaliland: Nation and State in the Horn of Africa* (New York: Longmans, 1980); also Brockett, "The British Protectorate."

37 Lewis, *A Modern History*, p. 44.

38 For the details of the debate between Foreign Office, the India Office, the Treasury, and the Indian government as to who should administer the Somali coast, see Brockett, "The British Protectorate," ch. 5.

39 Ibid., p. 145.

40 Colonial Office, *Treaties with Somali Tribes* n.p., n.d.

41 Quoted in Brockett, "The British Protectorate," p. 145.

42 Mohmood Mamdani, *Politics and Class Formation in Uganda* (New York: Monthly Review Press, 1976) ch. 2. See also Freund, *The Making of Contemporary Africa*, p. 138.

43 The British government of India clearly understood the cost involved in creating a new political structure, as the history of Indian colonization demonstrates.

44 Brockett, "The British Protectorate," p. 151.

45 Lewis, *A Modern History*, p. 48.

46 Ibid., p. 43.

47 Pankhurst, "The Trade of the Gulf of Aden Ports," p. 55.

48 Alamanni, quoted in ibid., p. 63.

49 The number of sheep and goats exported from the Somali coast in any one year was nowhere near the figures given by Alamanni even some forty years later. For instance, in 1926, a good trade year, only 126,280 sheep and goats were exported to Aden.

50 For a contrasting view of state involvement in the restructuring of precapitalist societies, see Mamdani, *Politics and Class Formation in Uganda*, ch. 2, and Joan Vincent, *Teso in Transformation: The Political Economy of Peasant and Class in Eastern Africa* (Berkeley and Los Angeles: University of California Press, 1982), ch. 8.

51 For the role of merchant capital in articulating different forms of production, see Karl Marx, *Capital* (New York: International Publishers, 1967), 3: 325.

52 Karl Marx, "The Future Results of the British Rule in India," in Karl Marx and Friedrich Engels, *On Colonialism: Articles from the "New York Tribune" and Other Writings* (New York: International Publishers, 1972), pp. 81–87.

53 Said Samatar, *Oral Poetry and Somali Nationalism: The Case of Sayyid Mohamed Abdille Hassan* (Cambridge: Cambridge University Press, 1982), p. 108.

54 The historic events leading to the rise of Menelik and the consequences of his policies for Somaliland are skillfully recorded in Lewis's *A Modern History of Somaliland*, ch. 3.

55 H. G. Marcus, *The Life and Times of Menelik II: Ethiopia, 1844–1913* (Oxford: Clarendon Press, 1975), pp. 180–85; Freund, *The Making of Contemporary Africa*, p. 105.

56 For fuller details and an explanation of this treaty and its impact on Somaliland, see Somali Republic, *The Somali Peninsula: A New Light on Imperial Motives* (London: n.p., 1962).

57 Brockett, "The British Protectorate," p. v.

58 Cassanelli, *The Shaping of Somali Society*, p. 190.

59 Margery Perham, *The Government of Ethiopia* (Evanston, Ill.: Northwestern University Press, 1969), p. 161.

60 Cassanelli, *The Shaping of Somali Society*, p. 200.

61 S. Samatar, *Oral Poetry*, p. 110.

62 Quoted ibid., p. 111.

63 For more details of the Sayyid's life and times, see Robert L. Hess, "The Poor Man of God—Mohamed Abdullah Hassan," in Norman R. Bennett, ed., *Leadership in Eastern Africa: Six Political Biographies* (Boston: Boston University Press, 1968), pp. 65–72. Also Lewis, *A Modern History*, ch. 4.

64 Richard C. Martin, *Islam* (Englewood Cliffs, N.J.: Prentice-Hall, 1982), p. 103.

65 Great Britain, *Correspondence Respecting the Rise of the Mullah Mohamed Abdullah Hassan 1899–1901*, British Sessional Papers, Cmd 597, 1901, no. 1, p. 7.

66 Toohyar Mohamed, quoted in Samatar, *Oral Poetry*, p. 112.

67 Lewis and Samatar have chronicled the means the Sayyid used to entice the support of other clans. See Lewis, *A Modern History*, pp. 68–70, and S. Samatar, *Oral Poetry*.

68 Lewis, *A Modern History*, p. 69.

69 H. R. Foxbourne, "The Story of Somaliland: British Lives Squandered and Treasury Wasted," *East Africa Pamphlet*, 8, no. 2 (1904): 9.

70 This materialist, not economistic, interpretation of the origins of the Somali resistence movement is at odds with the established Somali scholarship. My intent is not to deny the role played by religion in mobilizing the Dervishes, but to correct the historical record and give material life its proper weight.

71 For details see Great Britain, War Office, *Official History of the Operations in Somaliland, 1901–1904*, 2 vols (London: War Office, 1907). Also, *Correspondence Respecting Affairs in Somaliland* (London: Darling and Sons, 1910); D. Jardine, *The Mad Mullah of Somaliland* (London: Herbert Jenkins, 1923); S. Samatar, *Oral Poetry*; Lewis, *A Modern History*.

72 Lewis, *A Modern History*, p. 76.

73 In a recent article based on archieval research W. K. Durrill argues that Somalis in the extreme northeast of the Somali Peninsula suffered severe famine induced by pastoral commoditization before the colonial onslaught in the 1860s, 1870s, and 1880s. While Durrill's work is a welcome addition to Somali literature, this piece is based on slim historical sources, particularly inland sources in Somalia. See W. K. Durrill, "Atrocious Misery: The African Origins of Famine in Northern Somalia, 1839–1884," *American Historical Review* 91, no. 2 (1986): 287–306.

74 Part of the decline was due to the shift of trade away from Zeila to Djibouti because of the completion of the railroad link between Addis Ababa and Djibouti.

75 Colonial Office, *Somaliland: Report for 1914–15* (London: H. M. Stationery Office, 1915), p. 7.

76 Colonial Office, *Somaliland: Report for 1919–20* (London: H. M. Stationery Office, 1921), p. 5. See also Colonial Office, *Somaliland: Report for 1917–18* (London: H. M. Stationery Office, 1919), p. 4.

77 Colonial Office, *Somaliland: Report for 1920* (London: H. M. Stationery Office, 1922), p. 2.

78 Colonial Office, *Somaliland Reports for 1906–7 and 1907–8* (London: H. M. Stationery Office, 1907, 1908).

79 Let us assume, on the basis of trade figures from 1910 to 1920, that the *average* annual livestock exported during this period was 70,000 head of sheep and goats. Let us also assume that the size of an average pastoral family was 6 persons. The estimated population of the colony was 350,000 in 1920. This means that there were almost 60,000 families in the colony at the time. Therefore, on the average, each pastoral family traded 1.1 head of sheep and goats annually.

80 Colonial Office, *Somaliland: Report for 1918–19* (London: H. M. Stationery Office, 1920).

81 R. E. Drake-Brockman, *British Somaliland* (London: Hurst and Blackett, 1912), p. 67. See also C. V. A. Peel, *Somaliland* (London: F. E. Robinson, 1900), p. 155.

82 H. Golabian, "Development Strategies for Iran's Underdeveloped Rural and Nomadic Areas: Some Preliminary Thoughts and Ideas," *Ekistics* 45, no. 267 (1978): 88–95. Also Nadir Afshar Naderi, *The Settlement of Nomads and Its Social and Economic Implications* (Tehran: Tehran University, Institute for Social Studies and Research, 1971).

83 Stephen B. Baier, "African Merchants in the Colonial Period: A History of Commerce in Damagaran (Central Niger, 1880–1960)" (Ph.D. diss., University of Wisconsin, Madison, 1974). Cited in J. W. Sutter, "Commercial Strategies, Drought, and Monetary Pressure: Wo'daabe Nomads of Tanout Arrondissement, Niger" (Unpublished paper, Cornell University, 1979), p. 30.

84 Salzman, *Contemporary Nomadic and Pastoral Peoples*, p. xii.

85 Salmane Cisse, "Sedentarization of Nomadic Pastoralists and Pastoralization of Cultivators in Mali," in J. G. Galaty, D. Aronson, and P. C. Salzman,

eds., *The Future of Pastoral Peoples: Proceedings of a Conference Held in Nairobi, Kenya, 4–8 August 1980* (Ottawa: International Development Research Center, 1980), pp. 319, 312.

86 Communication between Somaliland governor and the Colonial Office, PRO, 52921, October 21, 1920.

87 PRO, CO 535/3876, paraphrase of a telegram from the Somaliland governor, January 21, 1921.

88 PRO, CO 535/65, 1921.

89 At one point there was even talk of withdrawing from Somaliland altogether. PRO, CO 535/69, 1921.

90 Colonial Office, *Annual Report on the Social and Economic Progress of the People of Somaliland for 1934* (London: H. M. Stationery Office, 1935), p. 12.

91 PRO, CO 535/65/29396, vol. 1, 1921.

92 PRO, CO 535/100/5886.

93 Ibid.

94 PRO, CO 535/38/46036.

95 Colonial Office, *Annual Report on the Social and Economic Progress of Somaliland for 1937* (London: H. M. Stationery Office, 1938), p. 15.

96 PRO, CO 535/72/59870, 1923.

97 Colonial Office, *Somaliland: Report for 1924* (London: H. M. Stationery Office, 1925), p. 10.

98 Colonial Office, Annual Reports, 1930–36.

99 Charles L. Geshekter, "Entrepreneurs, Livestock, and Politics: British Somaliland, 1920–1950" (Paper presented to the Joint Stanford University–University of California, Berkeley, Third Annual Conference, April 10, 1982). Most of the information in the paper is from oral sources.

100 Ibid., p. 7.

101 Colonial Office, *Report for 1937*, p. 29.

102 Colonial Office, *Somaliland: Report for 1930* (London: H. M. Stationery Office, 1931), p. 4.

103 PRO, CO 535/65/29396, vol. 1, 1921.

104 Colonial Office, *Somaliland: Report for 1925* (London: H. M. Stationery Office, 1926), p. 12.

105 Colonial Office, *Report for 1934*. For detailed information on agricultural experimentation and the possibilities for successful new crops, see Somaliland Protectorate, Agricultural Department, *Annual Report, 1930* (n.p., n.d.).

Chapter 3: Somali Colonial Political Economy, 1940–1960

1 Lord Rennell of Rodd, *British Military Administration of Occupied Territory in Africa during the Years 1941–1947* (London: H. M. Stationery Office, 1948) pp. 179–80.

2 Ibid., pp. 185 and 189.

3   D. C. Edwards, *A Survey of the Grazing Areas of British Somaliland* (Hargeisa: Department of Natural Resource, 1942).

4   The Glover Report. (No better citation is available to this author.)

5   *The Pastures of British Somaliland with Special Reference to the Glover Report and Future Policy* (Hargeisa, 1947), p. 19.

6   Ibid., p. 20. Glover's estimate may be close to the actual number of livestock in the protectorate, given the veterinary department's success in combatting epidemics. For off-take rates, see also Z. A. Konczacki, *The Economics of Pastorialism: A Case Study of Sub-Saharan Africa* (London: Frank Cass, 1978), p. 82.

7   Somaliland Protectorate, Department of Agriculture and Veterinary Services, *Annual Report for 1953* (Hargeisa, 1954), p. i.

8   This is suggested by Colonial Office, *Annual Report of Somaliland Protectorate for the Year 1949* (London: H. M. Stationery Office, 1950), p. 3, and *Report of the Committee of Inquiry into Pauperism in British Somaliland in 1945* (Hargeisa, 1945).

9   For example in 1952 only 7.2 percent of the protectorate's exports went to non-British countries, but in 1954 this figure was up to 10 percent, to 26.7 percent in 1956, and to 50.92 percent in 1959.

10   Swift, "The Development of Livestock Trading in a Pastoral Economy."

11   E. F. Peck, "The Veterinary History of the Somaliland Protectorate, 1924–60" (Unpublished manuscript, Rhodes House Library, 1962), p. 260.

12   Somaliland Protectorate, Department of Agricultural and Veterinary Service, *Annual Report for 1956* (Hargeisa, 1956), pp. 3–4.

13   See the debate on water tanks in the Protectorate Advisory Council as reported in *War Somali Sidihi* (The Somali Courier), July 31, 1954.

14   Somaliland Protectorate, Department of Agricultural and Veterinary Service, *Annual Report for 1950* (Hargeisa, 1951), p. 7.

15   Colonial Office, *Report for 1949*, p. 14, and Colonial Office, *Annual Report on Somaliland Protectorate for the Years 1954 and 1955* (London: H. M. Stationery Office, 1957), p. 14.

16   Somaliland Protectorate, Agricultural Department, *Annual Report for 1953*, p. 2.

17   Ibid.

18   *War Somali Sidihi*, February 12, 1955, p. 3.

19   For an exceptionally informative retheorization of the relationship between social structures, social relations, and environmental degradation, see P. M. Blaike, *The Political Economy of Soil Erosion in Developing Countries* (London: Longman, 1985).

20   Colonial Office, *Annual Report on the Somaliland Protectorate for the Years 1952 and 1953* (London: H. M. Stationery Office, 1954), p. 13. It was later suggested that in an average year, one acre of rain-fed farmland should produce 800 pounds of sorghum; see Colonial Office, *Report for 1954 and 1955*, p. 14.

21   Somaliland Protectorate, Agricultural Department, *Annual Report for 1950*,

p. 5. After all, the "nonpolitical" problem requires a solution with a political input.

22 British Somaliland Protectorate, *Annual Report on the Military Administration for the Year Ended 31st December, 1946* (Hargeisa, n.d.), p. 33.

23 Calvin Wixon, *Arabsiyo Soil and Water Conservation Project, Annual Report, 1963* (n.p.: USAID, n.d.). Wixon indicates that "a number of so-called Yemeni Farms were constructed for the Department by Yemeni Arabs" (p. 2).

24 Somaliland Protectorate, Agricultural Department, *Annual Report for 1953*, p. 12.

25 Somaliland Protectorate, Agricultural Department, *Annual Report for 1956*, p. i.

26 Colonial Office, *Annual Report on the Somaliland Protectorate for the Years 1958 and 1959* (London: H. M. Stationery Office, 1960), p. 22.

27 Colonial Office, *Report for 1954 and 1955*, p. 14.

28 The loans for the hire and purchase of bullocks were necessitated by the loss of oxen during the droughts of the 1940s and 1950s, and also by the increasing export of these animals, which diminished the number of oxen available for ploughing.

29 Somaliland Protectorate, Agricultural Department, *Annual Report for 1950*, p. 18.

30 Conversation with peasants in Galooley, 1984.

31 The 1954 and 1955 annual colonial report stated the problem this way: "The continual drift of nomads into towns and the consequent overcrowding has resulted in some health problems" (p. 20).

32 The Colonial Development and Welfare (CDW) Act of 1940 was an important part of the wartime British economic policy. As Britain's Asian empire began to unravel and as her competitive edge in world trade was lost to new industrial and commercial giants such as the United States, she had to find ways to cut her dollar deficits. This legislation was aimed at encouraging the production in her colonies of primary products which could be sold in dollar markets. The act was also seen as a way of building the capacity of the colonies to buy British goods. According to Iliffe, the calculated economic self-interest behind the act was also combined with some altruism, that is to say, with "guiding colonial peoples along the road to self-government." The act also helped to neutralize German war propaganda and American anti-imperialist rhetoric. The 1940 act made £120 million available for "development and welfare." For more details see, Iliffe, *A Modern History of Tanganyika*, ch. 14; N. Swainson, *The Development of Corporate Capitalism in Kenya, 1918–1977* (Berkeley and Los Angeles: University of California Press, 1980), pp. 22, 23, 105; R. M. A. van Zwanenberg, *An Economic History of Kenya and Uganda, 1800–1970* (New York: Macmillan, 1975), p. xxi. Apart from its strategic location, Somaliland had little else to offer to ease the pressure on the strained British economy. Towards the mid-1950s the skins which were exported to the U.S.A. (50%) began to encounter stiff

competition from artificial fabrics. The decline in demand for skins was compensated for in part by the increased livestock exports to oil-rich Saudi Arabia. Although it is difficult to put a price tag on the protectorate's strategic value, it is reasonable to suggest that altruism ranked high in the financial assistance offered by Britain.

33 See the desire in the Advisory Council as reported in the *War Somali Sidihi*, July 31, 1954.

34 Somaliland Protectorate, Department of Education, *Annual Report (Summary), 1956* (Hargeisa, 1956), pp. 21, 4.

35 Colonial Office, *Report for 1952 and 1953,* p. 16.

36 Ibid.

37 By 1954 members of the Protectorate Advisory Council were already complaining about the small classroom capacity of the protectorate's only two intermediate schools, which were unable to accommodate the students leaving the thirteen elementary schools. The administration's response foreshadowed a contemporary view about the role of elementary education which was reported in the protectorate's fortnightly newspaper: "The chairman [of the council] believed all the boys to be able to go back to the interior and their increased knowledge would help them to become more successful [herdsmen]" (*War Somali Sidihi,* July 31, 1954, p. 11).

38 Lewis, *A Modern History,* pp. 116–38.

39 There is a crying need for a critical historical study of colonial agrarian political economy in southern Somalia.

40 Thomas Hodgkin, *Nationalism in Colonial Africa* (New York: New York University Press, 1956), ch. 4.

41 Lewis, *A Modern History,* p. 22.

42 Ibid., p. 123.

43 The British, in particular, favored a united Somali territory (under the Bevin Plan). But all this changed with the onset of the cold war, as Italy was welcomed back to the Western camp.

44 Somali National Bank, *Report and Balance Sheet, 1962* (Mogadishu, 1963).

45 British Somaliland Protectorate, *Annual Report on the Military,* p. 1.

46 Colonial Office, *Report for 1954 and 1955,* p. 3.

47 Ibid.

48 Colonial Office, *Report for 1958 and 1959,* p. 4.

49 Colonial Office, *Report for the Somaliland Protectorate Constitutional Conference, May 1960* (London: H. M. Stationery Office, 1960).

50 Colonial Office, *Report for 1958 and 1959,* p. 15.

51 Gary Wasserman, *Politics of Decolonization: Kenya, Europeans, and the Land Issue, 1960–1965* (Cambridge: Cambridge University Press, 1976). Also Basil Davidson, *Let Freedom Come: Africa in Modern History* (Boston: Little, Brown, 1978), p. 259.

52 Freund, *The Making of Contemporary Africa,* p. xiii.

53 E.g., Hyden, *Beyond Ujamaa.*

54 A classic illustration of Henry Bernstein's "simple reproduction squeeze."

Chapter 4: The Civilian Postcolonial State and the Agrarian Sector, 1960–1969

1   Claude Ake, "Ideology and Objective Conditions," in Joel Barkan and John J. Okumu, *Politics and Public Policy in Kenya and Tanzania* (New York: Praeger, 1979), pp. 117–28.

2   Nora Hamilton suggests that "formal control of the state is distinct from control of the state." Control of the state refers to those class(es) who won or control the productive resource within a country upon which the state's fiscal strength depend. Hamilton, *The Limits of State Autonomy: Post-Revolutionary Mexico.* (Princeton: Princeton University Press, 1982).

3   Hamza Alavi, "The State in Post-Colonial Societies," pp. 59–81; Leys, *Underdevelopment in Kenya;* Colin Leys, "Capital Accumulation, Class Formation, and Dependence: The Significance of the Kenyan Case," *Socialist Register* (London: Merlin Press, 1979), pp. 241–66; Nicola Swainson, "State and Economy in Post-Colonial Kenya," *Canadian Journal of African Studies* 12, no. 3 (1978): 362–81; Michaela von Freyhold, "The Post-Colonial State and Its Tanzanian Version," *Review of African Political Economy* 8 (January–April 1977): 75–89.

4   Freyhold, "The Post-Colonial State," p. 76.

5   Leys, "Capital Accumulation."

6   Bates, *Markets and States in Africa,* pp. 96–97.

7   These issues are developed further in Abdi Samatar and Ahmed I. Samatar, "The Material Roots of the Suspended African State: Arguments from Somalia," *Journal of Modern African Studies,* 25, 4 (1987): 669–90.

8   Lewis, *A Modern History,* pp. 166–204.

9   Quoted in A. A. Castagno, Jr., *Somalia,* Carnegie Endowment for International Peace Series, no. 522 (New York: Carnegie Endowment for International Peace, 1959), p. 348.

10   Ibid., p. 14.

11   Colonial Office, *Report for 1958 and 1959,* p. 14.

12   Kitching, *Classes and Economic Change in Kenya,* p. 413.

13   The budget deficit declined significantly in 1962 and 1963 from that of 1961, largely because of the limit set by the British and Italian subsidy. See Somali Republic, *Government Activities from Independence until Today (July 1, 1960–December 31, 1963)* (Mogadishu, 1964), p. 88.

14   Ibid.

15   T. G. Shirname, *Report to the Government of Somalia on Food and Agricultural Economy,* Food and Agriculture Organization, Report no. 2088 (Rome, 1965), pp. 15–16.

16   Ibid., p. 17.

17   Ibid., p. 12.

18   Somali Republic, Planning and Coordinating Commission for Economic and Social Development, *First Five-Year Plan, 1963–1967* (Mogadishu, 1963), p. 42.

19   Somali Republic, *Government Activities,* p. 112.
20   Konczacki, *The Economics of Pastoralism,* p. 84.
21   Castagno, *Somalia,* p. 382.
22   Shirname, *Report to the Government of Somalia,* p. 7.
23   Ibid.
24   Ibid., p. 9.
25   Data from Tables 15 and 16.
26   Robert Shenton and Michael Watts note the same phenomenon in Nigeria. Shenton and Watts, "State and Agrarian Transformation in Nigeria," in Jonathan Barker, ed., *The Politics of Agriculture in Tropical Africa* (Beverly Hills: Sage, 1984), pp. 173–204.
27   Somali Republic, *Government Activities,* p. 83.
28   Lewis, *A Modern History,* p. 200.
29   Somali Republic, *Government Activities,* p. 91.
30   Somali Republic, *First Five-Year Plan,* pp. 150, 10.
31   Ibid., p. 23.
32   Ibid. p. 11.
33   Shirname, *Report to the Government of Somalia,* p. 14.
34   Somalia Republic, *First Five-Year Plan,* p. 23.
35   On the benefits of irrigation, see Ulrich Bauer, *Report to the Government of Somalia on the Marketing of Bananas,* Food and Agriculture Organization, Report no. TA 2362 (Rome, 1967), p. 5. On credit benefits, Somali National Bank, *Report and Balance Sheet, 1963,* p. 47. The bank indicated that the amount of 11.4 million Somali shillings was made available for loans to banana producers. Although the development plan did not specify who got access to credit, it is reasonable to assume that banana growers got the lion's share, since they were the only growers who had what the bank considered worthy collateral. See Somali Republic, *First Five-Year Plan,* pp. 138–39.
36   Bauer, *Marketing of Bananas,* p. 3.
37   Ibid., p. 15.
38   Somali Republic, *First Five-Year Plan,* p. 35.
39   Conversations I had with some of the peasants who live around the farm indicated that there existed no ties between the farm and the peasantry (interviews, March 8, 1984).
40   Somali Republic, *First Five-Year Plan,* pp. 37–41.
41   Ibid., p. 40.
42   Ibid., p. 38; USAID and Ministry of Agriculture, "Bonka Farmers' Training Center" (Unpublished manuscript, Baidoa, 1964).
43   Somali Republic, National Assembly, *Statement of Programme by H. E. Mohamed Ibrahim Egal* (Mogadishu, August 1967), p. 24.
44   Somali Republic, *First Five-Year Plan,* p. 42.
45   Ibid.
46   Ibid.
47   Somali Republic, Livestock Development Agency, *Annual Budget Statement of the Livestock Development Agency* (Mogadishu, September 2, 1966), p. 2.

48 Konczacki, *The Economics of Pastoralism*, p. 84.

49 Ibid., p. 91.

50 B. J. Hartley et al., *Agriculture and Water Survey: Livestock Development Survey*, Food and Agriculture Organization and United Nations Development Programme, Report no. MR/54396 (Rome, 1967), p. 47.

51 Konczacki, *The Economics of Pastoralism*, p. 85.

52 In the absence of information regarding retail prices of the commodities pastoralists bought, and regarding how much of the livestock price increases accrued to them, it is difficult to know whether the rise in livestock sales was a reflection of an attempt by pastoralists to maintain their previous consumption level or whether the terms of trade favored them and if a new "money-ethic" made them more secure and led them to market more livestock.

53 Hartley et al. *Livestock Development Survey*, pp. 11–12.

54 Somali Republic, Planning Commission, *Short-Term Development Programme, 1968–1970* (Mogadishu, August 1968), pp. 64–65.

55 Ibid. p. 29.

56 Ibid., pp. 1, 2, 10.

57 Somalia was exceptional in being able to secure most of the promised assistance. Up to 1969, she received 85.1 percent of her development expenditures from foreign sources, almost half of this being grants-in-aid. For more details see Ozay Mahmet, "Effectiveness of Foreign Aid: The Somali Case," *Journal of Modern African Studies* 9, no. 1 (1971): 31–47.

58 This was so in spite of the fact that the World Bank argued against further development of banana industry because of its poor long-term economic prospects. International Bank for Reconstruction and Development, *The Economy of the Trust Territory of Somaliland* (n.p., January 1957), p. 93.

59 Somali Republic, *First Five-Year Plan*, pp. 150–51.

60 Somali Republic, *Short-Term Development Programme*, p. 2.

61 I. M. Lewis, "The Politics of the 1969 Somali Coup," *Journal of Modern African Studies* 10, no. 3 (1972): 383–408.

62 Issa G. Shivji, *Class Struggle in Tanzania* (New York: Monthly Review Press, 1976); Claude Meillassoux, "A Class Analysis of the Bureaucratic Process in Mali," *Journal of Development Studies* 6, no. 2 (1970): 91–110; Mamdani, *Politics and Class Formation in Uganda;* John S. Saul, "Marketing Cooperatives in a Developing Country: The Case of Tanzania," in Peter Worsley, ed., *Two Blades of Grass: Rural Cooperatives and Agricultural Modernization* (Manchester: Manchester University Press, 1971).

63 Saul, "Marketing Cooperatives in a Developing Country," p. 350.

64 Shivji, *Class Struggle in Tanzania*, p. 49.

65 Ibid., p. 63.

66 Meillassoux, "A Class Analysis," p. 98.

67 Somali Republic, *The First Session of the National Advisory Council Held 20th–27th August 1968* (Mogadishu: Ministry of Interior, 1968), p. 2.

68 John S. Saul, *The State and Revolution in Eastern Africa* (New York: Monthly Review Press, 1979), p. 361.

69 Lewis, "The Politics of the 1969 Coup," p. 397.
70 Ibid.
71 Ibid., p. 399.
72 Ibid.
73 For an exceptionally thoughtful analysis of the authoritarian tendencies of the postcolonial peripheral capitalist state, see C. Y. Thomas, *The Rise of the Authoritarian State in Peripheral Societies* (New York: Monthly Review Press, 1984), pt. 2.
74 Source prefers to remain anonymous.
75 Samuel Decalo, *Coups and Army Rule in Africa: Studies in Military Style* (New Haven: Yale University Press, 1976), p. 7; Samuel Huntington, *Political Order in Changing Societies* (New Haven: Yale University Press, 1968); Morris Janowits, *The Military in Political Development of New Nations: An Essay in Comparative Analysis* (Chicago: University of Chicago Press, 1964).
76 Decalo, *Coups and Army Rule in Africa*, p. 14.
77 Ibid., p. 21.
78 Michael F. Lofchie, "The Ugandan Coup: Class Action by the Military," *Journal of Modern African Studies* 10, no. 1 (1972): 19–35.
79 Mamdani, *Politics and Class Formation in Uganda*, pp. 287, 288.
80 Ibid., p. 289.
81 Ibid.
82 Ahmed I. Samatar, "Self-Reliance in Theory and Practice: A Critique of the Somali Praxis, 1960–1980" (Ph.D. diss., University of Denver, 1984), pp. 202–3.
83 Ibid., p. 203.

Chapter 5: The Military and the Agrarian Sector, 1969–1984

1 Somali Democratic Republic Ministry of Planning and Coordination, *Five-Year Development Programme, 1974–1978* (Mogadishu, 1974), p. 28. Overseas donations supplied 67.4% of all development expenditures, while in the previous regimes that figure was close to 90%.
2 Basil Davidson, "Somalia: Towards Socialism," *Race and Class* 17, no. 1 (1975): 20–37.
3 Luigi Pestalozza, *The Somalian Revolution*, trans. Peter Glendening (Bari: Dedale Libni, 1974), p. 17.
4 Ahmed Samatar, "Self-Reliance in Theory and Practice," pp. 270–73.
5 Interview with G. M. A., former member of Gahileh District Revolutionary Council, February 10, 1984.
6 Ahmed Samatar, "Self-Reliance in Theory and Practice," pp. 274–76.
7 A woman state employee who was among the delegates told me that when the time came to elect Siyaad to his offices, the delegates went into a frenzy, dancing on the tables and trying to outdo one another.
8 I was witness to the same electoral fraud in the 1986 presidential elections.
9 Somali D. Republic, Ministry of Local Government and Rural Develop-

ment, *Somalia's Rural Development Strategy, 1981–1990* (Mogadishu, 1981), p. 14.

10 Ibid., p. 16.

11 Somali D. Republic, *Five-Year Development Programme, 1974–1978*, p. i.

12 Somali D. Republic, Ministry of Planning and Coordination, *Development Programme, 1971–1973* (Mogadishu, 1971), p. 6. See also Somali D. Republic, *Five-Year Development Programme, 1974–1978; Somali D. Republic, Five-Year Development Plans, 1982–1986* (Mogadishu, 1982); Somali D. Republic, *Rural Development Strategy, 1981–1990.*

13 Somali D. Republic, *Five-Year Development Programme, 1974–1978*, p. 51.

14 Dan Aronson, "Kinsmen and Comrades: Towards a Class Analysis of the Somali Pastoral Sector," *Nomadic Peoples* 7 (November 1980): 14–23.

15 John Holtzman, "The Economics of Improving Animal Health and Livestock Marketing in Somalia" (USAID, Mogadishu, 1982), pp. 78–79.

16 Somali D. Republic, *Development Programme, 1971–1973*, p. 46.

17 Interview with a range management expert in the Central Range Project, Mogadishu, November 3, 1984.

18 Aronson, "Kinsmen and Comrades," p. 21.

19 A mid-term review of the Central Rangeland Project indicates major problems with project implementation; see World Bank, *Somalia: Central Rangelands Project: Documents Relating to Mid-Term Review* (Washington, D.C., May 1984).

20 Holtzman, "The Economics of Improving Animal Health," p. 22.

21 International Labor Organization, Jobs and Skills Program for Africa, *Rural-Urban Gap and Income Distribution: The Case of Somalia* (Addis Ababa, 1982), p. 10.

22 Vali Jamal, "Nomads and Farmers: Income and Poverty in Rural Somalia," in D. Ghai and S. Radwan, eds., *Agrarian Policies and Rural Poverty in Africa* (Geneva: International Labor Organization, 1983), p. 286. Jamal's figures for small ruminant exports differ from those in Table 25: he has 1,617,200 small ruminants for 1972 and 1,450,700 for 1978.

23 Ibid., p. 297.

24 Ibid., pp. 287 and 297.

25 E. Reusse, "Somalia's Nomadic Livestock Economy: Its Reponse to Profitable Export Opportunity," *World Animal Review*, no. 43 (1982): 2–11. A bank manager's statement of such a phenomenon cannot be a proof. Those who use the bank are the traders, not the overwhelming majority of pastoralists.

26 Holtzman, "The Economics of Improving Animal Health," p. 25.

27 Aronson, "Kinsmen and Comrades," pp. 20–21. See also Swift, "The Development of Livestock Trading in a Pastoral Economy," pp. 447–65.

28 See Central Bank of Somalia, *Annual Report 1985* (Mogadishu, 1985). And also, Abdi Samatar, L. Salisbury, and J. Bascom, "The Political Economy of Livestock Marketing in Somalia," *African Economic History* (forthcoming), and fieldnotes. For instance, the black-market exchange rate was 37–40 shillings to one American dollar in late summer 1983, while the official rate

was 12 shillings. Currently the former rate is over 100 shillings, while the latter is 37 shillings to the dollar.

29 Jamal indicates that in most years the pastoralists receive two-thirds of the full price. Jamal, "Nomads and Farmers," pp. 298–99.

30 Interviews with a customs agent and a trader engaged in this trade, Hargeisa, December 7 and 10, 1983.

31 During my first full morning in Hargeisa, in October 1983, I took a walk around town, and while I was standing under a big shady tree outside the Commercial Bank, I heard an argument between two men, standing not far from the gate of the bank. One was definitely a pastoralist; the other, I realized, was a *dilaal*—a livestock broker. The pastoralist wanted to see the trader who had bought his livestock but had not paid him yet. He said it had been almost two months since the transaction and that he could not afford to stay in town or come back to town frequently. The broker seemed not eager to irritate his friend, the trader.

32 Aronson, "Kinsmen and Comrades," p. 21.

33 Somali D. Republic, *Development Programme, 1971–73*, pp. 71, 20.

34 Somali D. Republic, *Agriculture in the Service of the Nation: More Production with More Efforts* (Mogadishu, 1974), p. ii.

35 Somali D. Republic, *Development Programme, 1971–73*, p. 73.

36 Interview with Mohamed Abdillahi, former agricultural extension officer, Fresno, December 1982.

37 Fieldnotes, November 1983–April 1984.

38 Somali D. Republic, *Five-Year Development Programme, 1974–78*, p. 20.

39 Ibid., pp. 79–80.

40 Calvin Wixon, *Arabsiyo Soil and Water Conservation Project: First Annual Report, Calendar Year 1963* (n.p.: USAID, n.d.).

41 World Bank, *Appraisal of the Northwest Agricultural Development Project: Somalia* (East Africa Project Department, Nairobi, May 1976), pp. i–ii.

42 Somali D. Republic Northwest Agricultural Development Project, *Report: Second National Farmers' Conference, Mogadishu, October 11–16, 1983* (Hargeisa, October 10, 1983), p. 3. In spite of the claim by the Ministry of Agriculture, this meeting, which I attended, was not a farmers' conference; rather, it was a reporting on the performance of their respective projects. A few farmers were brought in to give it a rustic look. It was concluded on the World Food Day, when foreign dignitaries were invited.

43 Ibid., p. 4.

44 I was allowed to make use of the project office facilities during my frequent but short visits to Hargeisa, for which I thank Dr. Farooqi and Osman Oomane.

45 Interview with a village assembly chairman. These payoffs are in addition to the provisions of food and other expenses such as cigarettes and kat by the peasants; in some cases these expenses could be as high as 400 Somali shillings a day.

46 Interview, Gabileh District, February 8, 1984.

47   Interview, Saarey, February 22, 1984.

48   Fieldnotes. I lived in the region during the first four years of the military regime and took part in some of the self-help schemes.

49   Hyden, *Beyond Ujamaa in Tanzania,* and *No Shortcuts to Progress: African Development Management in Perspective* (Berkeley and Los Angeles: University of California Press, 1983).

50   Fieldnotes. During my stay in rural Gabileh, I found out that the majority of the peasants I contacted had paid these "development contributions." These were on the average three to four times as much as the annual farm tax, which was 150 shillings in 1984.

51   Such strategies are discussed in Bruce F. Johnston and P. Kilby, *Agriculture and Structural Transformation* (New York, Oxford University Press, 1975).

52   In southern Somalia, kat was not imported until long after independence, and until recently, consumption was much lower than in the north.

53   World Bank, *Appraisal of the Northwest Project.* The Bank estimates that there are about 12,000 farmers in the region. This is a conservative estimate.

54   For the details of the criteria and the method used in the selection of these settlements and families, see the Preface.

55   This is contrary to the World Bank estimate, which suggests that almost one-third of the agricultural land in Gabileh District is fallow. The Bank forgets to consider two factors. First, these peasants own livestock and hence need grazing space. Second, peasants are unable to cultivate all of their land at the same time, owing to primitive technology and/or expensive and often unavailable tractor-hire. World Bank, *Appraisal of the Northwest Project,* annex 3, p. 3.

56   Amane Getahun and A. D. Krikorian, "Chat: Coffee's Rival from Harar, Ethiopia, I: Botany, Cultivation, and Use," *Economic Botany* 27 (October–December 1973): 353–77. Also, P. J. Greenway, "Kat," *East African Agricultural Journal* 13 (1947): 98–102, and fieldnotes, 1984.

57   The price of a bunch (a pound) of kat in 1972–73 was 3–5 shillings; in 1983–84 it had increased to 80–200 shillings.

58   The information in these paragraphs is based on interviews and conversations with peasants and my observations during the fieldwork.

59   Refugees from war-torn western Somaliland (Ogaden) constituted about 40% of the laborers.

60   In spite of my persistence, individuals refused to specify the amount of money they earned from kat or spent on a particular thing such as a wedding.

61   These biographies are based entirely on taped interviews with the particular individuals and conversations I had with other peasants who had known them well.

62   For more details on the kat eradication campaign see Abdi Samatar, "The Predatory State and the Peasantry: Reflections on Rural Development Policy in Somalia," *Africa Today* 32, no. 3 (1985): 41–56.

63   Somali D. Republic, *Tiro Koobka Ijo Qiimaynta Qaadka* (Mogadishu, September 1983).

64 Hyden, *No Shortcuts to Progress*, p. 7.

65 Ibid., p. 8.

66 Phillip Raikes, "Food Policy and Production in Mozambique since Indepen-
    dence," *Review of African Political Economy* 29 (1984): 95–107. See also
    the devastating critique by M. Mamdani, "A Great Leap Backward: A Re-
    view of Goran Hyden; *No Shortcuts to Progress*," *Eastern Africa Social Sci-
    ence Research Review* 1, no. 1 (1985): 79–92, and N. Kasfir, "Are African
    Peasants Self-Sufficient? A Review of Goran Hyden," *Development and
    Change* 17 (1986): 335–57.

67 Although such personal gains are common knowledge, nevertheless it is al-
    most impossible to document them.

68 Anne O. Krueger, "The Political Economy of the Rent-Seeking Society,"
    American Economic Review 64, no. 3 (1974): 291–303. Also Bates, *Markets
    and States*.

69 Michael J. Watts and Thomas J. Bassett, "Politics, the State, and Agrarian
    Development: A Comparative Study of Nigeria and the Ivory Coast," *Politi-
    cal Geography Quarterly* 5, no. 2 (1986): 103–27; M. Watts, "State, Oil,
    and Accumulation: From Boom to Crisis," *Environment and Planning: So-
    ciety and Space* 2 (1984): 403–28.

70 Currently, Somalia is one of the four countries in Africa which receive about
    50% of the total U.S. aid to Sub-Saharan Africa. The others are Zaire,
    Kenya, and Liberia. USAID, *Congressional Presentation, Fiscal Year 1982
    and 1986*, cited in Kevin Danaher, *Myths of African Hunger* (San Francisco:
    Institute for Food and Development, 1985).

71 Abdi Samatar, "Reproduction Crisis, Peripheral Capitalist Pastoralism, and
    the Social Differentiation of Livestock Merchants" (Unpublished manu-
    script, University of Iowa, 1988).

72 This figure is calculated from Central Bank of Somalia, *Annual Report and
    Statement of Accounts* (Mogadishu, 1981), p. 26.

73 Abdi Samatar and Ahmed I. Samatar, "The Material Roots of the Suspended
    African State."

74 Barry Bluestone, Bennett Harrison, and Lawrence Baker, *Corporate Flight:
    The Causes and Consequences of Economic Dislocation* (Washington, D.C.:
    A Progressive Alliance Book, March 1981), p. 14.

Chapter 6: The Long Transition

1 Richard Sandbrook, "The State and Economic Stagnation in Tropical Africa," *World Development* 14, no. 3 (1986): 319–32.

2 Sara Berry, "The Food Crisis and Agrarian Change in Africa," *African Studies Review* 27, no. 2 (1984): 59–112.

3 K. Marx, *Precapitalist Economic Formation*.

4 Lewis, *A Pastoral Democracy*; Laitin and Samatar, *Somalia: Nation in
   Search of a State*.

5 Swift, "Pastoral Development in Somalia," and "The Development of Live-

stock Trading"; Aronson, "Kinsmen and Comrades"; A. I. Samatar, *Socialist Somalia: Rhetoric and Reality* (London: Zed Books, 1988).

6 Hyden, *Beyond Ujamaa in Tanzania,* and *No Shortcuts to Progress*

7 G. Vergopoulous, cited in H. Mouzelis, "Capitalism and the Development of Agriculture," *Journal of Peasant Studies* 3, no. 4 (1976): 483–92.

8 H. Friedman, "Household Production and the National Economy: Concepts for the Analysis of Agrarian Formation," *Journal of Peasant Studies* 7, no. 2 (1980): 158–84.

9 C. Murry, "Class, Gender, and Household: The Development Cycle in Southern Africa," *Development and Change* 18, no. 2 (1987): 253–70.

10 V. I. Lenin, cited in V. Athreya et al., "Identification of Agrarian Classes: A Methodological Essay with Empirical Material from South Asia," *Journal of Peasant Studies* 14, no. 2 (1987): 147–90. Emphasis mine.

11 Abdi Samatar, L. Salisbury, and J. Bascom, "The Political Economy of Livestock Marketing in Somalia," *African Economic History* (Forthcoming, 1988).

12 R. Aminzade, *Class, Politics, and Early Industrial Capitalism: A Study of Mid-Nineteenth-Century Toulouse, France* (Albany: State University of New York Press, 1981).

13 J. E. Davis, "Capitalist Agricultural Development and the Exploitation of Propertied Laborer," in F. H. Buttle and H. Newby, eds., *The Rural Sociology of the Advanced Societies: Critical Perspectives* (Montclair, N.J.: Allanheld, Osmun, 1980); J. Wilson, "The Political Economy of Contract Farming," *Review of Radical Political Economics* 18, no. 4 (1986): 47–70.

14 A. V. Chayanov, *The Theory of Peasant Economy,* ed. D. Thorner et al. (Madison: University of Wisconsin Press, 1986).

15 Abdi Samatar, "Reproduction Crisis, Peripheral Capitalist Pastoralism, and the Social Differentiation of Livestock Merchants."

16 S. Berry, *Fathers Work for Their Sons: Accumulation, Mobility, and Class Formation in an Extended Yoruba Community* (Berkeley and Los Angeles: University of California Press, 1985).

17 Abdi Samatar, "Merchant Capital, International Livestock Trade, and Pastoral Development in Somalia," *Canadian Journal of African Studies,* XXI, no. 3 (1987): 335–74.

18 R. E. Drake-Brockman, *British Somaliland.*

19 A. Gramsci, *Selection from the Prison Notebooks,* trans. and ed. Q. Hoare and G. N. Smith (New York: International Publishers, 1971).

20 For a penetrating analysis of the state's relations to the productive process in peripheral societies see M. Burawoy, *The Politics of Production: Factory Regimes under Capitalism and Socialism* (London: New Left Books, 1985).

21 W. Hinton, *Fanshen: A Documentary of Revolution in a Chinese Village* (New York: Vintage Books, 1966). According to Hinton, "*Fanshen* . . . literally means 'to turn the body,' or 'to turn over.' For China's hundreds of millions of landless and land-poor peasants it meant to stand up, to throw off the landlord yoke, to gain land, stocks. . . . But it meant much more than this.

It meant to throw off superstition and study science" (p. viii). I use *fanshen* to mean "qualitative transformation."

22   R. Poulin, "A Study of the Recurrent Costs of Development Projects in Somalia" (Paper prepared for USAID by Development Alternatives, Inc., Mogadishu, March, 1987).

23   Jonathan Barker, Introduction, in Barker, *The Politics of Agriculture in Tropical Africa.*

24   Ahmed I. Samatar, "Somalia Impasse: State, Power, and Dissent Politics," *Third World Quarterly* 9, no. 3 (1987): 871–90.

Bibliography

Books and Essays

Ake, Claude. "Ideology and Objective Conditions." In Joel Barkan and J. J. Okumu, eds., *Politics and Public Policy in Kenya and Tanzania.* New York: Praeger, 1979.

Allen, Barbara, and Montell, W. L. *From Memory to History: Using Oral Sources in Local Historical Research.* Nashville: American Association for State and Local History, 1981.

Amin, Samir. *Unequal Development: An Essay on the Social Formation of Peripheral Capitalism.* New York: Monthly Review Press, 1976.

Aminzade, R. *Class, Politics, and Early Industrial Capitalism: A Study of Mid-Nineteenth-Century Toulouse, France.* Albany: State University of New York Press, 1981.

Apter, David. *The Politics of Modernization.* Chicago: University of Chicago Press, 1967.

Bates, Robert. *Essays on the Political Economy of Rural Africa.* Cambridge: Cambridge University Press, 1984.

Bates, Robert. *Markets and States in Tropical Africa.* Berkeley and Los Angeles: University of California Press, 1981.

Baran, Paul A. *The Political Economy of Growth.* New York: Monthly Review Press, 1957.

Barker, Jonathan. *The Politics of Agriculture in Tropical Africa.* Beverly Hills: Sage, 1984.

Bechhofer, Frank, and Elliott, Brian, eds. *The Petite Bourgeoisie: Comparative Studies of the Uneasy Stratum.* New York: St. Martin's, 1981.

Berg, R. J., and Whitaker, J. S., eds. *Strategies for African Development.* Berkeley and Los Angeles: University of California Press, 1986.

Bernstein, Henry. "Concepts for the Analysis of Contemporary Peasantries." In Gali, *The Political Economy of Rural Development* (q.v.).

Bernstein, H., and Campbell, B. K., eds. *Contradictions of Accumulation in Africa: Studies in Economy and State.* Beverly Hills: Sage, 1985.

Berry, Sara. *Fathers Work for their Sons: Accumulation, Mobility, and Class Formation in an Extended Yoruba Community.* Berkeley and Los Angeles: University of California Press, 1985.

Blaike, P. M. *The Political Economy of Soil Erosion in Developing Countries.* London: Longman, 1985.

Bluestone, Barry; Harrison, Bennett; and Baker, Lawrence. *Corporate Flight: The Causes and Consequences of Economic Dislocation.* Washington, D.C.: A Progressive Alliance Book, March 1981.

Burawoy, M. *The Politics of Production: Factory Regimes under Capitalism and Socialism*. London: New Left Books, 1985.

Burton, Richard. *First Footsteps in East Africa*. New York: Praeger, 1966.

Buttle, F. H., and Newby, H. *The Rural Sociology of the Advanced Societies: Critical Perspectives*. Montclair, N.J.: Allanheld, Osmun, 1980.

Cardoso, F. H., and Faletto, E. *Dependency and Development in Latin America*. Berkeley and Los Angeles: University of California Press, 1979.

Cassanelli, Lee V. *The Shaping of Somali Society: Reconstructing the History of a Pastoral People, 1600–1900*. Philadelphia: University of Pennsylvania Press, 1982.

Castagno, A. A., Jr. *Somalia*. New York: Carnegie Endowment for International Peace, 1959. Series, no. 522.

Chayanov, A. V. *The Theory of Peasant Economy*. Ed. D. Thorner et al. Madison: University of Wisconsin Press, 1986.

Chibnik, M., ed. *Farm Work and Fieldwork: American Agriculture in Anthropological Perspective*. Ithaca: Cornell University Press, 1987.

Colson, Elizabeth. "African Society at the Time of the Scramble." In L. H. Gann and P. J. Duignan, eds., *Colonialism in Africa, 1870–1960, vol. 1*.

Curzon, Lord. *Frontiers*. Oxford: Clarendon, 1907.

Dahl, Gundrun, and Hjort, Anders. *Pastoral Change and the Role of Drought*. Stockholm: Swedish Agency for Research Cooperation with Developing Countries, 1979.

Danaher, Kevin. *Myths of African Hunger*. San Francisco: Institute for Food and Development Policy, 1985.

Davidson, Basil. *Let Freedom Come: Africa in Modern History*. Boston: Little, Brown, 1978.

Davis, J. E. "Capitalist Agricultural Development and the Exploitation of Propertied Labor." In F. H. Buttle, and H. Newby, eds., *The Rural Sociology of Advanced Societies: Critical Perspectives*. Montclair, N.J.: Allanheld, Osum, 1980.

Decalo, Samuel. *Coups and Army Rule in Africa: Studies in Military Style*. New Haven: Yale University Press, 1976.

De Janvry, Alain. *The Agrarian Question and Reformism in Latin America*. Baltimore; Johns Hopkins University Press, 1981.

Deshler, W. "Native Cattle Keeping." In A. Leeds and A. P. Vayda, eds., *Man, Culture, and Animals*. American Association for the Advancement of Science Publication no. 78. Washington, D.C., 1965.

Drake-Brockman, R. E. *British Somaliland*. London: Hurst and Blackett, 1912.

Evans, Peter. *Dependent Development: The Alliance of Multinationals, the State, and Local Capital in Brazil*. Princeton: Princeton University Press, 1979.

Foster, George M. *Traditional Societies and Technological Change*. New York: Harper and Row, 1973.

Freeman-Grenville, G. S. P. *The East African Coast: Selected Documents from the First to the Earlier Nineteenth Century*. London: Rex Collins, 1975.

Freund, Bill. *The Making of Contemporary Africa: The Development of African Society since 1800*. Bloomington: Indiana University Press, 1984.

Galaty, J. G.; Aronson, D.; and Salzman, P. C., eds. *The Future of Pastoral Peoples: Proceedings of a Conference Held in Nairobi, Kenya, 4–8 August 1980.* Ottowa: International Development Research Center, 1980.

Gali, Rosemary, ed. *The Political Economy of Rural Development: Peasants, International Capital, and the State.* Binghamton: SUNY Press, 1981.

Gibbon, P., and Neocosmos, M. "Some Problems in the Political Economy of African Socialism." In Bernstein and Campbell, *Contradictions of Accumulation in Africa* (q.v.).

Goodman, D., and Redclift, M. *From Peasants to Proletarians: Capitalist Development and Agrarian Transition.* New York: St. Martin's, 1982.

Gramsci, A. *Selection from the Prison Notebooks.* Trans. and ed. Q. Hoare and G. N. Smith. New York: International Publishers, 1971.

Girffiths, J. F., ed. *World Survey of Climatology,* vol. 10: *Climates of Africa.* New York: Sevier, 1972.

Gulliver, P. H. *The Family Herds: A Study of Two Pastoral Tribes in East Africa, the Jie and Turkana.* London: Routledge and Kegan, 1955.

Gurley, John G. *China's Economy and the Maoist Strategy.* New York: Monthly Review Press, 1976.

Hamilton, Nora. *The Limits of State Autonomy: Post-Revolutionary Mexico.* Princeton: Princeton University Press, 1982.

Hart, Keith. *The Political Economy of West African Agriculture.* Cambridge: Cambridge University Press, 1981.

Harvey D. *The Urbanization of Capital: Studies in the History and Theory of Capitalist Urbanization.* Baltimore: Johns Hopkins University Press, 1985.

Hess, Robert L. "The Poor Man of God: Mohamed Abdullah Hassan." In Norman R. Bennett, ed., *Leadership in Eastern Africa: Six Political Biographies.* Boston: Boston University Press, 1968.

Hinton, W. *Fanshen: A Documentary of Revolution in a Chinese Village.* New York: Vintage, 1966.

Hodgkin, Thomas. *Nationalism in Colonial Africa.* New York: New York University Press, 1956.

Hoopes, J. *Oral History: An Introduction for Students.* Chapel Hill: University of North Carolina Press, 1979.

Hopkins, A. G. *An Economic History of West Africa.* New York: Columbia University Press, 1973.

Hortin, Robin. "Stateless Societies in the History of West Africa." In J. F. A. Ajayi and Michael Crowder, *History of West Africa.* New York: Columbia University Press, 1976.

Hunter, G. *Modernizing Peasant Societies: A Comparative Study in Asia and Africa.* New York: Oxford University Press, 1969.

Huntington, Samuel. *Political Order in Changing Societies.* New Haven: Yale University Press, 1968.

Hyden, Goran. *Beyond Ujamaa in Tanzania: Underdevelopment and the Uncaptured Peasantry.* Berkeley and Los Angeles: University of California Press, 1980.

Hyden, Goran. *No Shortcuts to Progress: African Development Management in*

Perspective. Berkeley and Los Angeles: University of California Press, 1983.

Iliffe, John I. *A Modern History of Tanganyika*. Cambridge: Cambridge University Press, 1978.

Jamal, Vali. "Nomads and Farmers: Income and Poverty in Rural Somalia." In D. Ghai and S. Radwan, eds., *Agrarian Policies and Rural Poverty in Africa*. Geneva; International Labor Organization, 1983.

Janowits, Morris. *The Military in the Political Development of New Nations: An Essay in Comparative Analysis*. Chicago: University of Chicago Press, 1964.

Jardin, D. *The Mad Mullah of Somaliland*. London: Herbert Jenkins, 1923.

Johnson, Douglass L. *The Nature of Nomadism: A Comparative Study of Pastoral Migration in Southwestern Asia and Northern Africa*. University of Chicago, Department of Geography Research Paper no. 118. Chicago, 1969.

Johnston, Bruce F., and Kilby, P. *Agriculture and Structural Transformation*. New York: Oxford University Press, 1975.

Kitching, Gavin. *Classes and Economic Change in Kenya: The Making of the African Petite-Bourgeoisie, 1905–1970*. New Haven: Yale University Press, 1980.

Kitching, Gavin. *Development and Underdevelopment in Historical Perspective: Populism, Nationalism and Industrialization*. New York: Methuen, 1982.

Konczacki, Z. A. *The Economics of Pastoralism: A Case Study of Sub-Saharan Africa*. London: Frank Cass, 1978.

Laitin, D. D., and Samatar, S. S. *Somalia: Nation in Search of a State*. Boulder, Colo.: Westview Press, 1987.

Laurence, Margret. *New Wind in A Dry Country*. New York: Alfred Knopf, 1964.

Lenin, V. I. *The Development of Capitalism in Russia*. Moscow: Progress Publishers, 1977.

Lenin, V. I. *State and Revolution*. New York: International Publishers, 1983.

Lewis, I. M. *Abaar: The Somali Drought*. London: International African Institute, 1975.

Lewis, I. M. "The Dynamics of Nomadism: Prospects for Sedentarization and Social Change." In T. Monod, ed., *Pastoralism in Tropical Africa*. London: Oxford University Press, 1975.

Lewis, I. M. "Lineage Continuity and Modern Commerce in Northern Somaliland." In Paul Bohannan and G. D. Dalton, eds., *Markets in Africa*. Evanston: Northwestern University Press, 1962.

Lewis, I. M. *A Modern History of Somaliland: Nation and State in the Horn of Africa*. New York: Longmans, 1980.

Lewis, I. M. *A Pastoral Democracy: A Study of Pastoralism and Politics among the Northern Somali of the Horn of Africa*. London: Oxford University Press, 1961.

Leys, Colin. *Underdevelopment in Kenya: The Political Economy of Neo-Colonialism, 1964–1971*. Berkeley and Los Angeles: University of California Press, 1975.

Mamdani, Mohmood. *Politics and Class Formation in Uganda*. New York: Monthly Review Press, 1976.

Marcus, H. G. *The Life and Times of Menelik II: Ethiopia, 1844–1913*. Oxford: Clarendon Press, 1975.

Markovitz, Irving I. *Power and Class in Africa: An Introduction to Change and Conflict in African Politics.* Englewood Cliffs, N.J.: Prentice-Hall, 1977.

Martin, Richard C. *Islam.* Englewood Cliffs, N.J.: Prentice-Hall, 1982.

Marx, Karl. *Capital.* Vols. 1 and 3. New York: International Publishers, 1967.

Marx, Karl. "The Future Results of the British Rule in India." In *Karl Marx and Friedrich Engels, On Colonialism: Articles from the "New York Tribune" and Other Writings.* New York: International Publishers, 1972.

Marx, Karl. *Pre-Capitalist Economic Formation.* 9th ed. Trans. Jack Cohen, ed. Eric J. Habsbawn. New York: International Publishers, 1980.

Meillassoux, Claude. *Maidens, Meals, and Money: Capitalism and the Domestic Community.* Cambridge: Cambridge University Press, 1981.

Miliband, Ralph. *The State in Capitalist Society: An Analysis of the Western System of Power.* New York: Basic Books, 1969.

Naderi, Nader Afshar. *The Settlement of Momads and Its Social and Economic Implications.* Tehran: Tehran University, Institute for Social Studies and Research, 1971.

Nash, Manning. *Primitive and Peasant Economic Systems.* San Francisco: Chandler, 1966.

Peel, C. V. A. *Somaliland.* London: F. E. Robinson, 1900.

Perham, Margery. *The Government of Ethiopia.* Evanston: Northwestern University Press, 1969.

Person, V. "Chronology and Oral Tradition." In M. A. Klein and G. W. Johnson, eds., *Prospectives on the African Past.* Boston: Little, Brown, 1972.

Pestalozza, Luigi. *The Somalian Revolution.* Trans. Peter Glendening. Bari: Dedale Libni, 1974.

Rigby, Peter. *Persistent Pastoralism: Nomadic Societies in Transition.* London: Zed Books, 1985.

Rodd, Lord Rennell of. *British Military Administration of Occupied Territory in Africa during the Years 1941–1947.* London: H. M. Stationery Office, 1948.

Rodney, Walter. *How Europe Underdeveloped Africa.* Washington, D.C.: Howard University Press, 1981.

Ruddle, Kenneth. *The Crisis in Dryland Pastoral Economies: An Essay in Applied Human Ecology.* N.p., 1979.

Salzman, Philip C., ed. *Contemporary Nomadic and Pastoral Peoples: Africa and Latin America.* Williamsburg: College of William and Mary, Department of Anthropology, 1982.

Samatar, Ahmed I. *Socialist Somalia: Rhetoric and Reality.* London: Zed Books, 1988.

Samatar, Said. *Oral Poetry and Somali Nationalism: The Case of Sayyid Mohamed Abdille Hassan.* Cambridge: Cambridge University Press, 1982.

Sandbrook, Richard. *The Politics of Basic Needs: Urban Aspects of Assaulting Poverty in Africa.* Toronto: University of Toronto Press, 1982.

Saul, John S. "Marketing Cooperatives in a Developing Country: The Case of Tanzania." In Peter Worsley, ed., *Two Blades of Grass: Rural Cooperative and Agricultural Modernization.* Manchester: Manchester University Press, 1971.

Saul, John S. *The State and Revolution in Eastern Africa.* New York: Monthly Review Press, 1979.

Saul, John S., and Woods, Roger. "African Peasantries." In G. Arrighi and J. S. Saul, eds., *Essays on the Political Economy of Africa.* New York: Monthly Review Press, 1973.

Sayer, Andrew. *Methods in Social Science: A Realist Approach.* London: Hutchinson, 1984.

Scott, James C. *The Moral Economy of the Peasant: Rebellion and Subsistence in Southeast Asia.* New Haven: Yale University Press, 1976.

Scott, James C. *Weapons of the Weak: Everyday Forms of Peasant Resistance.* New Haven: Yale University Press, 1985.

Shenton, Robert, and Watts, Michael. "State and Agrarian Transformation in Nigeria." In Barker, *The Politics of Agriculture in Tropical Africa* (q.v.).

Shivji, Issa G. *Class Struggle in Tanzania.* New York: Monthly Review Press, 1976.

Sik, E. *The History of Black Africa.* 2 vols. Budapest: Akademiai Kiado, 1966.

Skocpal, T. *State and Social Revolution: A Comparative Analysis of France, Russia, and China.* Cambridge: Cambridge University Press, 1977.

Stavrianos, L. S. *Global Rift: The Third World Comes of Age.* New York: Morrow, 1981.

Swainson, Nicola. *The Development of Corporate Capitalism in Kenya, 1918–1977.* Berkeley and Los Angeles: University of California Press, 1980.

Swift, Jeremy, "The Development of Livestock Trading in a Pastoral Economy: The Somali Case." In *Pastoral Production and Society.* Cambridge: Cambridge University Press, 1979.

Swift, Jeremy. "Pastoral Development in Somalia: Herding Cooperatives as a Strategy against Desertification and Famine." In Michael H. Glantz, ed., *Desertification: Environmental Degradation in and around Arid Lands.* Boulder, Colo.: Westview, 1977.

Thomas, C. Y. *The Rise of the Authoritarian State in Peripheral Societies.* New York: Monthly Review Press, 1984.

Tosh, John. *Clan Leaders and Colonial Chiefs in Lango: The Political History of an East African Stateless Society.* Oxford: Clarendon, 1978.

Touval, Saadia. *Somali Nationalism: International Politics and the Drive for Unity in the Horn of Africa.* Cambridge: Cambridge University Press, 1963.

Vansina, J.; Mauny, R.; and Thomas L. V. eds. *The Historian in Tropical Africa.* London: Oxford University Press, 1964.

Van Zwanenberg, R. M. A. *An Economic History of Kenya and Uganda, 1800–1970.* New York: Macmillan, 1975.

Vincent, Joan. *Teso in Transformation: The Political Economy of Peasant and Class in Eastern Africa.* Berkeley and Los Angeles: University of California Press, 1982.

Wasserman, Gary. *Politics of Decolonization: Kenya, Europeans, and the Land Issue, 1960–1965.* New York: Cambridge University Press, 1976.

Watts, Michael J. *Silent Violence: Food, Famine, and Peasantry in Northern Nigeria.* Berkeley and Los Angeles: University of California Press, 1983.

Yudelman, M. *Africans on the Land: Economic Problems of African Agricultural Development in Southern, Central, and Eastern Africa, with Special Reference to Southern Rhodesia.* Cambridge: Harvard University Press, 1964.

Articles, Papers, and Dissertations

Alavi, Hamza. "The State in Post-Colonial Societies: Pakistan and Bangladesh." *New Left Review* 74 (July–August 1972): 59–81.

Amin, Samin. "Underdevelopment and Dependence in Black Africa: Origins and Contemporary Forms." *Journal of Modern African Studies* 10, no. 4 (1972): 503–24.

Aronson, Dan. "Kinsmen and Comrades: Towards a Class Analysis of the Somali Pastoral Sector." *Nomadic Peoples* 7 (November 1980): 14–23.

Asad, T. "Equality in Nomadic Social System? Notes towards the Dissolution of an Anthropological Category." *Critique of Anthropology* 11 (1978): 57–65.

Athreya, V.; Boklin, G.; Djurfeldt, G. D.; and Lindberg, S. "Identification of Agrarian Classes: A Methodological Essay with Empirical Material from South Asia." *Journal of Peasant Studies* 14, no. 2 (1987): 147–90.

Baier, Stephen B. "African Merchants in the Colonial Period: A History of Commerce in Damagaran (Central Niger, 1880–1960)." Ph.D. diss., University of Wisconsin, Madison, 1974.

Bernstein, Henry. "Agrarian Crisis in Africa and Neo-Classical Populism." Paper presented at the Postgraduate Seminar on Peasants, Institute of Commonwealth Studies, University of London, March 15, 1985.

Berry, S. "The Food Crisis and Agrarian Change in Africa." *African Studies Review* 27, no. 2 (1984): 59–112.

Brockett, A. M. "The British Somaliland Protectorate to 1905." Ph.D. thesis, Lincoln College, Oxford, 1969.

Crowder, Michael. "Whose Dream Was It Anyway? Twenty-Five Years of African Independence." *African Affairs* 86, no. 324 (1987): 7–24.

Curle, A. T. "The Ruined Towns of Somaliland." *Antiquity* 2 (1937): 315–27.

Davidson, Basil. "Somalia: Towards Socialism." *Race and Class* 17, no. 1 (1975): 20–37.

Durrill, W. K. "Atrocious Misery: The African Origins of Famine in Northern Somalia." *American Historical Review* 91, no. 2 (1986): 287–306.

Fatoke, Aderemi S. O. "British Colonial Administration of Somaliland Protectorate, 1920–1960." Ph.D. diss., University of Illinois, Chicago, 1982.

Foxbourne, H. R. "The Story of Somaliland: British Lives Squandered and Treasury Wasted." *East Africa Pamphlet* 8, no. 2 (1904): 1–20.

Friedman, H. "Household Production and the National Economy: Concepts for the Analysis of Agrarian Formation." *Journal of Peasant Studies* 7, no. 2 (1980): 158–84.

Galbourne, Harry. "The Problem of the State in Backward Capitalist Societies." *African Development* 6, no. 1 (1981): 45–70.

Geshekter, Charles Lee. "British Imperialism in the Horn of Africa and the

Somalia Response, 1884–1899." Ph.D. diss., University of California, Los Angeles, 1972.

Geshekter, Charles L. "Entrepreneurs, Livestock, and Politics: British Somaliland, 1920–1950." Paper presented at the Joint Stanford University—University of California, Berkeley, Third Annual Conference on African Studies, April 10, 1982.

Getahun, Amane and Krikorian, A. D. "Chat: Coffee's Rival from Harar, Ethiopia, I: Botany, Cultivation, and Use." *Economic Botany* 27 (October–December 1973): 357–77.

Gilliland, H. B. "An Approach to the Problems of the Government of Nomadic Peoples with Special Reference to Experience in British Somaliland." *South African Geographical Journal* 29 (April 1947): 43–76.

Golabian, H. "Development Strategies for Iran's Underdeveloped Rural Nomadic Areas: Some Preliminary Thoughts and Ideas." *Ekistics* 45, no. 267 (1978): 88–95.

Greenway, P. J. "Kat." *East African Agricultural Journal* 13 (1947): 98–102.

Hedlund, Hans. "Contradictions in the Peripheralization of a Pastoral Society: The Maasai." *Review of African Political Economy* 15/16 (1979): 15–34.

Hersi, A. A. "The Arab Factor in Somali History." Ph.D. diss., University of California, Los Angeles, 1977.

Herskovits, Melville J. "The Cattle Complex in East Africa." *American Anthropologist* 28 (1926): 230–72, 361–88, 494–528, 633–64.

Holtzman, John. "The Economics of Improving Animal Health and Livestock Marketing in Somalia." Manuscript. Mogadishu: USAID, 1982.

Jacobs, Allan H. "African Pastoralists: Some General Remarks," *Anthropological Quarterly* 38 (1965): 144–54.

Johnson, Douglass L. "The Response of Pastoral Nomads to Dought in the Absence of Outside Intervention." N.p., Special Sahelian Office, December 19, 1973.

Kitching, Gavin. "The Role of the National Bourgeoisie in the Current Phase of Capitalist Development: Some Reflections." Unpublished manuscript, 1980.

Krueger, Anne O. "The Political Economy of Rent-Seeking Society." *American Economic Review* 64, no. 3 (1974): 291–303.

Lewis, I. M. "The Politics of the 1969 Somali Coup." *Journal of Modern African Studies* 10, no. 3 (1972): 383–408.

Leys, Colin. "Capital Accumulation, Class Formation, and Dependence: The Significance of the Kenya Case." *Socialist Register.* London: Merlin Press, 1979: 241–66.

Leys, Colin. "The 'Overdeveloped' Post-Colonial State: A Re-evaluation." *Review of African Political Economy* 5 (1981): 39–48.

Lofchie, Michael, and Commins, Steve. "Food Deficits and Agricultural Policies in Tropical Africa." *Journal of Modern African Studies* 20, no. 1 (1982): 1–26.

Lonsdale, John. "States and Social Processes in Africa: A Historiographical Survey." *African Studies Review* 24, nos. 2–3 (1981): 227–74.

Lonsdale, John, and Berman, Bruce. "Coping with the Contradictions: The Development of the Colonial State in Kenya, 1895–1914." *Journal of African History* 20 (1979): 487–505.

Mahmet, Ozay. "Effectiveness of Foreign Aid: The Somali Case." *Journal of Modern African Studies* 9, no. 1 (1971): 31–47.

Mamdani, M. "Extreme but not Exceptional: Towards an Analysis of the Agrarian Question in Uganda." *Journal of Peasant Studies* 14, no. 2 (1987): 191–225.

Martin, W. G., and Beittel, M. "The Hidden Abode of Reproduction: Conceptualizing Household in Southern Africa." *Development and Change* 18, no. 2 (1987): 215–34.

Meillassoux, Claude. "A Class Analysis of the Bureaucratic Process in Mali." *Journal of Development Studies* 6, no. 2 (1970): 91–110.

Mouzelis, H. "Capitalism and the Development of Agriculture." *Journal of Peasant Studies* 3, no. 4 (1976): 483–92.

Murry, C. "Class, Gender, and Household: The Development Cycle in Southern Africa." *Development and Change* 18, no. 2 (1987): 253–70.

Pankhurst, Richard. "The Trade of the Gulf of Aden Ports of Africa in the Nineteenth and Early Twentieth Centuries." *Journal of Ethiopian Studies* 3, no. 1 (1965): 36–82.

Peck, E. F. *The Veterinary History of the Somaliland Protectorate, 1924–60.* Unpublished manuscript. Rhodes House Library, 1962.

Poulin, R. "A Study of the Recurrent Costs of Development Projects in Somalia." Paper prepared for the United States Agency for International Development by Development Alternatives, Inc., Mogadishu, March, 1987.

Raikes, Phillip. "Food Policy and Production in Mozambique since Independence." *Review of African Political economy* 29 (1984): 85–107.

Ranger, Terrance. "Growing from the Roots: Reflections on Peasant Research in Central and Southern Africa." *Journal of Southern African History* 5, no. 1 (1978): 99–133.

Reusse, E. "Somalia's Nomadic Livestock Economy: Its Response to Profitable Export Opportunity." *World Animal Review*, no. 43 (1982): 2–11.

Samatar, Abdi. "Merchant, Capital, International Livestock Trade, and Pastoral Development in Somalia," *Canadian Journal of African Studies*, XXI, no. 3 (1987): 355–74.

Samatar, Abdi. "The Predatory State and the Peasantry: Reflections on Rural Development Policy in Somalia." *Africa Today* 32, no. 3 (1985): 41–56.

Samatar, Abdi. "Reproduction Crisis, Peripheral Capitalist Pastoralism, and the Social Differentiation of Livestock Merchants." Unpublished manuscript, University of Iowa, 1988.

Samatar, Abdi Salisbury, L., and Bascom, J. "The Political Economy of Livestock Marketing in Somalia." *African Economic History.*

Samatar, Abdi, and Samatar, Ahmed I. "The Material Roots of the Suspended African State: Arguments from Somalia." *Journal of Modern African Studies*, 25, no. 4 (1987): 669–90.

Samatar, Ahmed I. "Self-Reliance in Theory and Practice: A Critique of Somali Praxis, 1969–1980." Ph.D. dissertation, University of Denver, 1984.

Samatar, Ahmed I. "Somalia Impasse: State, Power, and Dissent Politics." *Third World Quarterly* 9, no. 3 (1987): 871–90.

Samatar, M. S., and Bullaleh, M. E. "The Effects of Kat on the National Economy." Paper presented at the Inter-Country Meeting on Health, Social, and Economic Aspects of Kat, Mogadishu, October 24–28, 1983.

Sandbrook, R. "the State and Economic Stagnation in Tropical Africa." *World Development* 14, no. 3 (1986): 319–32.

Sutter, J. W. "Commercial Strategies, Drought, and Monetary Pressure: *Wo'daabe* Nomads of Tanout *Arrondissement, Niger.*" Unpublished paper, Cornell University, 1979.

Swainson, N. "State and Economy in Post-Colonial Kenya." *Canadian Journal of African Studies* 12, no. 3 (1978): 362–81.

Vansina, Jan. "Recording the Oral History of Bakuba, I: Methods." *Journal of African History* 1, no. 1 (1960): 45–53.

Von Freyhold, Michaela. "The Post-Colonial State and Its Tanzanian Version." *Review of African Political Economy* 8 (January–April 1977): 75–89.

Watts, Michael J. "The Agrarian Question in Africa: What Is the Question?" *Canadian Journal of African Studies* 19, no. 2 (1985).

Watts, Michael J. "The Etiology of Hunger: The Evolution of Famine in a Sudano-Sahelian Region." *Mass Emergencies* 4 (1979): 95–104.

Watts, Michael J. "State, Oil, and Accumulation: From Boom to Crisis." *Environment and Planning: Society and Space* 2 (1984): 403–28.

Documents

Bauer, Ulrich. *Report to the Government of Somalia on the Marketing of Bananas.* Food and Agricultural Organization, Report no. TA 2362, Rome, 1967.

British Somaliland Protectorate. *Annual Report on the Military Administration for the Year Ended 31st December, 1946.* Hargesia, n.d.

British Somaliland Protectorate. *War Somali Sidihi* (The Somali Courier). Hargesia, 1954–57.

Edwards, D. C. *A Survey of the Grazing Areas of British Somaliland.* Hargesia: Department of Natural Resources, 1942.

Great Britain. *Correspondence Respecting the Rise of the Mullah Mohamed Abdullah Hassan in Somaliland and the Subsequent Military Operations, 1899–1901.* British Sessional Papers. Cmd 597, 1901, no. 1.

Great Britain, Colonial Office. *Treaties with Somali Tribes.* N.p., n.d.

——. *Somaliland: Report for 1904–5.* London: H. M. Stationery Officer, 1905.

——. *Somaliland: Report for 1906–7.* London: H. M. Stationery Office, 1907.

——. *Somaliland: Report for 1907–8.* London: H. M. Stationery Office, 1908.

——. *Somaliland: Report for 1914–15.* London: H. M. Stationery Office, 1915.

——. *Somaliland: Report for 1917–18.* London: H. M. Stationery Office, 1919.

——. *Somaliland: Report for 1918–19.* London: H. M. Stationery Office, 1920.

——. *Somaliland: Report for 1919–20.* London: H. M. Stationery Office, 1921.

——. *Somaliland: Report for 1920.* London: H. M. Stationery Office, 1922.

——. *Somaliland: Report for 1924.* London: H. M. Stationery Office, 1925.

——. *Somaliland: Report for 1928.* London: H. M. Stationery Office, 1928.

——. *Somaliland: Report for 1928.* London: H. M. Stationery Office, 1929.

———. *Annual Report on the Social and Economic Progress of the People of Somaliland for 1930.* London: H. M. Stationery Office, 1931.

———. *Annual Report on the Social and Economic Progress of the People of Somaliland for 1934.* London: H. M. Stationery Office, 1935.

———. *Annual Report on the Social and Economic Progress of the People of Somaliland for 1937.* London: H. M. Stationery Office, 1938.

———. *Annual Report on the Somaliland Protectorate for the Year 1948.* London: H. M. Stationery Office, 1949.

———. *Annual Report on the Somaliland Protectorate for the Year 1949.* London: H. M. Stationery Office, 1950.

———. *Annual Report on the Somaliland Protectorate for the Years 1952 and 1953.* London: H. M. Stationery Office, 1954.

———. *Somaliland Protectorate: Somalialnd Report for the Years, 1954 and 1955.* London: H. M. Stationery Office, 1957.

———. *Somaliland: Report for the Years 1958 and 1959. London: H. M. Stationery Office,* 1960.

———. *Report of the Somaliland Protectorate Constitutional Conference, May 1960.* London: H. M. Stationery Office, 1960.

Great Britain, Foreign Office. *European Captives among the Somali Tribes 1866–69.* Foreign and Commonwealth Library. London, n.d.

Great Britain, Public Record Office. PRO, CO 535/38/46036.

———. Telegram from Somaliland Governor. PRO, CO 535/3876, January 21, 1921.

———. Somali Grievances, PRO, CO 535/100/5886, 1933.

———. Communication between Somaliland Governor and the Colonial Office, PRO, PR.52921, October 21, 1920.

———. PRO CO 535/65, 1921 and PRO CO 535/69, 1921.

———. PRO CO 535/65, 29396, vol. 1, 1921.

———. Somaliland Protectorate. Swayne to Major Rayne: Tribal Structure: Loyalty of Somali Chiefs, December 9, 1938. CO 535/131/46171.

Great Britain, War Office. *Official History of the Operations in Somaliland, 1901–1904* Vol. 2. London: War Office, 1907.

Hartley, B. J., Box, T., Uhlig, A. H., and Pillai, C. *Agriculture and Water Survey: Livestock Development Survey.* United Nations Development Program and Food and Agricultural Organization, Report no. MR/54396. Rome, 1967.

International Bank for Reconstruction and Development. *The Economy of the Trust Territory of Somaliland.* Report of a Mission Organized by the IBRD at the Request of the Government of Italy. 1957.

International Labor Organization, Jobs and Skills Program for Africa. *Rural-Urban Gap and Income Distribution: The Case of Somalia.* Addis Ababa, 1982.

Shirname, T. G. *Report to the Government of Somalia on Food and Agricultural Economy.* Food and Agricultural Organization, Report no. 2088. Rome, 1965.

Somali National Bank. *Report and Balance Sheet, 1962.* Mogadishu, 1963.

Somaliland Protectorate, Department of Agricultural and Veterinary Services. *Annual Report for 1950.* Hargeisa, 1950.

————. *Annual Report for 1953.* Hargeisa, 1953.

————. *Annual Report for 1956.* Hargeisa, 1956.

Somaliland Protectorate, Department of Education. *Annual Report (Summary), 1956.* Hargeisa, 1956.

Somali Republic. *The First Session of the National Advisory Council Held 20th–27th August 1968.* Mogadishu: Ministry of Interior, 1968.

————, Livestock Development Agency. *Annual Budget Statement of the Livestock Development Agency.* Mogadishu, September 2, 1966.

————, Planning and Coordinating Commission for Economic and Social Development. *First Five-Year Plan, 1963–1967.* Mogadishu, 1963.

————. *Government Activities from Independence until Today (July 1, 1960–December 31, 1963).* Mogadishu, 1964.

————. *The Somali Peninsula: A New Light on Imperial Motives.* London, 1964.

————. National Assembly. *Statement of Programme by H. E. Mohamed Ibrahim Egal.* Mogadishu, August 1967.

————, Planning Commission. *Short-Term Development Programme, 1968–1970.* Mogadishu, August 1968.

Somali D. Republic. *Agriculture in the Service of the Nation: More Production with More Efforts.* Mogadishu, 1974.

————, *Tiro Koobka Iyo Qiimaynta Qaadka.* Mogadishu, September 1983.

————, Ministry of Local Government and Rural Development. *Somalia's Rural Development Strategy, 1981–1990.* Mogadishu, 1981.

————, Ministry of Planning and Coordination. *Development Programme, 1971–1973.* Mogadishu, 1974.

————, Ministry of Planning and Coordination. *Five-Year Development Programme, 1974–1978.* Mogadishu, 1974.

————, Ministry of Planning and Coordination. *Five-Year Development Plan, 1982–1986.* Mogadishu, 1982.

————, Northwest Agricultural Development Project. *Report: Second National Farmers' Conference, Mogadishu, October 11–16, 1983.* Hargeisa, December 10, 1983.

USAID and Somali Republic Ministry of Agriculture. "Bonka Farmers' Training Center." Unpublished manuscript, Baidoa, 1964.

Wilson, J. "The Political Economy of Contract Farming." *Review of Radical Political Economics* 18, no. 4 (1986): 44–70.

Wixon, Calvin. *Arabsiyo Soil and Water Conservation Project, Annual Report* (n.p.: USAID, n.d.).

World Bank. *Accelerated Development in Sub-Saharan Africa: An Agenda for Action.* Washington, D.C., 1981.

————. *Appraisal of the Northwest Agricultural Development Project: Somalia.* Nairobi: East Africa Project Department, 1976.

————. *Land Reform.* Washington, D.C., 1974.

Index

201

www.ingramcontent.com/pod-product-compliance
Lightning Source LLC
Chambersburg PA
CBHW060844280326
41934CB00007B/914